Chpter 9

HIGH TECHNOLOGY AND INTERNATIONAL COMPETITIVENESS

HIGH TECHNOLOGY
AND
INTERNATIONAL
COMPETITIVENESS

ROMESH DIWAN <u>AND</u>
CHANDANA CHAKRABORTY

Foreword by Zoltan J. Acs

Praeger Studies in American Industry

New York
Westport, Connecticut
London

Library of Congress Cataloging-in-Publication Data

Diwan, Romesh K.
    High technology and international competitiveness / Romesh Diwan
and Chandana Chakraborty ; foreword by Zolton J. Acs.
        p.   cm. — (Praeger studies in American industry)
    Includes bibliographical references and index.
    ISBN 0-275-93032-7 (pbk. : alk. paper)
    1. High technology industries—United States.   2. Technological
innovations—Economic aspects—United States.   3. Industrial
productivity—United States.   4. Competition, International.
I. Chakraborty, Chandana.   II. Title.   III. Series.
HC110.H53D58   1991
338.4'762'000973—dc20   90-27810

British Library Cataloguing in Publication Data is available.

Library of Congress Catalog Card Number: 90-27810
ISBN: 0-275-93032-7

First published in 1991

Praeger Publishers, One Madison Avenue, New York, NY 10010
An imprint of Greenwood Publishing Group, Inc.

Printed in the United States of America

The paper used in this book complies with the Permanent
Paper Standard issued by the National Information Standards
Organization (Z39.48—1984).

10 9 8 7 6 5 4 3 2 1

Contents

Tables and Graphs

TABLES

GRAPHS

Foreword

Zoltan J. Acs

For the better part of the twentieth century the United States enjoyed an unprecedented position as the world's leader in industrial production. The origin of this industrial predominance is found in the last century and can be traced to America's abundance of raw materials and a large internal market. This tremendous base of raw materials along with high levels of craft knowledge made the United States an industrial leader in material-based industries like steel, autos, and textiles until the mid-1960s.

America's unprecedented leadership in mass production industries was followed by a similar lead in high-technology industries after World War II. This lead in high-technology industries can be traced in part to the tremendous confidence that Americans gained after victory in the war. One manifestation of this victory was the dramatic increase in the number of American high school graduates that went on to college. A small but important fraction of these graduates went into the nation's research universities, resulting in a significant lead over other countries in scientific learning. However, the largest share of the new graduates went to work for American companies in their R&D programs. Thus, by the mid-1960s the American lead in high-technology industries, as well as in the older mass production industries, was taken as a matter of fact.

By the end of the 1970s, America's lead in mass production industries had eroded, and in another ten years several countries caught up in high-technology goods. The U.S. became a net importer of manufactured goods. The interesting question is, "What caused this broad convergence to take place?" I would suggest that the internationalization of markets following World War II eroded America's comparative advantage in mass produced goods. The historical basis for U.S. mineral abundance was much more a matter of early development rather than geological endowment. In addition, the internationalization of business further complicated international trade statistics. For example, while the U.S. share of manufactured exports (both material and knowledge-based) fell during the mid-1960s, the export share of U.S.-owned firms held up.

The U.S. decline in high-technology industries requires a more fine-grained analysis. It can be traced to the following: (1) technology became more generally available with the internationalization of markets to all those with the required skills and willingness to make the investment; (2) other industrial powers greatly increased their expenditures on research and development. Indeed, by the early 1980s several countries had surpassed the United States in the percentage of GNP expended on purely civilian research and development; and (3) the final reason for the convergence in high-technology industries was a sharp decline in the importance of spillover from military R&D to civilian technology. While this spillover gave significant advantages to the civilian economy in the 1950s, today it buys little outside the military sphere—thus a decline in U.S. productivity.

The decline in U.S. industrial predominance can then be traced in part to the internationalization of markets and the significant investment that other countries have made in both physical and human capital. This would clearly explain why both Germany and Japan, with excellent educational systems, have closed the technological gap with the U.S. during the last decade.

While some of what has been stated above has been well researched much of it remains conjecture because of a lack of data. *High Technology and International Competitiveness* by Professors Romesh Diwan and Chandana Chakraborty is one of the first systematic empirical studies to fill this gap in our understanding of what happened to our competitive advantage in high-technology industries. The study uses new data to test existing theories of productivity growth. Perhaps the most important finding in this study is that while in the mass production industries capital and labor were substitutes, in knowledge-based industries they are complements. The implication is that labor is an asset and not a cost of production in high-technology industries. This implies the need for cooperation between labor and capital in the production process. These results clearly demonstrate for the first time that countries that invest heavily in human capital and improve their industrial relations will come to dominate high-technology manufacturing and international trade. In summary, investment in education and international competitiveness are highly linked as we move toward the next century.

Preface and Acknowledgments

There is a growing consensus that the fundamental weakness in the U.S. economy comes from the difficulties of its manufacturing sector. For the past two decades, the United States has been losing its competitive strength in both domestic and international markets. This has meant a decline in the market shares and an erosion in the profitability of U.S. businesses. It has resulted in a shift in its trade balance from surplus to deficit. In the final analysis it has led to a stagnation, if not an actual fall, in the American standard of living. This at a time when a new techno-economic paradigm is emerging based on new technologies that have internationalized production processes and globalized markets for products. Represented by microelectronics, these are the high technologies with high R&D intensity and economies of scope instead of scale so that customization and batch production are economic. These are the technologies of the future, radically different from older technologies based on standardization and mass production techniques. The implications of high technologies are fundamentally different. This book is based on the assumption that the United States can gain back its competitive strength if it can concentrate on high technologies and make the necessary adjustments in its production and economic institutions. Indeed, high technology is its next frontier.

Accordingly, this book defines quantitatively the U.S. high technology sector and provides, for the first time, its time profile in terms of output and three inputs—capital, labor, and materials. Labor is further split into skilled and unskilled labor. These original time series data will be useful to other researchers. A high-technology industry is defined on the basis of two criteria—proportion of technologically oriented workers and ratio of R&D expenditures to sales. These industries are distinguished at the three-digit level of the Standard Industrial Classification Codes. Having quantified the high-technology sector, this book makes the first attempt to analyze the various dimensions of its production structure and growth: productivity, input substitution, and technological change. The analysis is done through the method of a translog cost function while R&D stock is used as a technology variable.

This book provides the first empirical results on productivity and technical change in the high-technology sector. We find that capital and skilled labor are complements and technological change is non-neutral. These are consistent with intuitive analyses. One of the major conclusions is that labor in this sector is not a cost but an asset. This is a radical conclusion. The book analyzes in some depth cultural, institutional, and policy implications of the proposition that labor is an asset. It provides concrete suggestions for institutional change to foster skill formation. The book also discusses the substance of the other conclusions regarding technological change and how it can be promoted. It relates applied and basic research to the innovative process in terms of invention, innovation, and diffusion. Here again, concrete suggestions about institutional and policy change are made that will maintain and promote basic science infrastructure, encourage collaborative efforts for investments in high technologies, and reduce risk. We hope the book will encourage debate, discussion, and further research on this important issue.

This book was a joint product in every sense of the term. It began as Chandana Chakraborty's doctoral dissertation, written under the supervision of Romesh Diwan and then revised and expanded over the years by us. We agreed on all the empirical work, methodology, results, ideas, interpretations, and policies. We each took primary responsibility for specific chapters. Together we reviewed the entire manuscript several times, making necessary revisions. Diwan oversaw the final preparation for publication.

Every researcher owes a debt of gratitude to those who have traveled ahead and made the path easy to travel. Among these path makers are the great minds who clarify issues, formulate paradigms, and develop methodologies and data sources. We are fortunate that so many have already accomplished such a large amount of research. We have been particularly influenced by the wisdom of Mahatma Gandhi; writings of John Kenneth Galbraith, Robert Reich, and Lester Thurow; paradigm formulations by Christopher Freeman and Carlotta Perez as well as Joseph Schumpeter; and methodological developments by Ernie Berndt, Zvi Griliches, and Dale Jorgensen.

The material from this book has been presented at a number of meetings and seminars: Eastern Economic Association annual meetings, Washington, D.C. (1987), Boston (1988), Baltimore (1989), and Cincinnati (1990); European Association for Research in Industrial Economics annual meetings, Madrid (1987) and Rotterdam (1988); Allied Social Science Association annual meetings, New York (1988), Atlanta, (1989), and Washington, D.C. (1990); Science Research Centre (WZB), Berlin (1988); Interdisciplinary Physics Colloquium at the Westinghouse R&D Centre, Pittsburgh (1988); Graduate Lecture Series, Drexel University (1988); Institute of Economic Growth, Delhi (1989); Jawahar Lal Nehru

University, New Delhi (1989); National Council of Applied Economic Research, New Delhi (1989); Indian Council for Research in International Economic Relations, New Delhi (1989); Athens University, Athens, Ohio (1989); and International Sociology Association, 12th World Congress, Madrid (1990). A number of people at these meetings have encouraged us and made helpful comments. It is impossible to list all of them and thank them individually. Financial support to Chandana Chakraborty from the Career Development Committee of Montclair State College for work during the summer of 1990 is gratefully acknowledged.

Zoltan Acs introduced us to these series and made significant suggestions that have helped us in our revisions. We are also thankful to many others on three different continents who read excerpts and helped in clarifying our ideas, particularly Mohammed Al Nofai, David Audretsch, Ravi Aulakh, Tahir Ayar, Mohyee Ayoub, Said Bawazer, Gurdarshan Bhalla, Ashok Bhargava, Bo Carlsson, Alok Chakarabarti, Suresh Desai, Banarsi Dhawan, Fareed Felenbam, Sushila Gidwani, John Gowdy, Damodar Gujerati, the late Madan Handa, Manshya Hu, Renu Kallianpur, Moussa Kourouma, Talat Mahmood, Ishaq Nadiri, Muzaffar Qureshi, Vaman Rao, Ingrid Rima, Saroj Sawhney, J. D. Sethi, Nar Bahadur Singh, Leo Sveikaskaus, John Tomer, Prem Vashishtha, and Donald Vitaliano.

We had the good fortune to have the expert advice of Professor Joyce Diwan, who spared precious time from her research on mitochondrial ion channels and spent many hours on the graphics and other technical details. Without her advice and support this study would have been impossible indeed.

1

Introduction

A HISTORICAL NOTE

The U.S. generally, and its manufacturing sector particularly, emerged after the Second World War as the most vibrant and growth-oriented economy and industry in the world. U.S. ingenuity, investments, and enterprise used the theoretical advances made in Great Britain and Europe to develop the most technologically advanced manufacturing sector.[1] A new techno-economic paradigm or technology regime based on techniques of mass production was emerging. Large market size; capacity to standardize products and processes; innovativeness in mass production techniques; management skills; a hard working and motivated work force, due in part to the U.S. immigration policy; and the ample supply of capital in the country enabled the United States to enter this technology regime and take the lead in virtually all manufacturing industries. Other countries modeled their technologies and techniques on those introduced and practiced here. With European industries and economies damaged by the War, the United States became the leading industrial country in the world; it was also the technological leader. Innovations were regularly introduced, new production techniques were developed, new assembly lines were set up, and mass production methods were extended to new fields. Its economic strength, stable dollar, technological lead, and military power provided the necessary direction and stability to an international economic order in which the United States was the undisputed leader. The U.S. manufacturing sector provided the production base for this leadership and was the major source of the high material standards of living in the country. For the two decades of the 1950s and 1960s, the U.S. economy operated at full employment while per capita income grew. Not only did the U.S. economy grow, the international economic order, formalized by U.S. leadership, also promoted full employment, stability, and growth in the industrialized countries of Europe.[2] These were the decades of affluence, peace, and prosperity.

The 1970s and 1980s, unfortunately, have not been as kind to either the international order or the U.S. economy. Growth rates in all industrialized countries have slowed, and unemployment has become a stable feature of these economies. The optimism of the past has given way to pessimism about the future. Today there is a general feeling of unease about the U.S. economy.[3] Once a major creditor, the United States has become the largest debtor nation in the world during the 1980s. Imports from other countries compete successfully in the domestic market. Large, conspicuous financial and real estate assets are being taken over by foreign corporations, creating news headlines.[4] U.S. companies are losing market share even in such sophisticated technological products as electronics—a product line that was introduced by the United States.[5]

The U.S. standard of living is under serious strain,[6] and people are asking why U.S. prosperity is eroding.[7] Evidence shows that wage rates have not kept pace with inflation so that real wage rates have declined. Family income has been maintained by the entry of additional family members into the labor market,[8] which has put a severe burden on family structure.[9] There is also a change in the composition of jobs. High paying jobs in the manufacturing sector have declined while there has been an increase in low paying service jobs.[10]

At the international level, the old world order has crumbled. The division between East and West has evaporated with fundamental changes in the Eastern European countries. The United Soviet Socialist Republic has its own serious problems and is grappling with perestroika.[11] At present there are serious questions about the sources of unease in the United States. Some of the basic problems relate to the nature of U.S. industrial structure, specifically in the manufacturing sector.

DECLINE IN THE MANUFACTURING SECTOR

For much of the twentieth century, U.S. manufacturing remained unchallenged in an environment in which capital and energy intensive industries, like steel, automobiles, chemicals, textiles, rubber, and electrical equipment concentrated on large-scale machine production in association with mostly unskilled labor to achieve extraordinary efficiency. High volume and new techniques brought unit costs down so that industries enjoyed economies of scale that were unachievable in earlier periods. Productivity increased continuously. These trends, however, have changed, adversely affecting the U.S. manufacturing sector.

Since the late 1960s, changes in the relative strength of U.S. manufacturing have been slowly unraveling. Performance has exhibited a downward trend, causing resources to be progressively idled. The proportion of capacity utilized in production reached 86 percent in 1965, averaged around 80 percent during the 1970s, and fell to less than 70 percent in 1982.[12] U.S. manufacturing has not returned to the utilization rate of 1965 so far. The decline in the rate of capacity utilization is rooted in the falling growth rate of manufacturing output. Over the period 1967–1982 manufacturing output grew at an annual average rate of 2.9 percent. A breakdown of the period into two subperiods, 1967–1973 and 1973–1982, reveals that over the second period, 1973–1982, the growth rate was half that achieved during the first period, 1967–1973. A similar trend is reflected in the growth of employment. From an average of 0.62 percent per year over the period 1967–1973, the employment growth rate declined continuously to only 0.4 percent per year in the period 1973–1982. This situation has not improved in the last six years. The manufacturing output share in the gross national product (GNP) has been declining continuously over the last 15 years. This share was 25 percent in 1970, but had declined to 20 percent by 1985.[13] The situation has not improved in recent years.

The declining growth rates of output and employment point to another factor: productivity. The 1970s were also a period of declining productivity, measured by output per unit of labor. For the period 1960–1973, the average annual percentage growth in productivity was 3.4, while for the period 1973–1983 this rate fell to 1.8.[14] There has been a resurgence of productivity growth in manufacturing during the post-1982 period; the estimate of this ratio for 1979–1986 provides a growth rate of 3.5 percent.[15] These numbers, however, conceal declining trends because the major source of this growth lies in only one industry, namely computers. If standard industrial classification (SIC) code 35 data are excluded, this growth rate falls sharply. In addition, the manufacturing sector suffered a great deal from the recession of 1981–1982 so that the growth rate for this period is biased upward.[16] These estimates are consistent with observed declining wage rates. Employers once offered wage earners a part of productivity gains in the form of higher wages, but with declining productivity, they have little incentive or resources to pay higher wages.

The picture remains the same if one looks at estimates of total factor productivity,[17] a ratio of the growth of output divided by the weighted sum of the growth of different inputs, namely capital, labor, and materials. Total factor productivity is interpreted as a measure of the efficiency of production—the higher the growth rate of total factor productivity, the larger the output being generated by the inputs. It has also been interpreted as a measure of technological change. A high total factor productivity growth rate implies a high rate of neutral technological change, suggesting that the output growth is taking place because inputs are better organized and reflect the latest techniques of production. Therefore, the recent decline in the total factor productivity growth rate suggests that either inputs are not being efficiently employed or capital equipment is not up to date because new techniques have not been incorporated. This decline is reported by both measures of productivity. Although estimates of productivity for U.S. manufacturing suggest a slight upturn for recent years, the general proposition still holds. Scholars generally agree about this decline;[18] some even consider the situation a crisis, particularly in the larger private business economy.[19]

In view of growing market globalization and international competitiveness, it is not only the historical decline in productivity in U.S. manufacturing that is a problem, but its comparative performance with other competing industrialized countries also paints a poor picture. Throughout the period 1950 to 1986, labor productivity growth rates in the United States lagged behind those of France, Germany, Japan, and even Great Britain,[20] making U.S. manufacturing less competitive.

The reduced competitiveness of U.S. manufacturing leads us to the question of capital investment. Capital investment in United States manufacturing has been low; estimates place it at around 10 percent of value added.[21] This value is low, particularly in view of the fact that in the last decade new technologies have become available that require larger investments of capital.[22] It is also argued that the United States is not spending a large enough share of its GNP on research and development (R&D). The national expenditure on R&D as a percentage of the GNP was 2.57 percent in 1970. In 1975 it fell to 2.20 percent and did not catch up until 1985. However, this estimate includes the R&D expenditures on both defense and civilian outputs, and it is the civilian R&D that is relevant for success and growth in manufacturing. The civilian R&D expenditures were only 1.63 percent of the GNP in 1971; although these have started inching up in the last few years, they remain less than 2 percent. This ratio is low,[23] particularly because technological change is now rapid and the R&D contribution is signifi- cant. Studies generally indicate that R&D contributes about 0.2 to 0.3 percent annually to productivity growth in the non-farm U.S. economy.[24] Since R&D has much larger impact on manufacturing, its contribution to U.S. manufacturing is larger; around 0.5 during the forty year period of 1948 to 1987.[25]

Various explanations of this phenomena include the thesis framed in terms of collusive behavior. The basic proposition here is that collusive collective action is directed toward distributive gains rather than increasing productivity.[26] As our society matures, collusive collective action becomes profitable and common, and the struggle moves from production and competition toward securing additional advantages in distribution of the given pie.[27] In such a maturing society, or in a society where growth rate is somewhat low, it becomes much more profitable to form coalitions for collusive action. Another explanation focuses on reduced levels of aggregate demand, which result in a reduction in capacity utilization. This, in turn, creates other related effects, such as, reduced levels of capital and knowledge formation.[28] Those who argue that the decline in U.S. manufacturing follows from microeconomic factors emphasize the sudden increase in oil prices in the early 1970s.[29] However, a controversy exists about the importance of this factor in explaining both the slow growth rate of the economy and a slowing down of the productivity, and the empirical evidence is not conclusive. The other microeconomic factor concerns the low rates of capital investment, which is not independent of the cost of oil since much of the technology in the mass produc- tion technological regime has been oil based. The nature of technological change in U.S. industry is generally capital using,[30] so increases in the price of oil and capital have the effect of reducing the rate of productivity growth.

At another level, a thesis with two variants, formulated in terms of technology, has been advanced to explain U.S. productivity slow down or decline. One variant deals with the nature of the technology of production alone; it argues that U.S. manufacturing has not followed the latest technologies, has lagged behind in technological change, and has missed some opportunities.[31] In its micro form, this argument cites reduced levels of capital investment and R&D expenditures. The second variant places technology in a broader context, according to which U.S. production culture is no more suitable to current changes in production technologies than are the consumption habits of its consumers.[32] With growing affluence, consumers want to be "different," meaning they demand customized goods that are not mass produced. New technologies, particularly in electronics and associated processes, have enabled efficient production, in low volume, of the goods demanded by more affluent consumers. The U.S. production culture, however, has not been able to adapt to such changes in the production structure.[33] This thesis can be formulated in terms of a new, emerging techno-economic paradigm or technology regime. Although the terms techno-economic paradigm and technology regime have been defined somewhat differently, they basically concern the same large set, and in this study we will use them interchangeably.

The explanation for the slow down in terms of the new paradigm is based on two propositions. First, the new techno-economic paradigm is significantly different from the old in that it has different threshold levels. Second, the United States does not have any special advantages in moving on the trajectories of this paradigm. On the contrary, U.S. manufacturing may even have certain disadvantages.[34] This study delves deeply into the nature of the new technologies in the United States and their relationship to the growth process.

EMERGING NEW TECHNOLOGY REGIME AND HIGH TECHNOLOGY

There is now a growing consensus that (1) manufacturing matters, in the sense that economic growth depends essentially on manufacturing and not on service industry, and (2) that high technologies are essential for the growth of manufacturing and the economy.[35] This consensus arises from four different perspectives: (1) Scientists and businesses involved in old technologies recognize that these technologies are in decay and cannot compete with newer technologies because the market has changed and because obsolescence has made their costs prohibitively high. (2) Those involved with new technologies find that new innovations are reducing production costs continuously so that it is easier to compete with the products of older technologies. (3) Markets for products based on newer technologies are growing faster because consumers seek customized products that mass production technology is not able to provide. (4) Imports of goods produced by newer technologies are competing successfully in the U.S. domestic market.

Forecasts suggest that new technologies are here to stay,[36] and all these perspectives support a search for still more new technologies.

A consensus that there is a radical change in the industrial function is building among scholars and practitioners. Some talk of the emergence of the Third Wave,[37] others discuss the era of the great divide,[38] still others talks in terms of techno-economic paradigms,[39] but the basic premise of all these theses is the same. In the last two decades, the time period when U.S. manufacturing started experiencing decline, a change has taken place that involves technology in an essential way. The narrowest of these ideas suggests that a new techno-economic paradigm or technology regime comes into being when the following three conditions are satisfied: (1) the price of the basic element in the new technology starts to fall continuously; (2) there is ample supply of this element so that its demand, and applications, do not face bottlenecks;[40] and (3) the technology is pervasive, in the sense that it has applications in all fields. Once these conditions are satisfied, the new technology becomes profitable and develops its own momentum through the institutionalization of the vested interests of people who gain from its growth. Soon it becomes a large business. Its trade associations gain lobbying power. Academic scientists find that working on its various facets is prestigious. Entrepreneurs and venture capital are attracted to it. And finally, society finds it justifiable to subsidize its supportive functions. Some argue that in the case of electronics, the new paradigm is already in place. Electronics is now a multi-billion dollar industry.

The question is what this new emerging techno-economic paradigm constitutes. Our contention is that high technologies form the primary technological base of this new emerging technology regime, which explains high growth and export rates in high technologies. Japan's economic miracle and its success in generating export surplus follow from its being at the leading edge of this new technology regime. A techno-economic paradigm is like an escalator—anyone who gets on first continues to be ahead simply because the escalator is moving. U.S. industry got on the mass production technology regime escalator in the 1950s and became the world power *par excellence*. Germany and Japan seem to have jumped on the escalator of this new high-technology paradigm and have been declared as the premier economic powers today.[41] It is the high technologies that have growth potential in the future, and over time they will become a larger and more important part of any competitive economy. Since the new technology regime is international in character and fosters global markets, the high technologies have to compete internationally. It is high technologies that provide international competitive strength to an economy. If this argument is accepted, U.S. manufacturing cannot maintain its competitive strength without incorporating high technologies. This paradigm shift has made high technologies essential to manufacturing and to the U.S. economy.

OBJECTIVE AND PLAN OF STUDY

If the future growth and competitive strength of the U.S. economy depends on the development of high-technology industries, it is essential to define the U.S.

high-technology (USHT) sector; similar to the U.S. manufacturing sector. At this stage, the USHT sector is a small but growing subset of U.S. manufacturing. Over time the USHT sector will become synonymous with the U.S. manufacturing sector or its equivalent. There are at present a few studies that quantitatively define the USHT sector on a primarily *ad hoc* basis and for different periods, and there is no one study that defines it consistently for a long period. This study aims to fill the gap. It is the first study, to our knowledge, that quantitatively, and consistently, defines the USHT sector for 1967–1982. Having developed this information on the USHT sector, the study analyzes its dynamics and production structure so that meaningful policies can be debated and formulated.

The plan of the study is as follows. Chapter 2 places the U.S. manufacturing sector in its historical and international context. It analyzes the effects of international competitiveness, formulates the thesis about the new technology regime in greater depth, discusses various criteria for defining high technologies, and develops a definition that identifies 25 industry groups of three-digit SIC industries as high-technology industries and studies their international competitiveness. Chapter 3 develops tools for analyzing productivity. It discusses both partial and total productivity concepts and various approaches to measuring them; namely econometric, index number, and nonparametric. From there it moves to conceptual and measurement issues in technological change, elaborating on embodied and non-embodied technological change. Since technological change follows from a production function, this chapter includes some of the properties of aggregate production functions, such as separability, the distinction between value added and gross output concepts, and input aggregation. Chapter 3 also discusses various forms of production functions, particularly constant and variable elasticity of substitution, and concludes with the advantages of a duality-based production function. Chapter 4 picks up the thread and discusses at length the translog function; the concept, econometric applications, extensions of it, dynamic disequilibrium models, and empirical applications of the index number method. Since the translog cost function is commonly used, chapter 5 develops the theoretical model based on it for analyzing the USHT sector. It elaborates on the different assumptions and restrictions of a cost function; namely, homogeneity, neutrality, separability, and homotheticity. Finally, chapter 5 develops estimation design and procedures. Chapter 6 develops the time series data set for the USHT sector. It explains the procedures adopted to quantify different quantities and prices of output and three inputs, capital, labor, and materials. Labor is further divided into skilled and unskilled labor. Having developed the time series data set for output and inputs, chapter 6 discusses trends in these variables, their growth rates, and the sources of output growth. One of the findings of this study is that materials forms an important part of the USHT sector. Accordingly, it quantifies the sources of growth both for labor and material productivity. It ends by quantifying partial and total factor productivity. Chapter 7 provides quantitative estimates of the application of the translog cost function to the output and input time series data for the USHT sector. Given these estimates, partial elasticity of substitution between factor inputs are quantified for the whole period and analyzed for four different periods; namely 1967–1969, 1969–1973, 1973–1979, and 1979–1982. The periods 1969–1973 and 1973–1979 are two business cycles; 1967–1969 is the upswing phase of a business cycle and 1979–1982 the downswing. The elasticities of substitution and factor demand are compared for different periods. The chapter identifies and quantifies the nature of technological change. Three conclusions emerge: (1) materials are the most important cost factor, (2) capital and labor are complements, and (3) technological change is embodied in inputs. The dynamics of the USHT sector is assessed from the estimates on the production structure. Chapters 8 and 9 analyze, in detail, the implications of these conclusions in terms of policies to encourage skill formation and promote technological change. Chapter 8 looks at the capital-labor complementarity that makes labor an asset instead of a cost so that skill formation through education and training becomes an important policy objective. Capital-labor complementarity also involves different perceptions both by labor about its self-worth and by management regarding labor's involvement in decision making. Instead of confrontation, relations have to move toward cooperation and encompass changes in the institutional framework that fosters team work. Chapter 9 deals with issues that promote technological change. It formulates a process of technological change based on invention, innovation, and diffusion of technologies. All technological change requires R&D and the basic research that has been declining recently needs to be encouraged. Chapter 9 discusses policies to promote research and development and develops a proposal for the U.S. government to promote technological change. Chapter 10 summarizes conclusions.

NOTES

1. Reich (1983) provides a well-articulated argument on this issue. He also gives evidence of the adoption by the United States of the many inventions made in these countries.

2. It is interesting to note that during this period, economists talked of growth theories. The underlying emphasis was not on the business cycle but on continuous growth.

3. The *New York Times* and other media constantly bring out stories concerning this unease; the Japanese are outcompeting us, families are breaking down, we fear recession, the American dream is evaporating. Terkel (1988) surveyed a large number of Americans and collected their feelings in his book *The Great Divide: Second Thoughts on The American Dream*. The book focuses on this unease that is both a cause and an effect of the growing divide. He summarizes in a note. "The Great Divide bespeaks more than the deepening chasm between the haves—and have-somewhats—and have-nots. It is the rift of race that, at times, appears to close and then casually widens; not unrelated to having and not having. It is the split in the sphere of the worship, rendering unto Caesar what may not rightfully be his and unto God what may not spiritually be His. It is the cleft that has cut us off, one from the other and, indeed, from our very selves. It is the breach that has cut off past from present" (p. vii, Avon Edition).

4. The purchase of Columbia Pictures by Sony and a majority share in the Rockefeller Building in New York by Mitsubishi not only carried large headlines in all media but also led to a lot of comment, which still continues.

5. The *New York Times* Business Section, dated January 5, 1989, had the top page headline, "US Share Declines in Electronics; Fall called 'Startling.' "

6. A number of essays in Starr (1988) refer to and comment on this fact. The focus of many of these essays is on how to bring the United States back on track and improve its standards of living.

7. As recently as January 9, 1989, the *New York Times* carried an editorial with the sub-title, "Why is U.S. Prosperity Eroding?"

8. These conclusions follow from the data on wages and family incomes provided by the Bureau of Labor Statistics. Family income in 1970 was $27,862, whereas in 1980 it was $27,974. In the following five years it inched up a little to $28,269. (These are all in 1986 dollars.) *Statistical Abstract of the United States*, 1988, table 699, page 427. By comparison, the weekly wage rate in manufacturing in constant dollars was $222.9 in 1976 and $222.2 in 1986. It went up in 1978 and fell since then. *Ibid.*, table 468, page 392.

9. There has been an increase in both divorce rates and single parent family households.

10. Incidentally, this was one of the topics for discussion between the two major contenders during the 1988 election campaign. Dukakis maintained that there are not enough high-paying jobs. In 1960, the weekly wage in private non-agriculture and in manufacturing was mostly similar. In 1980, the weekly wage in manufacturing was about 22 percent higher than in private non-agriculture. *Ibid.*, table 468, page 392.

11. Diwan and Desai (1990a) discuss some of the implications and probabilities of successful perestroika in terms of the principles of Gandhian economics.

12. Reich (1983). In case one argues that 1982 was a recession year, the declining trend has continued. The capacity utilization ratio for 1985 is 80.

13. In 1986 this share is 19 percent. *Statistical Abstract of the United States*, 1988, table 1240, page 700.

14. *U.S. Bureau of Labor Statistics*, 1985.

15. Bailey and Charkrabarti (1988), page 5.

16. Bailey and Charkabarti (1988) also point out that estimation of productivity estimates starts from an aggregate and is broken down into industries thereby creating some possibilities of bias. On the other hand, we are comparing similar estimates over time so that these biases should not effect the trend.

17. *U.S. Bureau of Labor Statistics*, 1985.

18. According to Griliches (1988) "*A number of facts are not in dispute.* Around 1974–1975, output growth and associated productivity measures dropped sharply in the United States and in most other western industrialized nations and continued at rather low rates for most of the rest of the 1970s," p. 9 (emphasis added).

19. According to Bailey and Chakrabarti (1988), "Productivity growth in the U.S. economy has collapsed in recent years, and *the size of the collapse has the dimension of a crisis.* In the private business sector, output per hour of labor (one standard measure of productivity) grew 3.3 percent a year between 1948 and 1965 but slumped to 1.4 percent a year between 1965 and 1985. Had growth continued at its pre 1965 rate, U.S. output in 1985 would have been 45 percent higher than it actually was, with no additional labor used in production," p. 1 (emphasis added).

20. Bailey and Charkabarti (1988), p. 5. The U.S. productivity was a shade higher than that of Great Britain during the short period 1973–1979. For the remaining period it has been lower.

21. Magaziner and Reich (1983) place it at 9 percent in 1970 and 10 percent in 1978.

The *U.S. Bureau of Labor Statistics* places it at 10 percent for 1965–1973 and 11 percent for 1974–1982.

22. This may be because of the fact that U.S. industry in the last two decades has been particularly affected by mergers, which have resulted in the locking up of large sums of financial resources in take over bids thereby making the capital investment difficult. Also, multinationals have been transferring some of their manufacturing facilities in poor countries to take advantages of lower wage costs.

23. These details are contained in *Science and Engineering Indicators—1987*, National Science Board (1987), tables 4.2 and 4.3, pp. 236 and 237.

24. Griliches (1980).

25. U.S. Department of Labor, Bureau of Labor Statistics (1989), p. 28, table 18.

26. Olson (1982, 1988) is the most articulate exponent of this thesis.

27. The coalitions for collusive collective action "have an incentive to press for special privileges and monopoly. . . . A society dense with these coalitions concerned with distributional struggle instead of production is like a china shop filled with wrestlers battling over its contents and breaking more than they carry away" Olson (1988), p. 59.

28. Griliches (1988) makes this point.

29. Jorgenson (1988b) develops this thesis.

30. Jorgenson (1988a).

31. "Looking at the evidence we conclude that, although the scientific frontiers have continued to advance, *some technological opportunities were indeed missed*" Bailey and Chakrabarti (1988), pp. 11–12 (emphasis added).

32. Reich (1983) and Diwan (1990) articulate this thesis.

33. The concept of production culture extends to the institutional framework and the rules of the game within these institutions. Reich (1987), Piore and Sable (1984), and Dertouzos et al. (1989), among others, refer to cultural issues in production and the needed changes therein.

34. Diwan (1989) refers to some of these disadvantages.

35. National Research Council study (1986) speaks of this concensus. Tyson et al. (1988) discuss the importance of manufacturing and high technologies.

36. Naisbitt (1982) talks of megatrends that lean in this direction.

37. Toffler (1980).

38. Piore and Sabel (1984).

39. Freeman and Perez (1988).

40. This is not to say that quantity and price of such products do not go through a cycle. On the contrary, these suffer from far larger cyclical movements.

41. Reich (1987) discusses the rise of the Japanese-American corporation. The implication of the Japanese-American corporation is that Japanese capital is so much enmeshed with American economic production and activity that it may be difficult to distinguish what is truly American. The argument is made that it is the Japanese who are in the driver's seat and the Americans are simply passengers. Japanese design the product, and the U.S. supplies unskilled cheap labor.

2

International Competitiveness
and U.S. Manufacturing

INTERNATIONAL COMPETITIVENESS

One of the major changes that has taken place in the past two decades is the globalization of markets. Market globalization means that a particular product, specifically in the manufacturing sector, is produced and sold in many different parts and countries of the world. The production process itself has been divided so that parts of a complex product are manufactured in different countries and then assembled in another country, which exports or distributes this product to still different countries. Manufacturing forms a large part of the U.S. trade, and 60 percent of its manufactured goods are exported to the industrialized countries (this trend has increased a little in more recent years).[1] The United States, therefore, is quite susceptible to the influence of market globalization. Market globalization is both a cause and an effect of U.S. market penetration. Products from other countries have penetrated U.S. markets in large quantities. The import-penetration ratio in the United States was 6 percent in 1972, a decade later, in 1982, it had gone up to 8.5 percent, and by 1986 it was close to 12 percent.[2] This penetration is deeper in individual commodities and products. In one of the more important U.S. industries, namely automobiles, the penetration ratio has more than doubled—in 1972, it was 13.6 percent, in 1982 it grew to 26.7 percent, and in 1986 it was close to 28 percent.[3] This is a significant penetration of the U.S. market, particularly given that the U.S. automobile industry was perhaps the largest in the world. Had Japanese not allowed a voluntary quota policy that limited their export of automobiles to a ceiling of 2 million, these import penetration ratios would be still higher. Market globalization may also explain changes in U.S. import structure. In 1965, machinery and transport equipment formed 14 percent of total U.S. imports. In 1986, this ratio had jumped to 42 percent,[4] providing one explanation of the growing deficit in U.S. manufactures trade. The U.S. trade in manufactures had a positive balance of about $19 billion in 1980, but this balance has changed to a whopping deficit of $107 billion in 1984.

Although the United States trades with all the industrialized countries, both old and new, and its largest trading partner is its neighbor in the north, namely Canada, its primary competitors in the global market are Japan and West Germany—both countries that were destroyed in World War II and resurrected by financial and economic help from the United States. It is instructive to compare some of the relevant economic performance indices of the United States with these two competitors. Table 2.1 reports the trade balance in manufactures for the United States, Japan, and West Germany for 15 years, 1970–1984, in billions of U.S. dollars. This table provides a vivid comparative picture of U.S. strengths and weakness in international competitiveness. Japan's trade balance has been positive throughout and its rate of growth phenomenal. In 1970, its trade balance was +$12.5 billion; slightly less than that of West Germany. By 1984, this positive trade balance zoomed to +$170.7 billion, slightly less than twice that of West Germany. By comparison, the U.S. trade balance was just positive, merely +$3.4 billion in 1970, and by 1984, had catapulted to a deficit as large as the Japanese surplus, −$107.5 billion. The contrast could not be sharper.[5] Some argue that the trade balance was highly affected by the value of the dollar, a picture somewhat accentuated by the overvalued dollar; however, the overvalued dollar cannot explain the continuous unfavorable trade balance in manufactures. The reasons lie elsewhere. When one compares the trade in manufacturing between U.S. and Japan, one finds that Japan has been exporting more to the United States. This is now a well-accepted fact, and the trade figures tell the story. In 1980, the United States exports to Japan were worth $13 billion, whereas imports from Japan were worth $32 billion. The situation worsened in 1985— U.S. exports were worth only $16 billion while imports amounted to $70 billion.[6] It is obvious that Japanese goods are in demand in the United States and that Japan can compete favorably in the U.S. domestic market. The converse is also true—U.S. goods are not popular in the Japanese market and U.S. industry does not compete well there.

If one producer in a market can sell while another cannot, the theory of competition suggests that the seller is successful because of comparatively lower costs. In real-world markets, it is not so simple to identify all the cost elements; the products are never the same and consumers are neither rational nor fully informed. This argument, however, is sufficiently persuasive to make further pursuit of the concept worthwhile. Some argue that one of the major costs in manufacturing is labor.[7] Labor costs, however, are not necessarily proportionately related to wage rate, although the wage rate forms an integral part of labor costs. It is possible for wage costs to be higher in a production unit where the wage rate is lower, and vice versa. The theory of competition suggests that one reason why the United States cannot compete is because its wage costs are higher. Table 2.2 provides information on labor costs for the United States and six other industrialized countries for the 15-year period, 1970–1984. The labor costs have been made comparative by taking the labor costs of other countries as a percentage of U.S. labor costs in manufacturing. Labor costs in the West European countries, West Germany, France, Italy, and the United Kingdom, were higher than those of the United States for the 1970s and labor costs in West Germany and the United Kingdom in 1980 were one and a half to one and three-fourth times those of the United States. Since 1980, these West European countries and Japan have been reducing their labor costs so that by 1984 the labor costs in all the countries except the United Kingdom were lower than those in the United States. The only country whose labor costs have gone up since 1975 is Korea, but Korean labor costs were very low to start with. This table presents the conclusion that the competitors have been following practices to lower their costs and have been successful in doing so.

The other side of this cost comparison looks into changes in productivity. Productivity is the flip side of labor costs with the important difference that it does not depend on price, and therefore, market data. Instead it is a physical and technological measure. Whereas labor costs are part of the production process, productivity is the end result that takes into consideration all the other factors in operation. Generally, productivity is defined as labor-productivity, which is an output-labor quantity ratio.[8] Table 2.3 presents estimates of average annual rates of growth of labor productivity, defined as output per hour in manufacturing, for the United States and five other countries, Canada, France, West Germany, Japan, and the United Kingdom. These rates of productivity growth have been estimated for two periods, 1960–1973 and 1973–1983. The year 1973 has been chosen because it was the peak year and one in which a major change took place as a result of a sudden, large increase in the price of oil, which affected manufacturing industries in all countries. Two conclusions stand out. First, the productivity growth rates have been consistently higher for every country in the period 1960–1973 compared to 1973–1983. Second, the productivity growth rates for the United States have been equal to or lower than those of the other five countries for both periods. Thus during the period 1960–1973, the rate of productivity growth in Japan and Germany was approximately 3 and 1.5 times that of the United States, respectively. In the period 1973–1983, these ratios had moved up to 3.7 and 2 times, which is consistent with the observations from labor-costs data. Both these tables suggest that the competitive position of the U.S. vis-à-vis its competitors has been deteriorating over these 15 years.

The standard neoclassical production theory identifies two factors of production—labor and capital. We have already looked at labor costs. Although labor productivity takes into consideration the overall effect of capital, it is instructive to compare capital growth in the different countries. Table 2.4 presents capital investment in manufacturing as a ratio of total output for the United States and four other countries and for the two periods 1965–1973 and 1974–1982 as well as for the whole period of 1965–1982.[9] The ratios for the whole period define the technological structure of manufacturing in a country, which is liable to be stable over time and less affected by year to year fluctuations. Looking at the whole period, it is clear that the capital investment-output ratio in U.S. manufacturing is the lowest compared to France, West Germany, Japan, and United Kingdom. The Japanese capital investment output ratio is twice that of the United States.[10] When this period is divided into two subperiods, one notices a small tendency for this ratio to decline in virtually all other countries except the United States; the rise in the United States, however, is too slight to change the picture in any way. Many argue that the United States needs to promote capital investment in manufacturing, and many macroeconomic policies relate to incentives for capital investment.

The extension of the neoclassical theory of production involves consideration of another form of capital—knowledge. Many economists argue that R&D and the skill intensity of the labor force are also important factors that need to be taken into account. The United States started the policy of mass education quite some time ago. The government and private industry have been involved in investments in both public and private R&D. Table 2.5 places the expenditure on R&D in an international context.[11] The data is presented for 15 years for the United States and four other countries and related to the R&D expenditures as a percentage of GNP. One clear conclusion emerges. The R&D-GNP ratio in the United States has been sliding continuously. It was above 3 percent in 1964, but is now far below that. On the other hand, this ratio has been continually increasing in other industrialized countries. In 1985 this ratio was highest in Japan. West Germany has more or less caught up with the United States, and France is not far off. The aggregate R&D-GNP ratio, however, is not a good measure in so far as it includes defence expenditures. For purposes of competitiveness, the R&D expenditures devoted to commercial purposes is what is relevant. Both West Germany and Japan have very limited defence postures and expenditures. When this fact is taken into consideration, the R&D relative advantage becomes all the more favorable to West Germany and Japan. The table also gives non-defense R&D expenditure-GNP ratios. In terms of these ratios, Japan and Germany are far ahead; they spent as much as 2.75 and 2.53 percent of GNP while the U.S. ratio was only 1.85 in 1985. France also spent as much as U.S. on non-defense R&D.

EFFECTS OF INTERNATIONAL COMPETITION

As we have seen above, when compared with other industrialized countries, the labor costs in the United States have not declined as fast, the productivity rate has been lower, and the capital investment-output and R&D expenditure-GNP ratios have been lower than its competitors. There has, therefore, been a relative decline in U.S. manufacturing. This decline is rooted in the changes in the global market. Prior to 1965, foreign trade did not figure significantly in the U.S. economy. Only a small part of manufactured goods were traded internationally and an equally small proportion of foreign production entered the United States. This situation has changed dramatically. In 1980, 19 percent of the goods made by U.S. manufacturers were exported and more than 22 percent of the goods consumed in the United States were imported. But these figures understate the new importance of foreign competition. They show only where U.S. manufacturers had already been tested in the U.S. economy and emphasize the vastly widened scope of global competition. The most telling statistic is that by 1980 more than 70 percent of all goods produced in the United States were actively competing with foreign made goods. The United States has become a part of the world market.

American producers have not fared well in this new contest. Beginning in the mid-1960s, foreign imports have claimed an increasing share of the American market. By 1981, America was importing almost 26 percent of its cars; 25 percents of its steel; 60 percent of its televisions, radios, and tape recorders; 13 percent of its calculators; 27 percent of its metal forming machine tools; 35 percent of its textile machinery; and 53 percent of its numerically controlled machine tools. Twenty years ago, imports accounted for less than 10 percent of the U.S. market for each of these products. Between 1970 and 1980 imports from developing nations increased almost tenfold: from $3.5 billion to $30 billion. Similarly, during the 1970s the share of American manufactured goods in total world sales declined by 23 percent while every other industrialized nation, except Britain, maintained or expanded its share. Japan's share rose from 6 to 10.5 percent. The developing nations, as a group, expanded their share to 10 percent of the world trade in manufactured products by the mid-1970s, up from just 4 percent a few years before. By 1980 their share had increased to 13 percent. The diminishing U.S. presence in the international market has been particularly marked in capital-intensive, high-volume industries. Since 1963, the U.S. proportion of world automobiles sales has declined by one third, of industrial machinery by 10 percent, of telecommunication machinery by 50 percent, and of metal working machinery by 55 percent.

The growth of the developing countries' world market share has several related causes. Beginning with the General Agreement on Tariffs and Trade in 1947, industrialized nations gradually reduced their tariff levels, often granting special preference to developing countries. Also, the developing countries have gained easy access to international capital through the World Bank.[12] Technology has also moved fluidly across the globe. Developing countries can now acquire the world's most modern steel-rolling mills, paper machines, computer controlled machine tools, or fertilizer plants, and can get training and technical supervision to accompany the new production facilities. The global channels of sales and marketing have also opened up. The growth of large-scale retail outlets in industrialized nations has given the developing countries an efficient way to distribute their wares. These changes in the mid-1960s have enabled developing countries to move quickly into global industries. The globe is fast becoming a single market place. Goods are being made wherever they can be made cheapest,

regardless of national boundaries. The most efficient places for mass production
of standardized commodities are now the developing countries. Over a period
only of 15 years many of the developing countries have begun to specialize in
high-volume production, featuring long runs of standardized products. Their
production costs are lower than those of the United States, both because the
workers are paid lower wages and because their governments provide favored
access to cheap materials.

The trend of the change under way in U.S. manufacturing has now become
clear. First, industries like basic steel, automobile, consumer electronics, rubber,
and petrochemical industries, have become uncompetitive in the world market.
Second, now that the production can be fragmented into separate, globally scat-
tered operations, whole segments of other industries are becoming uncompetitive. Whatever the final product, those parts of U.S. production requiring
high-volume production processes and unsophisticated workers can be accomplished more cheaply in developing countries. And automation, far from halting
this trend, has actually accentuated it by making these countries better suited to
standardized production. Consequently, what began in the 1960s as a gradual
shift became by the late 1970s a major structural change in the world economy.
Assembly operations are being established in developing countries at a rapid
pace. The U.S. manufacturing base in these industries is eroding precipitously.
The United States must either halt this trend or seek new industries and technologies in which it has a competitive edge and in which it can maintain its base. This
is what the current debate is all about. Halting the eroding trend is a comparatively difficult task. Also it implies a lowering of the wage rate and of the
standards of living. Many argue about the desirability of seeking new industries,
which leads us to the question of what new industries or technologies there are
and how these new technologies are affecting international competitiveness?

It is argued in some quarters that some new technologies have come to the
surface in the past two decades that have made major changes in the modes of
production.[13] Some are suggesting that there are new trends, megatrends, that
are transforming our very living and life styles.[14] Others suggest that the industrial system is now on its way out,[15] particularly the model of industrialism and
the system of mass production.[16] Mass production involves producing standardized commodities in high volume, which requires that the production be separated from consumption. The development of the market and the market economy, the hallmark of this civilization, has required standardization, specialization,
synchronization, concentration, maximization, and centralization. The logic of
the system has been to produce the largest number of commodities to gain
economies of scale in order to make maximum profits. The emphasis has been on
the massive: mass production, mass education, mass media, mass transport, et
cetera. This system of production required institutions consistent with it, and the
three key social institutions of the mass production society have been the nuclear
family, the factory-style school, and giant corporations. The ideas that gave it
shape have been based on three scientific principles: progress is linear, survival

of the fittest, and nature is for exploitation. The energy base of this civilization has been non-renewable oil and petroleum. The genesis of the mass production is the factory or assembly line.[17] Mass production depended on massive capital investment, and labor has been treated as a complement to this capital. Some argue that this system is a source of the U.S. decline.[18] Since this system affects every country in the world, the decline is not only in the United States but also everywhere else.[19] However, the decline in the United States is relatively more pronounced because the United States had reached the highest level of mass production civilization.[20] If this argument is valid, then the industrial system is in a problematical situation and the regime of mass production may be coming to an end.[21] At a somewhat less broad and more concrete level, it is being argued that there is a change in the techno-economic paradigm. A paradigm is basically a world view, or an understanding of the world by an explicit theory. The techno-economic paradigm attempts to define the world in terms of a technology and the socio-economic institutions consistent with and supportive of such a technology.[22] The system idea carries the concept of such a paradigm to its logical conclusion. Thus viewed, mass production formed a techno-economic paradigm in which the United States was the most successful.[23] It can be added in passing, that some have compared the slow down or stagnation of the 1970s and 1980s with the downswing of the Kondratiev business cycle.[24] This idea about large business cycles is not inconsistent with changes in the techno-economic paradigm. There is now a growing consensus that the mass production technology defined by smoke stacks or sunset industries has little future, and that it is because of the decline of these mass production technologies that the United States is experiencing difficulties of adjustment, just as England and other similar countries faced adjustment problems with the ascendancy of the mass production technology paradigm.

NEW TECHNOLOGIES AND RELATED INSTITUTIONS

Some observers are suggesting that we are now in a period of some new major innovations, such as microelectronics and bio-technologies. The question is whether or not these new innovations can usher in a new techno-economic paradigm. A techno-economic paradigm is much different from innovations in the sense that it is much more comprehensive. One can distinguish among three types of innovation-related changes.[25] First are the ordinary innovations that simply improve on the existing products and processes. These are incremental changes and follow from the day to day improvements in the production process. At their most trivial level, these are merely the changes in packaging and color that are so much encouraged by the forces of monopolistic competition. At a certain meaningful level, these changes involve R&D, and some improvements, implied by the logic of cost, are in the nature of developments in the process of diffusion.[26] In the U.S. context such changes have primarily involved scaling-up plants and equipments and improvements for specific purposes. These are not innovations in the true sense—although, they do involve changes in techniques and technology—because individually these changes do not amount to much. The economic logic behind these technological changes, however, is important because they are the product of an institutional set up made up of large bureaucratic corporations. They, therefore, do not reflect Keynesian "animal spirits" or acts of Schumpeterian "innovators" or "entrepreneurs." On the other hand, collectively, they can, and do, seem to produce visible change. Since these changes are motivated by cost considerations, they improve productivity by reducing input-output ratios.

The second group of changes are the proper innovations, the innovations that Schumpeter had in mind.[27] These result from advances in knowledge and, although not created by specific R&D, do involve R&D intensively. These are fluke affairs resulting from university research or an application of some new theory. By their very nature, they are not continuous improvements but are instead disjointed and discontinuous. Once a basic idea has been discovered and some of its applications look promising, there is deliberate and focussed research to work out applications; here R&D becomes intensive and necessary. It is still a hit and miss affair. The profit or cost motivation is not effective in ensuring the supply of these innovations, which depend, in a fundamental way, on public awareness and government support.[28] Not only are these innovations distributed discontinuously but their distribution over different sectors and activities is also uneven. However, their impact is large in so far as they open up whole new products with new markets and new processes with new suppliers. Because of their large impact, these innovations also require large investments. It is these innovations that Schumpeter thought could lead to long waves of growth. At this point, it is necessary to make a distinction between these innovations and their relationship to the process of technological change. There is no doubt that a growth process would require these innovations; they are a necessary condition. However, by themselves, such innovations are not a sufficient condition for growth. Even a cluster of these innovations, by themselves, are not sufficient to produce continuous growth.[29]

To understand the growth process we need something more, something that congeals these innovations into a positive force, which leads us to the techno-economic paradigm. The radical inventions, combined with the first category of small technological changes, placed in an institutional environment becomes a self-propagating process. When this happens, there is a techno-economic paradigm. The essential conditions for this to happen are that some of the innovations must have three properties.[30] First, the effect of the innovations must be to reduce the price of a commodity or process, *continuously*. Second, the supply of such commodities or processes affected by these innovations should be virtually *unlimited*. Third, the effect of these innovations should be *pervasive* in promoting more innovations and in their application in other and different sectors of the economy. These properties ensure cost reductions in the goods and processes in which the innovations are involved. Their pervasiveness enlarges old markets

and establishes new ones. Cost reduction and enlarged markets together provide
the necessary condition for a self-propagating process. The sufficient condition is
that socio-economic institutions must also be consistent with this process. Institutional framework, in this context, embraces a very large spectrum containing
a wide variety of institutions: economic, international, national, political, and
social. It begins with the individual and family and expands to the international.
It involves rules of the game, logic of production, social welfare, community,
locality, and the like. What the techno-economic paradigm means, then, is the
technology of production, its continuous upgrade, and the institutions that promote it. It is the institutional framework that ensures the growth process; it is
necessary for the diffusion process to start and continue. As these innovations
take hold of the production system, the organization of production becomes
crucial for successful production and marketing of the new goods. The organization not only has to ensure that the production process continues efficiently but
also must be able to recognize major innovations and their various ramifications.
As this process spreads from one sector to another, the whole society is engaged
and has to be prepared to accept the rules of the game and the logic of such
production. Some argue that the success of the United States during the expan-
sionary phase of the mass-production techno-economic paradigm was primarily
due to its institutional framework: its nuclear family and mobile labor force, its
materialism and the resulting demand to have a materialist standard of living. For
obvious reasons, such a process is a gradual one; a society takes a good deal of
time to change its values, its social set up, its rewards and punishments, and the
other rules of the game.

It is now recognized that a new techno-economic paradigm is in place, one that
is international in character and based fundamentally on microelectronic, or
information-based, technologies. These technologies are intrinsically different
from the mass-production ones based on oil. This technology satisfies all three
conditions: (1) The price of the chip has been continuously falling. (2) The
supply of chips is available in as large a supply as desired. Scientific discoveries
and concomitant innovations in the memory capacity of chips are in full swing.
The miniaturizing process is already packing a chip with memory that would
have taken large space only a few years ago. (3) Microchips are now embedded
in a multitude of consumer and producer goods; they are pervasive indeed. The
production system for microchips, microelectronics, and related technologies is
vastly different from the continuous-flow and assembly-line factory of mass-
production technologies. The ideal type of a production system in microelectronics is an integrative one; integrating various functions of design, management, production, and marketing. The labor requirements are for broader
multi-purpose basic technical skills instead of the narrow specialization of the
earlier era. Instead of homogeneity, the work process seeks diversity and flexibility. In view of the radically different nature of this production system, the success
of the new techno-economic paradigm requires different social and economic
institutions; e.g., team work instead of individual work, cooperation instead of

competition or confrontation, loyalty instead of mobility, decentralization instead of hierarchy, small instead of large.

Because of the falling prices, pervasiveness of use, and sufficiently large supplies, the cost structure of the new technologies gives them an edge over the old ones. There is a potential for quantum jumps in productivity as an industry moves from the old to the new paradigm.[31] This jump in productivity, however, is possible only if the socio-economic system encourages diffusion of these technologies. Productivity growth follows from the establishment of the techno-economic paradigm. Such a crystallization results in a major change. There is a new "best practice" form of organization at both the plant and the firm level.[32] There is a major emphasis on science and technology, both at the R&D level and in schools and colleges. The new techno-economic paradigm is based on the idea that scientific discoveries, as against their applications, are a continuous process so that there is an added emphasis on R&D at all levels,[33] which is reflected in the U.S. press today. A constant comparing of U.S. education and learning levels in science with those in Japan and Germany, even with the Union of Soviet Socialist Republics, is pointing out that science education in the United States is highly deficient. The new paradigm involves a less specialized but more technologically oriented work force with greater breadth in technological education to fulfill the needs of a different skill profile. All this productive process spills into, and integrates with, the consumption needs and habits of society so that goods produced by new technologies are required. The product mix is undergoing a change.[34] Once these side effects come into play they further encourage capital investment in the direction of the new paradigm technologies. Supportive government policies cannot lag too far behind because new vested interests are forming and growing that influence policies in favor of providing appropriate subsidies and externalities to promote new technologies. A new socio-institutional framework is required and is coming into operation.[35]

The new techno-paradigm is international in character, in the sense that the new technologies can be, and have been, introduced into many different countries. Since this paradigm is still in the initial stages of its development and establishment, many countries have the opportunity to enter into the related technologies. Reductions in the cost of communication, itself dependent on the cost of the microelectronics, has made integration of the market easier and spread of the paradigm international. This paradigm is based, in an essential way, on (1) scientific knowledge, (2) skill and experience of the work force, (3) capital costs, and (4) locational advantages. Accordingly, it presents different entry levels for small and large firms in one country as well as for different countries.[36] The four different threshold levels for entry into new production technologies are (1) traditional investment costs, (2) level of scientific and technological knowledge, (3) degree of skills and experience, and (4) geographical and locational advantages. By contrast, investment costs alone defined entry levels in the old mass-production technologies. Looking into threshold levels for entry into new technologies reveals that investment costs are the least important, which follows partly from the nature of new technologies and the continuously falling price of its essential ingredients and partly because the markets are new and still not fully developed. It is thus not accidental that small companies have been able to get ahead in new technologies.[37] Scientific and technological knowledge is determined by the macroeconomic policies of an economy, which provide investments in education in the society at large. Most industrialized countries have well-developed educational systems so that a particular country does not have a special advantage in this respect. Similarly, skills and experience do not provide any great advantage to any particular country because the threshold levels of skill and experience is low since these technologies are in the initial stages of growth. The new technologies are promoting global markets because of their accessibility and different threshold levels.

Given the shift to this new techno-economic paradigm and its international character, U.S. industry is finding that it must both move into these new technologies and face competition at the international level. The new technologies are sometimes called sunrise industries or "high-tech" industries; "high technologies" for short to distinguish them from the existing mass-production or "low technologies." The question is whether or not high tech can be a solution to the problems of U.S. manufacturing. This one poses a number of other questions. How are industries classified into high- and low-tech industries? What are the characteristics of the high-tech sector of U.S. manufacturing? How does the United States compare with its competitors in this high-tech sector? What is the nature of productivity and cost structure in this high-tech sector?

DEFINING HIGH-TECHNOLOGY INDUSTRIES

In view of the emergence of a new techno-economic paradigm, a shift of the industrial base toward high-technology industries merits attention and is being argued by persuasive groups.[38] The advantages of high-technology industries are being recognized. Over the last few years the topic, and the role, of high-technology industries in economic recovery as well as in world market competition has emerged from near obscurity to become a national economic policy debate. Accordingly, efforts are being made to track closely the developments in these industries. Increasing importance is being attached to the implications of these developments for productivity, international competition, national defence, and the general standard of living. Although it is recognized that high technology is necessary for the vitality of the U.S. manufacturing sector, it is still not clear what one means by high technology. How does one define high-technology industries? How are the high-technology industries different from other industries? These are not simple questions. The term high-technology connotes different industries and activities to different groups of people. For state and local economic development planners, it means emerging growth industries that have the potential to provide the solution for high localized unemployment. For entrepreneurs, these indicate new products and new process, often labor-saving processes. In congressional and political circles, the term implies the promise of both economic recovery and achievement of competitive success. In the midst of all these different meanings, an unavoidable fact emerges: we lack a standard definition of what high-technology industries constitute.[39]

Before we attempt to classify industries as high tech, let us ask what the need is to classify an industry as high tech in the first place. It seems to us that the need to classify certain industries as high tech arises from the fact that the rate of technological change is continuously increasing. The advances in science and their applications are causing fundamental changes in both products and processes. This follows from the pervasiveness of the new technologies. While some industries are better able to increase their efficiency by incorporating these advanced scientific principles in their products and processes, others are not able to do so. In view of major and continuous advances in science and related technologies, the former industries are radically different from the latter group of traditional industries based on mass-production techniques. These traditional industries applied earlier scientific principles and are inhibited by their structures from incorporating new scientific advances. This is a significant point and needs elaboration. To incorporate advances in technology, any industry has to accept two realities: (1) these advances are major and, therefore, involve major shifts in capital and complementary skills, and (2) these advances involve a continuous attention to change. In other words, these are not simple scientific advances. Instead, these advances are continuous and their directions are unforeseen. The technological applications, therefore, also need to be continuous. For example, the microchip is changing so fast and adding complexity and memory continuously. Production processes for chip-producing industry are thus undergoing serious changes.[40] These processes cannot be programmed according to a fixed set of rules covering all contingencies. Instead, production in this industry requires high-level skills to cope with the unanticipated problems, and opportunities, that may arise. This is clearly not the case in traditional industries. Production efficiency in traditional industries can be better increased by scaling up of the old techniques than by adopting new ones. Thus, the unit costs of producing simple, standardized products like cotton textiles, basic steel, or rubber generally decline more with long production runs than with improvements in the production processes. Manufactures of these products, therefore, do well to emphasize large capacity, cheap labor, and cheap materials rather than the incorporation of advances in scientific principles. Once one recognizes the complexity and continuity of scientific and related technological advances, the need to identify and classify high-technology industries becomes obvious.

In the literature on industry studies, high-technology industries have been loosely defined. Experts differ about the constituents of these groups of industries. In the case of some industries, such as those that manufacture microchips, computers, telecommunications, aeroplanes, electronic components, new drugs, and medicine, a majority of the experts agree. The disagreement arises only at the edge of the set and not at its core. The general perception among most researchers is that industries defining the high-technology division must involve some degree of sophistication. What remains unclear, however, are (1) the required degree of sophistication, (2) whether the sophistication should reflect itself at the product level or in the process or both, and (3) what the indices are for identifying technological sophistication. It seems that technological sophistication has to be both at the process and product level. Although it may sometimes be difficult to separate a product from a process, products and processes are highly interrelated. It is not an easy task to identify the degree of technological sophistication involved in either a product or a process. In empirical studies, technological sophistication is usually defined with reference to an index that can be simply determined, in a way nullifying the idea about the degree of sophistication. A variety of indices have been suggested in the literature.

A close look at published research and reports on high technology prepared by different federal and state government agencies indicates that the three criteria generally used to classify industries as high tech are (1) research and development expenditures as a percentage of sales, (2) the use of scientific and technological personnel relative to total employment, and (3) the perceived degree of technological sophistication of the product produced by an industry. Virtually all the definitions suggested so far are based on one or a combination of these measures. The techniques used to combine them varies between definitions. The proposed definitions, however, can be divided into two major groups: (1) product-based definitions and (2) industry-based definitions.

PRODUCT-BASED DEFINITIONS

The impetus to develop a high-technology classification of industries has come from the need to look into trade in technology intensive goods and commodities. In a 1977 study National Science Foundation (NSF) data was used on "applied R&D expenditures by product field" with U.S. Department of Commerce (DOC) data on the value of product shipments by standard industrial classification (SIC) codes as a basis for developing data on R&D intensive products. These were called R&D intensities. The underlying assumption of this statistical exercise is that R&D reflects technological sophistication so that high R&D intensity signifies new and high technologies. These intensities were calculated for the period 1968–1970. R. Kelly ranked products by R&D intensity, classified them by technology, and designated the first quartile of these R&D intensive products as high-technology goods.[41] Subsequently, this analysis was refined to classify product groups into above average R&D intensities as technology intensive goods. On the basis of this definition, the following products were defined as technology intensive: aircrafts and parts (SIC 372); office, computing, and accounting machines (SIC 357); electric transmission and distribution equipment (SIC 361–362); electrical industrial apparatus, communication equipment, and electronic components (SIC 283); plastic materials synthetics (SIC 282); engines and turbines (SIC 351); agricultural chemicals (SIC 287); professional, scientific, and measuring instruments (SIC 381–82); industrial chemicals (SIC 281); and radio and television receiving equipment (SIC 365). Basically this methodology was used to specifically identify technology intensive product groups for trade purposes using the standard international trade classification (SITC) instead of SIC codes, and more recent data series.[42] R&D intensities were determined with SITC codes, facilitating comparisons of international trade data. Interestingly, the only major difference between this extension and the earlier study was the elimination of automobiles (SITC 732) from the list of high-tech industries.

Another approach involving a review of the U.S. government's SIC codes manual was made by a state agency in 1979.[43] This definition identified 20 industrial groups as high tech, based on a perceived degree of technological sophistication of the products. A list of these industries is given in Table 2.6. This list includes such industries as industrial inorganic chemicals, plastics and synthetic resins, drugs, and engines and turbines. These industries are defined as high tech by the earlier definition as well. However, this list also includes some of the services listed in the 73 and 89 two-digit SIC codes, such as, computer programming services, commercial R&D laboratories, business management and consulting services, and engineering and architectural services. One complication of this approach is the difficulty of defining "degree of sophistication," which, of necessity, involves subjective judgment. This subjective judgment is conditioned not only by investigator bias but also by the objective of the analysis. If, for example, one is interested in the implications of high tech for capital and labor requirements for a state, technological complexity rather than sophistication may be considered appropriate and relevant. Complexity is justified as a form of sophistication and used to classify high-tech industries.[44] It is because of subjectivity in identifying sophistication that such a classification ends up including services in an industrial classification.[45] These two definitions discussed above lead to different classifications; one includes a particular industry while the other excludes it. If an objective of the analysis is to concentrate on an industry *per se,* a classification scheme of the second kind may not be helpful.

In 1979, the Congressional Office of Technology Assessment (OTA) used a much broader and more complex approach to define high-tech firms and industries.[46] They described companies engaged in design, development, and introduction of new products and manufacturing processes involving systematic application of science and technology as high-technology firms. The study points out that such companies typically use state-of-the-art techniques; have a high proportion of R&D costs; employ a high proportion of scientific, engineering, and technical personnel; and serve small and specialized markets. It is not clear if these companies deal with only products in the manufacturing sector or in any activity whatsoever including agriculture, services, or the like. The emphasis in this definition is on companies and not on products. One may argue that these companies will, *ipso facto,* contribute to the high-tech industrial sector. Whether these relate to the industrial sector is a matter of fact and not of assumption. What is not obvious is if, and how, they relate to the industrial sector. Another problem with this approach regards the weights that may be given to various factors involved. At what level does a particular factor become relevant? It is a useful approach when one studies a particular region and a particular industrial park, but loses its usefulness when comparisons have to be made with different industries and different regions. Aggregation would suffer from the fallacy of gross categories.

Another, and comparatively recent, approach has used input-output analysis, R&D expenditure, and shipment data by product groups to develop an index of technology intensity.[47] Using the input-output matrix and the value of R&D embodied in the various inputs used in the final product, the percentage of R&D embodied in the final product was determined. An estimate of total R&D was made, based on direct R&D expenditures on product development and indirect R&D expenditures contributed by inputs. The products were then ranked according to the total R&D-shipment intensity. Products with significant R&D intensities were designated as high-technology products. There is a certain amount of subjectivity associated with the concept of a "significant level" of R&D intensity. These were defined as products with "above the average" R&D intensities. Although this procedure seems reasonable and practical, it lacks the finesse of a principle.

The most recent approach to product-defined high-technology classification comes from a study for the Center of Economic Studies of the Bureau of the Census.[48] Once again, the need for such a study arose from the observation that the U.S. trade in high-tech industries showed a deficit in 1986. This brought the concept of high-tech into further focus. The general perception is that the high-tech sector has a favorable trade balance, but trade data on high-tech industries seem to contradict this general perception. Could the contradiction be caused by measurement errors? The study attempts to identify advanced technology products and analyzes the U.S. trade balance for these products. This study differs from other DOC studies in that it does not use any data on R&D or make an attempt to develop an index of technology intensities. The basic premise of this study is that such indices, particularly in the aggregate form, make the untenable assumption that all products in a group have the same intensities. The study also breaks new ground by using information from scientists and technologists as to what they consider to be high-tech products. On the basis of interviews with scientists and technologists, it defines what it calls "advanced or high-technology fields."[49] These are: biotechnology, life sciences (medical), optoelectronics, computers and telecommunications, electronics, computer-integrated manufacturing, materials design, aerospace, and weapons and nuclear technology. Given these high-technology fields, the next step is to identify products, processes, and breakthroughs that can be considered on the leading edge of their fields. Based on this information about fields and breakthroughs, every product traded in international trade was examined to determine if it contained "significant" amounts of leading edge technologies. In other words, the classifying investigator asked if these products embody some of these leading edge technologies in an essential way. The level of significance was, for obvious reasons, left to the investigators to decide on a case-by-case basis.[50] Recognizing that this classification system is liable to be affected by the judgments of individual investigators,[51] the researchers took steps to reduce this possible source of bias by reviewing the data with trade experts and by comparing it with other measures in other agencies of the U.S. DOC. There are, however, some other problems. The data relate only to products and not processes, resulting in a partial rather than a complete listing of high-technology industries. Even the ten fields selected are not comprehensive, a few others are equally relevant and advanced, for example, composite materials. Perhaps the classification is useful, particularly in view of the extensive details on seven-digit SIC longitudinal data that the Census Bureau has; however, when these products are aggregated at four-, three-, and two-digit SIC industries, some of the advantages of detail are lost.

INDUSTRY-BASED DEFINITIONS

For larger policy purposes, a definition of high tech that spans a whole industry rather than a product is needed. This macro approach seeks to describe a high-technology industrial sector. Of course, given high-tech products, one can aggregate these into industries by the method of industrial classification, which is the micro approach. Which of these two approaches is better depends on a number of factors; for example, the purpose of the classification scheme, the criteria for such a classification, the limitations of time and resources, and the complexity and dynamics of technological change. Both approaches can play a useful role. The macro approach of defining a whole industry as a high-tech industry is a comparatively easy task and is the least sensitive to minor changes in products so that estimates based on this approach are more robust. On the other hand, because all products in an industry are not high tech, the macro approach is liable to overestimate the size of the high-tech sector. The second, or the micro, approach is very detailed. Accordingly, it is liable to be comparatively more accurate. However, it requires a very large data base and a good deal of time. Another difficulty with the micro approach is its sensitivity to small changes in definitions and criteria. Different investigators can easily end up with different values of a high-tech sector. Since the need for such classifications is generally felt by government departments with time pressures and labor time limitations, it is not surprising that the first, or macro, approach has generally been the rule.

In an effort to identify technology intensive trade, two-digit SIC-based definition of high-technology industries was developed.[52] Scientific and engineering manpower, R&D expenditures, and relative level of skilled workers were used as criteria for defining categories of industries concerned. As a result, the following industries were classified as technology intensive or high-tech industries: Chemicals (SIC 28), non-electrical machinery (SIC 35), electrical machinery (SIC 36), transport equipment (SIC 37), and instruments (SIC 38). Basically, there are five two-digit SIC industries, namely SIC 28 and SIC 35–38. Even for 1975, this is too small a subset. The National Science Foundation followed a similar approach,[53] basing their definition on the number of scientists and engineers employed in R&D and company R&D expenditures as a percentage of sales by two-digit SIC codes. The NSF criteria differ, although slightly, from the earlier approach. The major difference is the consideration of scientists and engineers for R&D purposes. As a result of this change, transportation (SIC 37) falls from the class of high-tech industries. The remaining four SIC industries identified earlier are consistent with this definition as well.

Recently another study has defined high-technology industries as those "possessing above average levels of scientific and engineering skills and capabilities, compared to other industries, and currently experiencing the accelerated technological growth associated with the germination and evolution stages along their respective S curves."[54] The choice of criteria for defining high-tech industries is based on the following argument. For traditional industries, the rate of increase in S-curve, which measures technological growth over time, falters after the evolution phase is passed. For high-tech industries, on the other hand, investments in R&D and consequent expansion in the scientific knowledge base leads to the creation of a new S-curve. This argument is consistent with the idea of a new technology paradigm. Trends in R&D and number of scientists and engineers per 1,000 employees within an industry were used as indicators of trends in an industry's technological growth. Following identification of variables, the definition was applied to 25 U.S. industry groups consisting of either two- or three-digit SIC industries. Nine industry groups were classified as high-tech industries, including drugs and medicine (SIC 283); petroleum refining (SIC 29); office, computing, and accounting equipment (SIC 366); electronic components (SIC 367); other electronic equipment (SIC 261–64, 369); aircraft and missiles (SIC 372, 376); scientific and mechanical measuring equipment (SIC 381–82); and capital, surgical, photographic, and other equipment (SIC 383–87). Compared with earlier definitions, the difference here is that this group of high-tech industries includes SIC 29 and SIC 261–64. There are two possible reasons for this extension of the set defining high-tech industries. First, it follows from the hypothesis of the techno-economic regimes. As this regime spreads, more industries are coming under its purview so that the coverage increases with time. Second, the definition itself is broader, because (1) it considers only one criterion based on R&D scientists and engineers and (2) the dividing line is an average.

The most recent definition of high-tech industry is based on occupational profiles.[55] High-tech industries are defined as those in which the proportion of engineers, engineering technicians, computer scientists, life scientists, and mathematicians exceeds the manufacturing average. The object here is to identify as many occupations dealing with new technologies as possible in the hope that these occupations reflect the technological capacity of an industry to capture technological complexities and expertise needed for development of new and technologically advanced products. Although this criterion delves into great detail at the occupation level, it actually broadens the category that defines high-tech industries because of the inclusion of technicians along with engineers and scientists. It is not surprising that this criterion yields a much larger category of high-tech industries, a list of 29 three-digit SIC manufacturing industries, which are listed in Table 2.7. Compared with earlier ones, this list is the most comprehensive, including all the high-tech industries defined by earlier definitions as well as added ones. It is a much larger list and also the most recent. Here again, the spread of the techno-economic regime has led to more industries using new technologies.

For the purpose of identifying high-tech industries, the criterion of scientific and technological personnel has been widely used, and the concept of scientific and technological personnel is a wide one. It includes a number of different occupational categories, not all of which are directly related to the development and application of new scientific principles, which, in the last analysis, is the distinguishing characteristic of high-tech industries. For example, computer operators, computer service technicians, and other high-tech machinery repairers may well be, and many times are, considered as technological personnel. The increased proportion of such workers can be attributed to many factors other than the technological sophistication involved in the products and processes of the industry concerned. Moreover, their work does not involve any in-depth knowledge of theories and principles of science and engineering underlying advancement of technology. If this is true, they would not be a good basis for identifying high-tech industries. There is, however, a counter argument. Not all high-tech industrial work has been, or needs to be, done by only engineers and scientists. Some sophisticated technological work can be reduced to simple tasks. Although these simple tasks by themselves may not define high tech, they may be an integral part of high tech.

R&D expenditures as a percentage of total industry sales is another widely used measure of high-tech industries. The R in R&D consists of two components: basic and applied research. Basic research refers to scientific explorations for advancing knowledge and pushing its frontiers. Most of this work is undertaken by scientists within universities and research institutions; only a small portion of the research done in industrial organizations falls into this category. Instead, applied research makes up the majority of industrial research. Applied research is loosely defined as an application of scientific and engineering principles with the clear objective of obtaining economic returns. It is not easy to distinguish between these two parts of R in R&D, although it is well recognized that applied and basic research are different. Publicly funded research, sponsored by the NSF, the National Institute of Health (NIH), and other government agencies, was once carried out primarily in the universities and dealt generally with basic research, but in recent years the distinction between applied and basic has been blurred as these agencies have shifted funding in favor of applied research.[56] The D in R&D refers to development—development of products and processes. For purposes of meeting the market, research proceeds from an idea to a concrete and narrow principle and to its test in terms of materials that eventually form the product. Development then identifies those areas of principles that can be translated into products and processes with a market potential. The object, and hope, is that these will eventually become commercial products and processes. Since markets, by their very nature, are uncertain, the movement from products and processes with a market potential to actual commercial products and processes involves uncertainty and risk; the development process is therefore risky and costly. In view of its involvement with scientific and technological knowledge and its eventual application in commercial products and processes, R&D activity provides a significant quantifiable proxy for level of technology in an industry. R&D activity is conventionally measured by categorical expenditures rather than by actual measured effort. Accordingly, R&D expenditures provide a good measure for industries in the early stages of a product development cycle. On the other hand, this measure has the disadvantage of not identifying mature and stable industries that should be considered high tech.[57] Another difficulty with this measure is associated with fluctuations caused by changing economic conditions. Cyclical changes in the economy, variations in public fiscal policies dealing with taxes and subsidies, and direct government expenditures cause variations in R&D spending. A reliable measure of R&D expenditures would require the ability to isolate the effects of technological achievement in an industry from those arising out of other economic factors, particularly in a dynamic economy.

OUR DEFINITION OF HIGH TECHNOLOGY

We have suggested above a number of problems with each criterion for the identification of high-tech industries, which suggests that the best proxy for the technological intensity of specific products or industries has yet to be determined. Even if a general agreement on measures of high-technology intensity were reached, the very nature of technological change would preclude a final definition of specific products or industries as high technology, because technology is constantly changing. Although the alternative criteria discussed so far don't provide a good basis for defining high-technology industries, individually, they do contain important elements relating to characteristics of high technology. R&D expenditures and scientific and technological personnel, *jointly,* reflect major features in new and continuous scientific innovations being incorporated in products and processes.

The Bureau of Labor Statistics (BLS) has developed three different definitions of high-tech industries.[58] These three specific definitions consider an industry as high-tech if (1) its technology-oriented workers account for a proportion of total employment that is at least one and a half times the average of all industries; (2) the ratio of R&D expenditures to net sales are at least twice the average for all industries; and (3) it satisfies two conditions: (a) its proportion of technology-

oriented workers is equal to or greater than the average for all manufacturing
industries, and (b) its ratio of R&D expenditures to sales is close or above the
average of all manufacturing industries. It seems to us that the third part of the
definition is superior to alternative definitions for several reasons. First, the
criterion used is a stringent one; it encompasses the requirements of both scientists
and technicians on the one hand and R&D expenditures on the other, as a basis for
technological achievement. Consequently, it relates to and compares with high-
tech industries classified by other definitions discussed earlier. Second, the
measure of scientists and technicians used in this definition is comprehensive since
it includes occupational categories that meet high-technology needs. The specific
categories included in the measure are engineers, life and physical scientists,
mathematical specialists, engineering and science technicians, and computer
specialists. Since most of these professions are certified by national boards, there
is a degree of consistency across occupational categories. Third, data needed for
this definition are provided by the NSF and BLS on a regular basis. These data are
comparatively more standardized, comprehensive, and reliable. Fourth, a ranking
procedure that picks up the top half of two distributions is least arbitrary. In view of
these advantages, we have used this definition to identify high-tech industries. The
industries included in our definition of the high-technology manufacturing sector
are listed in Table 2.8.[59]

TRADE PERFORMANCE—HIGH TECH VERSUS U.S. MANUFACTURING

An important question is whether and to what extent high tech plays an
important role in the competitive strength of U.S. manufacturing. The U.S. trade
balance in manufacturing and high-tech industries is given in Table 2.9. It is clear
that the overall trade balance in manufacturing has deteriorated steadily.[60] In
1972, the United States even experienced a deficit; however, the manufacturing
trade balance recovered in 1973 and showed some strength till 1975, but it seems
that this strength was not sustainable. Starting in 1976, the trade balance slid
downward and continued a decline till 1980. Recent data suggest that this balance has continued to decline further. It moved from a surplus of $12 billion in
1980 to a whopping deficit of $107 billion in 1985. The situation has not
improved in the past 3 to 4 years; instead the deficit has persisted at an alarmingly high level.

By comparison, the United States had a trade surplus in high-technology
industries throughout the entire period of 20 years. It is generally believed that
high-technology goods provide the cutting edge of international competitiveness
and contribute significantly to economic growth as well as to trade performance.[61] A number of studies have claimed that (1) the high-technology sector
of the U.S. economy has grown much faster over the last decade and a half than
the more mature industrial sectors; (2) a growing percentage of U.S. manufacturing exports contain high technology products; and (3) while U.S. trade balance in

low-technology products has deteriorated, trade balance in high-technology products has remained positive, except in recent years[62] (it was only in 1986 that there has been a deficit in this balance). Starting in 1968, the trade balance in high-technology industries has exceeded the trade balance in manufacturing for every year. In many years, this surplus in high-technology trade was the strength in the overall manufacturing trade balance, especially in 1972 and 1973 when total manufacturing experienced trade deficits. The drop in high-technology trade balance in 1972 coincided with the trade deficit in the manufacturing industry. Following a slight decline in 1976 and 1977, the high-technology trade balance continued to grow until 1980. The 1980s have not been good to this balance; although still positive, it started sliding down. By 1985, this balance fell to $7 billion from a balance of $30 billion in 1980, and in 1986, this balance became a deficit. The decline in the trade balance has not resulted from a decline in exports. The major culprit has been an increase in imports. Between 1980 and 1985 imports virtually doubled while exports maintained their normal growth.

Looking into growth rates of exports and imports betters an understanding of the trade balance. To estimate growth rates, we selected four periods; namely 1962–1969, 1969–1976, 1976–1980, and 1980–1985. Because of a well-defined trend in exports and imports reflected in the trade balance, the conclusions are not sensitive to selection of a time period for analytical purposes. Although the time periods we have selected are, *prima facie,* somewhat arbitrary, the empirical evidence does not change. The quantitative magnitudes are basically illustrative and illuminate the general thesis. The estimated annual growth rates for these periods for both exports and imports and for the two sectors, manufacturing and high tech, are given in Table 2.10. The table shows that the rates of growth of imports in manufacturing have always outpaced those of exports. Not only have import growth rates been higher, they are higher by a large magnitude—more than double in the earlier period and virtually 10 times as large during the 1980s. During the 1980s the growth rates of exports were mostly stagnant; a mere 2 percent growth rate while imports grew at 24 percent per year. Some argue that the high growth rates of imports reflect the pull of growing U.S. demand and the overvalued U.S. dollar. No doubt the U.S. dollar was overvalued and the U.S. economy did experience early recovery from the 1982 recession; however, these two reasons are not sufficient to explain the growth in imports. After catching up with the growth rates of other countries, and after a decline in the value of the dollar, the trade deficit has persisted; exports have done well but imports have continued to grow at a fast rate. The high growth rates of imports also reflect a deterioration in the U.S. competitive position. U.S. domestic costs and productivity performances have also contributed to increasing imports. In the high-tech sector, the United States started with an advantageous position; high levels of exports and few imports. In 1962, for example, imports of high tech formed only 25 percent of the exports of high-tech products. As late as 1980, imports were only half as great as exports. The situation worsened in the 1980s, however, when exports virtually stagnated while imports grew at very high non-historical rates. The trade balance was, naturally, undone. Part of the reason why, even in the high-tech sector, the United States has been experiencing high import growth rates may lie in the nature of the new techno-economic paradigm. As new technologies have spread, the old industries resisted new innovations and the resulting changes. While other entrants have joined the global market, U.S. industry has remained behind; the rate of growth of technological change and innovations has lagged in the United States.[63] The U.S. recovery and overvalued dollar have accentuated this effect; however, macroeconomic policies are not the villain in the first place. The problem seems to be that U.S. industries, even high-tech industries, have not kept pace with new technologies.[64] Since the new paradigm involves different entry levels for different factors, it seems that U.S. industry may actually have a disadvantage in introducing new technologies since U.S. industry is not starting from a clean slate but may have to unlearn some of the practices it has been accustomed to. Unlearning too has costs, and these may be part of transaction costs.[65]

That the problem of U.S. industry lies in its competitiveness becomes more evident when we look at the market shares of U.S. high-technology products in total world exports. Table 2.11 presents the market share of the high-tech sector as well as that of individual two- and three-digit SIC code industries classified as high tech. Looking at the aggregate sector, we notice that the market share has dropped from 28 percent in 1965 to 24 percent in 1980. This is a large drop considering that the U.S. market is a large part of the global market. As we look into individual industries we notice that the fall in the U.S. market share is not precipitated by a few industries; instead it is spread over virtually all industries. It is clear from this table that the market share has been declining in every industry. This may be a reflection of the earlier suggestion that the United States is unable to introduce and maintain new technologies. Also, U.S. industry has not developed the necessary, related institutions to make use of new innovations and technologies. This is a serious situation. The United States has an institutional base for the most complex and advanced knowledge about technologies and techniques and possesses all the information and know-how to organize production as well as the necessary materials and resources, yet U.S. industry is losing its market share. And empirical evidence suggests that these problems are becoming more serious over time. An explanation that seems both logical and consistent is that the United States is experiencing problems of adjustment to new technologies and to the new paradigm.[66] It is useful to further analyze the issue of competitiveness.

HIGH TECH AND INTERNATIONAL COMPETITIVENESS

The new techno-economic paradigm involves a whole range of new technologies and new products that have a global market and a production process spread over different countries. Because of its newness, international spread, and continuous change, there are different threshold levels for entry into various product markets. Instead of one country having the lead, different countries may lead in different products. Thus all trading countries both export and import high-technology goods. In this respect the new paradigm differs from the classical theory of trade and practice wherein one country specializes in the production of a particular commodity. The United States has had the advantage of being industrially most developed with its export network perfected and extended all over the globe, of having a lot of new industrial knowledge spin off from its defence industry, and of having the largest market. We would therefore expect the United States to be a leader in new technologies and new products. Although it still remains the leading exporter of high-technology manufactures, as we have seen in the previous section, the United States has been losing its market share and experiencing a trade deficit in manufactures and a declining trade surplus in high-tech industries. It is worth examining how it fares with its other competitors, basically, Japan, Germany, and France.

Table 2.12 presents the value of high-technology net exports for 14 industrialized countries, the Organization for Economic Cooperation and Development (OECD), the United States, Japan, and West Germany. We have not included France in this table because its net exports have been slim. As expected, the United States led the major countries in absolute value of high-technology exports for the whole period. The U.S. net exports of high-technology goods were $3.6 billion in 1962, virtually more than half of all net exports of the 14 industrialized countries. In 1980, the United States still had the largest value of net exports; $30.5 billion out of $70.3 billion for the 14 industrialized countries. However, the ratio has fallen and there are other players in the field, particularly Japan. Dramatic change in the Japanese competitive position regarding high-technology surplus is indicated in its expanding bilateral balance with the United States. From a deficit in these products in 1968, Japan moved to a surplus of $3.0 billion in 1980. This surplus—about one seventh of Japan's global high-technology trade surplus—is approximately equal to the U.S. surplus in these products combined with that of France and Germany. The situation has worsened during 1980, even though Japan agreed to accept voluntary quotas in exports to the United States.

The surplus generated in high-technology trade is significant for the United States. Nonetheless, a substantial portion of this surplus has been due to only two industries. In 1980 more than 50 percent of the U.S. surplus in high-technology trade was from aircraft and computer related products. This portion has been increasing since 1965, suggesting that other high-technology industries have been relatively less successful in the international market.

To analyze the changing picture in net exports, it helps to study the rates of growth of exports. Table 2.13 provides annual growth rates of exports of high-technology products for the four periods, 1962–1969, 1969–1974, 1974–1977, and 1977–1980, for 14 industrialized countries, the OECD, the United States, Japan, West Germany, and France. A number of observations follow from this table. (1) The rates of growth of exports are reasonably high; from a minimum of

10 percent to a maximum of 28 percent. This is consistent with and supportive of the hypothesis about a new techno-economic paradigm. (2) Comparatively, the U.S. growth rates are the lowest. In absolute terms, these are respectable. One may, however, argue that the reason for these low rates of growth may be the large size of U.S. industry, but considering these are growth rates of high-technology goods this argument is not tenable. A better explanation seems to lie in a general decline of U.S. competitiveness. (3) Japanese growth rates are the highest; Japan is considered the leading producer of high-technology products.

The conclusion is that U.S. competitive strength has been declining. Two direct measures of relative competitive strength are the ratio of imports to exports and export market share in world and third-country markets. The ratio of imports to exports makes different countries comparable. The import-export ratio summarizes growth in imports and exports. Since the new paradigm implies greater trade, the *a priori* expectation is for both imports and exports to grow. However growth rates of exports and imports will differ. A country fully adjusted to the new technologies will have higher growth rates of exports and its import-export ratio will decline. A country that does not adjust to the new paradigm will experience higher rates of growth of imports so that this ratio will increase. Table 2.14 gives these ratios for four competitors; the United States, Japan, West Germany, and France for the period 1962–1980. The following conclusions emerge from this table. (1) This ratio has been increasing both for the United States and West Germany. The United States imported 22 percent of its exports of high-tech goods in 1962. Eighteen years later, this ratio had more than doubled, to 52 percent. There has been a generally steady upward trend. West Germany also followed a similar trend; although the rate of growth of this ratio is lower for West Germany compared with the United States. (2) In the case of France, this ratio describes an inverted U-shaped curve. The ratio rose in the 1960s, reached a peak, and declined in 1970s. An explanation may be that France had to import high technology to start the production process in high-tech industries. In other words, entry into high tech in France has been through imports. (3) This ratio has been steadily falling for Japan; from 88 percent in 1962 to 34 percent in 1980. This is consistent with other evidence on Japan.

The weakening of the U.S. competitive strength and the strengthening of other competitors is also reflected in other measures of competitiveness. Table 2.15 provides information on export market shares of the four competing countries, the United States, Japan, West Germany, and France, over the two decades, in terms of market share (1) in the world market and (2) in the third-country market. The world market share is defined as a country's exports divided by the total world exports; that is, the sum of all exports in the world. The third-country market share is defined differently. It is obtained as a country's exports divided by the total exports to the third countries, which are all other countries minus the countries that are being compared. The idea behind the third-country market is that all the competing countries are equal and face similar, if not same, trading conditions. The third-country market may be a better measure of competitive strength.[67] Looking at these two shares in the table, we find that the U.S. share is the largest in the world market. This share was close to one third in 1962. However, over the two decades it has declined, so that by 1980 it was close to one fourth. The next largest share in the world market is held by West Germany; between one fifth and one sixth. West Germany's world market share has not changed over the two decades. The Japanese share started low; in 1962, it was around 4 percent, however, it has been rising fast. By 1980 it had grown to more than one tenth. The French share has been around 8 percent and has inched up to 9 percent over these two decades. We can analyze the changes in these shares by looking into the third-country market shares. These shares provide some interesting insights. Here again the U.S. share is the largest, but declining. It is larger than that of the world market, which is understandable and expected because the United States has a very large influence in the world and particularly in Third-World countries. Interestingly, this comparison suggests that the United States has difficulty selling in the domestic markets of its competitors. That the United States is unable to sell in Japanese market has been discussed.[68] It is not clear how well the U.S. has been doing with the other two competitors.[69] The Japanese share of the third-country markets is quite small, around 5 percent, and has not changed over the two decades, making it clear that Japan is not a major competitor in this market.[70] Considering that Japanese share of the world market has been increasing rapidly while its share in third-country markets has remained stationary, it follows that Japan has been exporting mostly to industrialized and other competing countries. Both West Germany and France have increased their share in third-country markets so that their joint share now approaches the U.S. share—they are major U.S. competitors in the third-country market.

CONCLUSIONS

The quantitative information presented here confirms the view that the United States has historically had a competitive advantage in high-technology production. Several indicators reveal that high-technology industries have been a source of strength in the overall U.S. manufacturing trade balance. The products of these industries comprise an increasing proportion of U.S. exports. There has been a trade surplus in high-technology products over virtually the whole period. The United States still maintains a strong competitive advantage in high-technology trade and exports; it is still the largest exporter in terms of both world trade and in the third-country market.

In recent years, however, there has been a noticeable shift in the pattern of trade in high-technology products. There are several indications that U.S. dominance in world trade of high-technology products is beginning to erode. The United States market share both in world exports and third-country exports has been declining. The primary source of competition is Japan in the world market and West Germany and France in the third-country market.

Table 2.1
Trade Balance in Manufacturing (Billions of U.S. Dollars)

	(Billions of U.S.Dollars)		
YEAR	U.S.	JAPAN	WEST GERMANY
1970	3.4	12.5	13.3
1975	19.9	41.7	38.7
1980	18.8	93.7	63.1
1984	-107.5	107.7	59.5

Source: U.S. International Trade Administration (*Industrial Outlook,* 1986).

Table 2.2
Foreign Labor Cost (Percentage of U.S. Labor Costs)

COUNTRY	1970	1975	1980	1984
France	63	103	112	65
West Germany	85	136	157	95
Italy	75	123	115	84
Japan	53	92	79	60
Korea	--	39	63	56
U.K.	86	120	177	105
U.S.	100	100	100	100

Source: National Research Council (1986).

Table 2.3
Output per Hour in Manufacturing (Average Annual Percent Change)

COUNTRY	1960-1973	1973-1983
Canada	4.7	1.8
France	6.5	4.6
West Germany	5.7	3.7
Japan	10.5	6.8
U.K.	4.3	2.4
U.S.	3.4	1.8

Source: U.S. Bureau of Labor Statistics (1985).

Table 2.4
Capital Investment—Output Ratio in Manufacturing (Constant U.S. Dollars)

PERIOD	FRANCE	W. GERMANY	JAPAN	U.K.	U.S.
1965-1982	15.1	12.8	21.2	13.6	10.5
1965-1973	16.5	14.3	25.3	14.3	10.0
1974-1982	13.6	11.2	17.1	13.0	11.1

Source: U.S. Bureau of Labor Statistics (1985).

Table 2.5
R&D-GNP Ratio

YEAR	FRANCE	W. GERMANY	JAPAN	U.S.
A: R&D-GNP RATIO				
1970	1.91	2.10	1.85	2.57
1975	1.80	2.22	1.96	2.20
1980	1.84	2.42	2.22	2.29
1985	2.31	2.67	2.77	2.69
B: NON DEFENSE R&D-GNP RATIO				
1971	NA	2.03	1.83	1.65
1975	1.46	2.08	1.95	1.63
1980	1.43	2.30	2.21	1.79
1985	1.85	2.53	2.75	1.86

Source: Science and Engineering Indicators (1987).

Table 2.6
High-Technology Industries—Product-Based Definition

SIC#	INDUSTRY
281	Industrial Inorganic Chemicals
282	Plastics and Synthetic Resins
283	Drugs
351	Engines and Turbines
357	Office Computing Machines
361	Electrical Transmission Equipment
362	Electrical Industrial Appratus
366	Communication Equipment
367	Electric Components and Assembly
372	Aircraft and Parts
376	Space Vehicles and Guided Missiles
381	Eng, Lab, and Scientific and Research Equipment
382	Measuring Controlling Instruments
383	Optical Instruments
385	Photographic Equipment
737	Computer Programming Services
7391,7397	Commercial and R&D Labs
7392	Business Management and Consulting Services
891	Engineering and Architectural Services
892	Non Profit Educational, Scientific and Research Orgn

Source: Vandyopadhyaya (1987), p. 46.

Table 2.7
High-Tech Industries—Occupational Mix–Based Definition

SIC#	INDUSTRY
281	Industrial Organic Chemicals
282	Plastic Materials and Synthetics
283	Drugs
284	Soaps
285	Paints and Varnishes
286	Industrial Organic Chemicals
287	Agricultural Chemicals
289	Miscellaneous Chemicals
303	Reclaimed Rubber
348	Ordinances
351	Engines and Turbines
353	Construction Equipment
354	Metal Working Machinery
356	General Industrial Machinery
357	Office Computing Machines
361	Electrical Transmission Equipment
362	Electrical Industrial Appratus
365	Radio and TV Receiving Equipment
367	Electrical Components and Accessories
373	Aircraft and Parts
374	Railroad Equipment
376	Guided Missiles and Space Vehicles
381	Industrial Inorganic Chemicals
382	Measuring and Controlling Instruments
383	Optical Instruments
384	Surgical and Medical Instruments
386	Photographic Equipment

Source: Vandyopadhyaya (1987), p. 45.

Table 2.8
High-Technology Industries—Our Definition

SIC#	INDUSTRY
281	Industrial Inorganic Chemicals
282	Plastics, Materials, and Synthetics
284	Soaps, Cleaners, and Toilet Preparations
285	Paints and Allied Products
286	Industrial Organic Chemicals
287	Agricultural Chemicals
289	Miscellaneous Chemical Products
291	Petroleum Refinng
348	Ordinances and Accessories
351	Engines and Turbines
355	Special Industrial Machinery
357	Office, Computing, and Accounting Machines
361	Elec. Transmission and Distributional Equipment
362	Electrical Industrial Appratus
365	Radio and TV Receiving Equipment
366	Communication Equipment
367	Electronic Components and Accessories
369	Miscellaneous Electrical Machinery
372	Aircrafts and Parts
376	Guided Missiles and Space Vehicles
381	Eng., Lab., Scientific, and Research Instruments
382	Measuring and Controlling Instruments
383	Optical Instruments and Lenses
384	Surgical and Medical Instruments
386	Photographic Equipment

Source: Vandyopadhyaya (1987), p. 47.

Table 2.9
Trade Balance in Manufacturing and High-Tech Industries (Billions of Current Dollars)

Year	Manufacturing			High Technology		
	X	M	B	X	M	B
1962	13.7	6.9	6.8	4.6	1.0	3.6
1970	29.7	25.9	3.4	12.2	5.0	7.3
1980	116.6	118.8	-2.1	51.0	27.2	23.8
1985	178.6	289.8	-111.2	66.6	59.9	6.7

Note: X = Exports, M = Imports, B = Trade Balance.

Source: U.S. Department of Commerce, International Trade Administration, *Assessment of U.S. Competitiveness in High-Technology Industries,* 1983; U.S. Department of Commerce, International Trade Administration, *U.S. Industrial Outlook,* 1988, 1989.

Table 2.10
Average Annual Growth Rates (Percentages)

Sector	1962-1969	1969-1976	1976-1980	1980-1985
TOTAL MANUFACTURING				
EXPORTS	9.8	16.2	15.2	2.2
IMPORTS	18.1	15.8	20.7	44.0
HIGH-TECHNOLOGY INDUSTRIES				
EXPORTS	10.3	16.5	18.1	1.5
IMPORTS	22.4	21.0	23.7	36.5

Source: U.S. Department of Commerce; same as Table 2.9.

Table 2.11
World Market Share of U.S. High-Tech Industries (Percentages)

INDUSTRY	SIC CODE	1965	1970	1980
High-Technology Industries		28.0	27.4	23.9
Industrial Chemicals	281,86	24.4	22.7	17.6
Plastics and Synthetics	282	20.0	12.5	13.9
Other Chemicals	284,85,87	16.7	20.0	30.3
Engines,Turbine, and Parts	351,55	31.3	28.1	28.3
Office, Comp., and Accounting Mach.	357	35.7	38.1	36.2
Elec. Equip. and Components	361-2,65,69	23.8	22.1	17.1
Comm. Equip. and Electron. Comp.	366,67	20.4	20.2	16.3
Aircraft and Parts	372	50.0	60.8	51.2
Guided Missiles and Space	376	43.1	40.2	39.5
Prof. and Scient. Instruments	381-2,86	35.7	33.3	30.6
Opt. and Med. Instruments	383-85	20.6	17.9	15.1

Source: U.S. Department of Commerce, International Trade Administration, *Assessment of U.S. Competitiveness in High-Technology Industries,* GPO, 1983.

Table 2.12
Net Exports of High-Technology Products (Billions of U.S. Dollars)

Country	1962	1970	1980
14 Industrial Countries	6.2	13.1	70.3
OECD Countries	5.5	9.7	58.9
U.S.	3.6	7.3	30.5
Japan	0.1	1.9	21.3
West Germany	1.7	3.9	15.7

Source: U.S. Department of Commerce, International Trade Administration, *U.S. High-Technology Trade and Competitiveness,* GPO, 1984.

Table 2.13
Average Annual Growth Rates of High-Tech Exports

Country	1962-1969	1969-1974	1974-1977	1977-1980
14 Industrialised countries	17.4	13.9	22.5	17.1
OECD Countries	14.7	22.7	17.2	20.0
U.S	10.3	19.2	16.0	19.7
Japan	27.3	28.3	22.6	22.2
West Germany	14.9	25.2	18.2	17.2
France	19.5	24.1	18.9	20.9

Source: U.S. Department of Commerce, International Trade Administration; same as
Table 2.12.

Table 2.14
Import-Export Ratios in High-Tech Trade (Percentages)

Country	1962	1970	1980
U.S.	22.2	40.5	51.8
Japan	88.7	51.6	34.5
West Germany	38.0	51.6	66.2
France	73.9	101.4	97.6

Source: U.S. Department of Commerce, International Trade Administration; same as
Table 2.12.

Table 2.15
Market Shares of High-Tech Exports (Percentages)

Year	U.S.	Japan	West Germany	France
A: World Market Shares				
1962	30.3	4.1	17.6	7.7
1970	27.6	9.6	18.0	7.8
1980	23.9	12.3	17.5	9.0
B: Third-Country Market Shares				
1962	38.4	4.6	8.5	7.2
1970	38.6	6.9	13.2	10.6
1980	32.9	5.8	16.0	12.1

Source: U.S. Department of Commerce, International Trade Administration, *Assessment of U.S. Competitiveness in High-Technology Industries,* 1983.

NOTES

1. In 1986, industrialized countries accounted for 63 percent of U.S. exports and developing countries 36 percent. *World Development Report,* 1988, table 14. p. 249.

2. *Survey of Current Business* 67. no. 9, September 1987.

3. *Ibid.* The penetration ratio is measured by an import-shipment ratio.

4. *World Development Report,* 1988, table 13, p. 247.

5. Astute observers recognized this trend early; one can understand why Vogel (1979) titled his book: *Japan: No. 1: Lessons for America.*

6. If one believes in the idea that flag follows trade, it may suggest one reason why *New York Times* editorials talk of "Japan bashing."

7. Labor costs are generally defined as the ratio of the wage bill to value added.

8. Although it seems obvious, the measurement of the quantity of labor and output are beset with a number of serious problems, particularly if one considers an aggregate such as total manufacturing.

9. The number of countries for which these comparative rates are being presented is shrinking because detailed data are generally not easily available and because the definition and measurement of data on capital is replete with complex theoretical and statistical problems.

10. Jorgenson and Kuroda (1985b) consider this as an explanation of Japan's "catching up" process.

11. There are theoretical questions about the meaning of R&D expenditures and what such expenditures measure. On the other hand, it has now become a part of the accepted tradition in the literature on productivity to compare R&D expenditures.

12. There is however the other point of view that the World Bank is not helpful to the

developing countries in gaining capital and technology. On the contrary, the World Bank and International Monetary Fund (IMF) policies promote products of developed countries' industry in the markets of developing countries. There is a good deal of literature on this issue, which is well represented by Payer (1982). A large number of issues are involved here. Diwan (1971a) discusses development and poverty. Diwan (1973) and Diwan and Marwah (1976) analyze trade between unequal partners. Diwan (1981) questions the impact of transfers of hard technology on human rights. Diwan and Livingston (1979) discuss the technological implications of development policies.

13. This idea is consistent with another thesis that speaks of a major civilization change. This thesis has been articulated in a number of different versions. The most comprehensive version relates to the emergence of the "Third Wave." It is discussed at great length in Toffler (1980).

14. Naisbitt (1982) forecasts some details of the changes in life styles that will emerge in the near and not too distant future.

15. Piore and Sabel (1984) have outlined the decline of the industrialized societies. Reich (1983) argues that mass production technologies form the sunset industries.

16. Gandhi (1962) was one of the very early observers of the strengths and weaknesses of the industrial way of life. He placed the whole issue in perspective by distinguishing between "mass production" and "production by masses." Some of these ideas are formulated in economic terms in Diwan and Lutz (1987) and Diwan (1982, 1985a, 1985b, 1987).

17. "In one Second Wave country after another, social inventors, believing the factory to be the most advanced and efficient agency for production, tried to embody its principles in other organisations as well. Schools, hospitals, prisons, government bureaucracies, and other organizations thus took on many of the characteristics of the factory—its division of labor, its hierarchical structure and its metallic impersonality" Toffler (1980), p. 31, Bantam edition.

18. "Our claim is that the present deterioration in economic performance results from the limits of the model of industrial development that is founded on mass production: the use of special-purpose (product-specific) machines and of semi skilled workers to produce standardized goods. We argue that the technologies and operating procedures of most modern corporations; the forms of labor-market control defined by many labor movements; the instruments of macroeconomic control developed by bureaucrats and economists in the welfare states; and the rules of the international monetary and trading systems established immediately after World War II—all must be modified, perhaps even discarded, if the chronic economic diseases of our time are to be cured" Piore and Sabel (1984), p. 4.

19. This is consistent with an observations by Griliches (1988). "This drop in productivity growth was actually larger, in absolute terms, in some other countries (such as Canada, Japan, and Sweden) than in the United States, making explanations for these events which rely heavily on especially U.S. based causes or arguments somewhat less plausible. Whether the productivity slow down has come to an end in the mid 1980s is still very much in dispute. So too is the possibility that the slowdown actually started earlier, in the mid 1960s, as is implied by some of the more inclusive, multifactor productivity measures," p. 9. "Of course, there may not be a single cause-one murderer. Perhaps it is more like the *Murder on the Orient Express*—they all did it! From the longer run point of view there are still lingering doubts about the crime itself: perhaps the 1970s were not so abnormal after all. Maybe it is the inexplicably high growth rates in 1950s and early 1960s that are the real puzzle" p. 19.

20. It is interesting to note that perceptive observers point out the nuances of industrialism without any statistics or economic training. Paul Theroux, a novelist, writing on the basis of his travels comes to the conclusion, "Writing my diary that night, I generalized on this, concluding that every large hotel at which I stayed in England was run down or badly managed—overpriced, understaffed, and dirty, the staff overworked and slow; and all the smaller places were preferable, smallest always the best. The English were great craftsmen but poor mass-producers of goods. They were brilliant at running a corner shop, but were failures when they tried their hand at supermarkets. . . . The English do small things well and big things badly" Theroux (1985) p. 208. This may be one of the reasons why English productivity has suffered the most in the post–second-world-war period when mass production and its concomitant civilization has been at its zenith.

21. "However one chooses to evaluate the fading present, it is vital to understand that the industrial game is over, its energies spent, the force of the Second Wave diminishing everywhere as the next wave of change begins. Two changes, by themselves, make the 'normal' continuation of industrialization no longer possible. First, we have reached a turning point in the war against nature. The biosphere will simply no longer tolerate the industrial assault. Second, we can no longer rely indefinitely on non-renewable energy, until now the main subsidy of industrial development" Toffler (1980), p. 122, Bantam edition.

22. "Certain types of technical change—defined as changes in 'techno-economic paradigm'—have such widespread consequences for all sectors of the economy that their diffusion is accompanied by a major structural crisis of adjustment, in which social and institutional changes are necessary to bring about a better 'match' between the new technology and the system of social management of the economy" Freeman and Perez (1988), p. 38.

23. Reich (1983) articulates this argument. This paradigm is well explained in the comparative statement that the United States is a nation of "salesmen" while England is one of "shopkeepers."

24. Kondratiev business cycles that span 50 to 80 years are embedded deep in economic literature. Very little empirical work has been done on these long cycles. All the same, economists bring them out, as if from the woods, whenever the situation warrants. Kondratiev cycles are quite consistent, and so is the current situation, with Schumpeter's idea about "long waves" (1939). After the Great Depression theories of the business cycle were particularly relevant and every important economist suggested some explanation about the cycle. The business cycle, as a topic for research and analysis, has fallen into disuse in the sustained growth after the Second World War. Whether the current slow down will bring this subject back into fashion is anybody's guess. The success of Batra (1989), forecasting depression, suggests such a possibility.

25. Freeman and Perez (1988) have identified in detail various distinctions in technological change from the empirical work in the Science Policy Research Unit at Sussex University, based on Schumpeter's distinction between invention, innovation, and diffusion. Qureshi and Diwan (1990) discuss the implications of these distinctions. Diwan and Desai (1990b) analyze its implications for U.S. business.

26. It has been suggested that these types of changes have been the most common in the United States in the 1960s and 1970s.

27. Freeman and Perez (1988) call these "radical innovations." They distinguish these from "incremental innovations," which corresponds to our first category.

28. It is these innovations that explain the high rate of return to public R&D.

29. Freeman and Perez (1988) make a further distinction between radical innovations and technology systems. Their technology system is a combination of the two types of the innovations suggested above with some related changes and some clusters of radical innovations. Logically, and intrinsically, the technology system is not really different from its parts. The distinction between radical innovation and the technology system is a useful one for taxonomy purposes; it is not of much help for analytical purposes.

30. We follow Freeman and Perez (1988), Diwan (1989), and Diwan and Deasi (1990b) for a discussion of the techno-economic paradigm.

31. The levels and growth rates of productivity in new technologies in Japanese manufacturing have been particularly high, due, it has been suggested, to the fact that Japan has followed practices that encourage these technologies. See for example, Vogel (1979) who discusses it in detail. It may be explained by the fact that the Japanese have adopted the new techno-economic paradigm in their production process. Diwan (1988) articulates some of the implications of the new technology regimes in terms of decision making processes.

32. This may explain the large, and still growing, literature on Japanese management techniques discussed in Tomer (1987). Diwan (1985a) argues the success of the Japanese system as a result of its management system based on an institutionalization of a joint family system.

33. The R&D expenditures in Japan and West Germany have been growing at an accelerated rate. These increases are not accidental; they are consistent with and follow from the implications of the new techno-economic paradigm.

34. This may explain the success of Japanese exports in the U.S. domestic market.

35. "The onset of prolonged recessionary trends indicate the increasing degree of mismatch between the techno-economic sub-systems and the old socio-institutional framework" Freeman and Perez (1988), p. 59.

36. "It is clear that there is no single price tag for production technologies nor is it solely determined by the supplier. Furthermore, the absolute threshold level is not limited to the price of technology. It includes minimum levels of scientific and technical knowledge, practical experience and locational advantages" Perez and Soete (1988), p. 470.

37. Diwan (1989) discusses the relevance of small businesses in the new techno-economic paradigm and suggests why small firms have a comparative advantage in entering new technologies.

38. The report of the National Research Council (1986) provides an important consensus on this issue among policy makers, engineers and scientists, and business executives.

39. One need not be too concerered about this lack of one accepted definition. The progress of science has always followed when different groups of people have identified differing observation sets by similar terms. The process of open discussion, over a period of time, develops a consensus about definition. For example, it took economists some 20 years before the Second World War to settle down to an acceptable definition of the term "savings"; after a long debate and hundreds of articles.

40. It has been argued that this continuous and unpredictable change is one of the explanations for large cyclical changes, or swings, in this industry.

41. Kelly (1977) provides further details. By this method she was able to account for the overstatement in technology-intensive trade that occurs when a broader definition of high tech is used.

42. Aho and Rosen (1981) provide details on this study.

43. This approach is detailed in the U.S. Department of Commerce (1983).

44. Vinson and Harrington (1979) use an index based on technological complexity for analysing high tech in Massachussetts.

45. It is possible to argue that the standard industrial classification is consistent with the old mass-production paradigm. The new paradigm would involve a different industrial classification in which the distinction between services and industries may not be significant. Diwan (1989) discusses problems of the relevance of standard economic and statistical categories for flexible manufacturing phenomena; it is equally true of high-tech industries.

46. U.S. Congress, OTA (1982). Their concern has been regional development instead of trade or industrial growth.

47. Davis (1982) contains the necessary details.

48. Abbott et al. (1989) have done the study for the Bureau of the Census, Department of Commerce.

49. The interviews were not conducted by the DOC itself but were conducted earlier by others. This study used different sources to identify these fields.

50. This procedure may seem far more subjective than it actually is. It has been pointed out that these analysts are fully conversant with the data sources on a day-to-day basis so that they are competent to classify the data according to technological intensity. Similar judgments are also made by such analysts when they assign individual establishments and products to particular industries for SIC code purposes.

51. The report recognises this possibility. In its own language, "This implies that another set of analysts, working with the same data, may identify a somewhat different list of advanced technology products" Abbot et al. (1989), p. 7.

52. Boretsky (1975) defines trade in high-tech industries instead of in products, although such a distinction between products and industries is sometimes somewhat spurious.

53. National Science Foundation (1978).

54. Lawson (1982), p. 12.

55. Markusen et al. (1986) provides details of the definition and the occupational profiles.

56. It is now widely discussed that funding for basic research in the United States is declining so fast that it is jeopardizing the U.S. lead in this area.

57. Markusen et al. (1986) found that by this criterion, petroleum and chemicals do not qualify as high-tech industries, partly because the criterion is based on a ratio, the denomintor of which is sales. In mature industries, sales are generally large so that this ratio becomes deflated. Such a ratio in a ranking based on these ratios results in placing these industries at the lower end of the distribution.

58. U.S. Department of Labor, Bureau of Labor Statistics (1982).

59. Vandyopadhyaya (1987) was the first to develop this list.

60. Tyson et al. (1988) argue that economic problems of the trade deficit and U.S. manufacturing can be solved only if U.S. industry moves agressively toward the high-tech sector.

61. Aho and Rosen (1981) have done quantitative research on high-technology industries that provides evidence in support of this proposition.

62. Recent studies suggest that the trade balance in high-tech goods has also become negative. One of the reasons for the Abbott et al. (1989) study has been to examine this proposition. They claim that trade balance in high-tech industries is still positive, and that the problem arises from the difficulties of measurement of high-tech products.

63. We have already commented above on the lack of R&D growth in the United States.

64. Some have suggested that the U.S. high-tech sector is high tech in name only, that it lacks the essential institutional framework associated with high-tech industries elsewhere, such as a cooperative management system. Bailey and Chakrabarti (1988) also imply this.

65. Williamson (1975) makes a persuasive case for the inefficiencies of large businesses due to high transaction costs. Unlearning skills and changing managemnt styles and methods will further increase these transaction costs.

66. In a broader sense, this relates to the arguments about management and cultural change well articulated by different authors in Starr (1988).

67. Trade cannot be easily separated from politics. Different third-country markets are liable to be differentially influenced by the politics of different countries. The United States used to have, and still has, an advantage in these markets in so far as these are defined by Third-World country governments, particularly in South America, where U.S. political and military influence is quite large.

68. The debate about opening Japanese markets to U.S. products has been particularly intense in U.S. political circles, and was one of the planks in the 1988 presidential politics. The U.S. Congress passed the 1988 Omnibus Trade Act with a Super 301 provision by which U.S. trade representatives are required to identify unfair trade partners. In 1989, Japan was classified as an unfair trade partner. Since then, negotiations, extending over a year, have been carried on to formulate mutually agreeable policies in the two countries so as to reduce friction in trade relations.

69. There is a growing feeling of frustration about exports to some of the Common Market countries; the friction caused by beef hormones is the most recent.

70. This is liable to change. Japan is emerging as the largest donor to Third-World countries. As its level of giving goes up, its influence also increases, which eventually will be reflected in its exports to this part of the world.

3

Productivity Concepts and Measures

INTRODUCTION

Productivity in the broadest sense is concerned with the overall effectiveness and efficiency of resources in the production process. Changes in productivity may best be conceived as both the cause and the consequence of dynamism inherent in a modern economy; for example, advancement in technology, development of human skill, accumulation of human and physical capital, changes in institutional arrangements, etc. Measurement and interpretation of productivity behavior at the microeconomic and macroeconomic levels is a complex task. Yet interest in the measurement and analysis of productivity has intensified more rapidly than ever before over the past two decades and a half, perhaps because of the alarming trend of slackening productivity in the United States.[1]

During the immediate postwar years, pressure to recover from the devastation caused by the war, and the subsequent job of reconstruction, played a significant role in spurring interest in productivity analysis. With rapid advancement in transportation and communication, disparities in standards of living among nations and levels and rates of change in productivity were brought vividly to the notice of a widening group of observers. Differential productivity changes make their impact felt on a myriad of interrelated factors; for example, relative exchange rates and movements in price levels. Recognition of these facts led governmental authorities of almost every developed nation to make a drive to catch up or stay ahead in economic development. Such drive consequently increased the demand for better information on production, resources, and productivity levels.

The growing demand for information on productivity was met, and stimulated further, through the workings of the United Nations and other international organizations. Under the guidance of these organizations, population censuses and income and product accountings were established for the first time in many countries. The research of a growing number of economists and statisticians, as well as management and engineering experts, on production and productivity data, methodology, theory, and policy also contributed toward building such an information base. The role played by these researchers was further strengthened by the formation of different international organizations. For example, the International Association for Research in Income and Wealth was established in 1947. In addition, specialized institutional support for the measurement, analysis, and promotion of productivity was provided by the establishment of productivity centers in many nations during the 1950s. In the 1960s, representatives of these centers began meeting in international forums organized by the Asian Productivity Organization and the European Associations of National Productivity Centers.[2]

With a growing information base and need to explain productivity slow downs, understanding the behavior of productivity measures through time, the conceptual foundations of productivity analysis, and the linkage between productivity performance and other major forces in the economy became increasingly important. Special attention was focused on the study of international differences in levels and rates of increases in productivity. Through the joint efforts of the national commission, government agencies, private organizations, and university researchers, enormous progress has been made in productivity studies over the last two decades. The important task for us is to bring together the findings of different studies in a systematic form. Only through a proper understanding of the causal factors, and the economic consequences of their dynamic nature, can policies be formulated, and implemented to enhance productivity to a desirable extent.

PRODUCTIVITY CONCEPTS

The significance of productivity and interpretation of its behavior derives mainly from two concerns—economic efficiency and economic welfare[3]—both of which are meaningful to economic development. Although these concerns are closely related to each other they are not the same. The economic welfare of the members of a society is dependent on the efficiency with which its resources are combined. However, efficiency is only one of the many factors underlying welfare. The volume and quality of the resources made available to the work force are also crucial in determining welfare in an economy. The concept of economic welfare while encompassing concern for economic efficiency, goes far beyond it.

These conceptual differences imply that the productivity concepts and measurements most appropriate to each objective also differ. Unawareness of these differences can, and often does, lead to misunderstanding what a particular productivity measure means. Appropriateness of different productivity measures are defined in terms of specific objectives. Although a series of productivity measures are available, the most commonly known concept defines the relationship of output to associated inputs. The total productivity measure relates output to all the inputs classes in production; whereas, the partial productivity measure relates output separately to each major class of inputs.

LABOR PRODUCTIVITY

Of the partial productivity measures, labor productivity, or output in relation to labor hour, is the most commonly used. Labor productivity is the ratio of the aggregate amount of real output (Q) produced by a firm, industry, or nation, in a given period, to the aggregate number of work hours (L) employed in producing this real output. This is the output per work hour, Q/L, and is generally reported in the official productivity statistics of the United States and other countries in the form of rates of change of index numbers. This productivity index most often enters public discussions of economic efficiency, growth, inflation, and a country's international economic status.

As is apparent from this definition, labor productivity cannot be the most appropriate concept for all these purposes. It certainly is not appropriate for measuring efficiency in the use of resources. Output per work hour would rise, for example, even in the absence of any change in efficiency, if labor were aided by more capital goods, equipment, and inventory stocks. If both efficiency and capital input per labor hour rose, labor productivity would go up more than could be accounted for by efficiency; it would reflect, in addition, the substitution of capital for labor. In other words, a rise in output per work hour in such a case reflects the composite effect of both kinds of increase. It is partly for this reason that a nation's output per work hour is considered an appropriate productivity measure only when the objective is to attain economic welfare.

A number of refinements of this productivity measure have been suggested by economists over the years. Some economists prefer to take account of the changes in terms of trade with other countries particularly when trade defines a significant share of the GNP. A relevant example is the sharp increase in import prices relative to export prices that occurred when the Organization of Petroleum Exporting Countries (OPEC) raised crude oil prices in 1973 and again in 1979. Statistics of U.S. productivity growth rates for 1973–1979 reveal that changes in the terms of trade certainly affected the economy adversely during this period. Accordingly, the concerned group of economists argued that continuous unidirectional changes in terms of trade, even if small in magnitude, can have a substantial impact on the economy and hence should be taken into account in formulating productivity measurements.[4] Another group is concerned with the distinction between gross domestic product and gross national product as a measure of output in defining productivity. According to this group, when labor productivity is measured by gross domestic product instead of gross national product, per work hour, a crucial factor is omitted that biases the productivity measure. This crucial factor is the net flow of income, to or from other countries, earned on international capital investments. When net flow of income is significant, this omission could result in entirely misleading information. As suggested by scholars dealing with this issue, a simple modification of conventional productivity measures can yield the desired result under such circumstances.

A number of economists argue in favor of taking into consideration changes in the conditions under which people live and work. These conditions refer to environment and quality of working life. Some suggest that deterioration in these conditions be considered "negative outputs" and be included in productivity measurements. The recommended method estimates the expenditure for different regulatory activities such as pollution abatement, worker safety, and health. These expenditures are treated as factors adversely affecting labor productivity.

All these refinements imply that labor productivity, broadly or narrowly defined, is not the only effective measure of economic welfare. If economic welfare is measured by per capita output, as it commonly is, labor productivity defines one of its important elements. Productivity measures derived by relating output to other inputs, such as capital goods, land and natural resources, materials, and energy also provide useful information.

TOTAL FACTOR PRODUCTIVITY (TFP)

When analyzing the impact on productivity from the economic efficiency point of view, the effects of any change that takes place in the proportions among different inputs must be excluded. As noted earlier, if efficiency remains unchanged and capital is substituted for labor, the result will be a decline in output per unit of capital, on the one hand, and a rise in output per unit of work hour on the other. Both these effects need to be taken into account in interpreting efficiency. A simple way around this problem averages changes in output per unit of each separate input; that is, averaging different partial productivity measures. Each of these partial productivity measures would obviously have to be weighted by its share in total output. Such weighted averages provide a measure of output per unit of total inputs, which is known as total factor productivity. The significance of the total factor productivity lies in its ability to measure changes in efficiency with unchanged factor proportions.

The conventional method of calculating total factor productivity is straightforward; output is related to total input in use. In other words, total factor productivity is conventionally defined as the ratio of "quantity of output produced" to a "weighted combination of quantities of different input factors used." Denoting total factor productivity by A and the level of output by Q, we have

$$A = \frac{Q}{\Sigma W_i x_i},$$

where x_i is the quantity of input factor i and W_i is some appropriate weight.

The idea of comparing output with total input was conceived precisely in order to provide a measure of efficiency that was more appropriate than labor productivity. Prior to World War II, the concept of total factor productivity was virtually unheard of. Indeed, there was very little quantitative data on capital and other inputs in a form suited to productivity measurement. It took a good deal of research on the theoretical, econometric, and data problems involved to open the way for total factor productivity measurements. A series of studies of economic growth conducted at the National Bureau of Economic Research in the 1950s, in particular, played a significant role in generating contemporary interest in total factor productivity measurement. By today, to most economists the term productivity means total factor productivity. Non-economists, on the other hand, still consider productivity as labor productivity.

The first official index comparing national output with an aggregate input concept broader than work hours was published in 1983 by the U.S. Bureau of Labor Statistics (BLS), and the BLS remains the only agency providing information on total factor productivity at an economy level. However, many issues still remain to be resolved. The total factor productivity measure derived and used by economists relates output not to total input but to something less because, in the input measure, not all the inputs are covered and those that are covered are not covered fully. For this reason, these measures are sometimes designated by the less definitive term, "multifactor productivity"; the BLS follows this nomenclature. Regardless of whether the adopted measures are designated as total or multifactor productivity, because of conceptual differences, differences in the input factors covered and the availability of necessary data, various measures provide different estimates.

In summary, viewed from the point of view of economic efficiency, total factor productivity appears to be the most appropriate measure. Output per work hour—or any other partial productivity measure, such as output per unit of capital goods, materials, land, or energy—provides only an incomplete story, even though it conveys a great deal of information about the production process. Partial productivity measures provide a story in which effects of changes in efficiency are intertwined with those in input compositions. However, data on the number of persons and number of work hours have been collected by most countries over longer time periods than have data on other inputs. Indices of labor productivity are easily available, while other productivity indices are not. For this practical reason, labor productivity has been and continues to be taken to measure efficiency in the use of resources generally, often with little modification.

EXISTING APPROACHES TO THE MEASUREMENT OF TFP

Since its inception, the TFP measure has gone through various stages of refinement and application, and there is now a large literature on the subject.[5] A close look at this literature reveals that a change in TFP, which is also called technical change, is interpreted either as (1) the rate of change of an index of outputs divided by an index of inputs[6] or (2) a shift in a production function.[7] Regardless of the ways of interpreting this concept, methods developed for measuring technological change can broadly be divided into three groups—the econometric approach, the index number approach, and the nonparametric approach. These approaches along with different subapproaches within them are briefly reviewed below. We interpret a change in TFP as a shift in an underlying production function, or production possibilities set.[8]

ECONOMETRIC APPROACH

The econometric approach to the measurement of technological change consists of estimation of a well-behaved production or cost function. If data on output produced during period t, Q^t, and the input set used during period t, $x^t = (x_1^t, x_2^t, x_N^t)$, are available, then one need only assume a conventional functional form for the production function f, and estimate the parameters that characterize f by using a regression equation

$$Q^t = f(x^t, t) + \text{error}. \tag{3.1}$$

A conventional measure of technological change during period t is $\partial \ln f(x^t, t)/\partial t$, the percentage change in output due to an increment of time. The general consensus is that it is useful to assume a functional form for f that can provide a second-order approximation to an arbitrary twice continuously differentiable production function. An example of such a functional form, which is widely in use, is the translog form.

The econometric approach for measuring shifts in the production function is as follows. Given that a producer faces a positive vector of input prices, $p^t = (p_1^t, p_2^t, \ldots, p_N^t) > O_N$, where O_N is a null vector of 1*N dimension, during period t, and minimizes costs in the competitive market, a producer's cost function C can be defined by solving the following constrained cost minimization problem:

$$C(Q^t, p^t, t) = \min_x \{p^t x: f(x, t) \geq Q^t, x \geq O_N\}. \tag{3.2}$$

Note that $x > O_N$ is a non-negative vector of input quantities and $p^t \cdot x = \sum_{n=1}^{N} p_n^t x_n$ denotes the product between the vectors p^t and x.

Obviously C is completely determined by f. We also have the following useful result by Shephard's Lemma:

$$x^t = \Delta_p C(Q^t, p^t, t), \tag{3.3}$$

where $\Delta_p C(Q^t, p^t, t) = [\partial C/\partial p_1, \partial C/\partial p_2, \ldots, \partial C/\partial p_N]$ is the vector of partial derivatives of C with respect to the components of p. The producer's system of input demand equations can be obtained by differentiating the cost function with respect to input prices. The cost function described above can be extended to the multiple output case with little difficulty. We simply include the additional outputs in the input vector. If we assume a functional form for the cost function and differentiate with respect to the input prices, then the parameters in the cost function can be estimated statistically by adding error terms to equation (3.3). A functional form for the cost function C can provide a second-order approximation to an arbitrary cost function, which is useful.[9] The advantage of this approach to measuring technological progress over the regression equation approach suggested above, and implied in equation (3.1), is that the system of equations in (3.3) has more degrees of freedom in a statistical sense. However, there is one major shortcoming of this approach; it requires the stringent assumption of competitive behavior on the part of a producer with respect to inputs.

INDEX NUMBER APPROACH

We turn now to a method for measuring shifts in a production function that does not require any assumption about its functional form—the index number approach. Among the various index number approaches, the generally accepted one is the "Divisia" approach.[10] The Divisia approach assumes that data are available not only at discrete points of time but at every moment of time t, where t ranges over a closed interval.

Let $Q(t) = f[x(t),t]$ be output at time t and let $x(t) = [x_1(t), x_2(t), \ldots, x_N^t]$ denote the vector of inputs utilized at time t. If the production function exhibits neutral technological change, then it can be written as $F[x(t), t] = A(t)f[x(t)]$, where $A(t)$ is a shift parameter for the production function F at time t. If we differentiate the identity $Q(t) = A(t)fx(t)$ with respect to time, divide by $Q(t)$, and replace the terms $A(t)\partial f[x(t)]/\partial x_n$ by $p_n(t)$, the nth input price at time t, we obtain the following identity:

$$\frac{DA(t)}{A(t)} = \frac{DQ(t)}{Q(t)} - \sum_{n=1}^{N} S_n(t)\frac{Dx_n(t)}{x_n(t)}, \qquad (3.4)$$

where D is an operator and denotes a derivative with respect to time. The nth input share is defined as $S_n(t) = p_n(t)x_n(t)/Q(t)$.

If $DA(t)/A(t) = 0$, then $A(t)$ is a constant for all t, and there is no exogenous shift in the production function; there is no technological progress and no increase in total factor productivity.

This analysis assumes a single output, but an extension of the approach to multiple output can be, and has been, made.[11] Starting with the assumption that the joint cost function C defined by (3.2) is differentiable for each time unit t, differentiating the identity $\Sigma p_n(t)x_n(t) = C\{Q(t), p(t), t\}$ with respect to time t, assuming competitive profit maximization behavior, which implies that equations (3.2) and (3.3) hold good for each instant of time t, and dividing both sides of the identity by $C\{Q(t), \mathbf{p}(t), t\}$, one obtains the following expression for shift in the cost function:

$$\partial \ln C\{\mathbf{Q}(t),\mathbf{p}(t),t\}/dt = \sum_{n=1}^{N} \frac{p_n(t)x_n(t)Dx_n(t)}{\mathbf{p}(t)\mathbf{x}(t)x_n(t)} - \sum_{m=1}^{M} \frac{P_{qm}(t)Q_m(t)DQ_m(t)}{\mathbf{p}_q(t)\mathbf{Q}(t)Q_m(t)}, \quad (3.5)$$

where $\mathbf{p}(t)\mathbf{x}(t) = \Sigma\, p_n(t)x_n(t) = C\{\mathbf{Q}(t), \mathbf{p}(t),t\}$, $\mathbf{p}_q(t) = (p_{q1}, p_{q2}, \ldots, p_{qM})$, is an output price vector, Q_m = output, $m = 1, 2, \ldots, M$, and $\mathbf{p}_q(t)\mathbf{Q}(t) = \Sigma\, p_q(t)Q_m(t)$ = value of output. If there is technological progress in the economy, then the partial derivative of the cost function with respect to its last argument will not be positive and hence $\partial \ln C\{\mathbf{Q}(t),\mathbf{p}(t), T\}/\partial t < 0$. The left-hand side of the expression in equation (3.5) represents the percentage rate of cost increase unexplained by changes in inputs and outputs.

The problem with the Divisia approach is that economic data on $\mathbf{x}(t)$, $\mathbf{p}(t)$, and $\mathbf{Q}(t)$ do not come in continuous form, they are instead available in discrete form. Thus continuous time formulae (3.4) and (3.5) have to be approximated using discrete time data. There are many ways to achieve such approximation using discrete data; however, the Divisia approach does not yield unique estimates of total factor productivity when applied to discrete economic data.

In the econometric approach one has to approximate the firm's true production or cost function with a particular functional form. In the Divisia approach, we have to approximate the continuous time derivative with discrete differences. The exact index number approach also involves an approximation. Assuming a relevant production or joint cost function to be of a certain functional form, this approach defines index numbers that are consistent with the assumed functional form.[12] Among different index numbers, one based on the translog cost function, namely, the Tornquist-Theil-Translog index, is commonly used. Starting with a translog function of the following form:

$$\ln C(\mathbf{Q}^t,\mathbf{p}^t,t) = a_0 + \sum a_m \ln Q_m{}^t + \frac{1}{2}\sum\sum a_{mk} \ln Q_m{}^t \ln Q_k{}^t + \sum a_{mt} \ln t \ln Q_m{}^t$$

$$+ \sum b_n \ln p_n{}^t + \frac{1}{2}\sum\sum b_{ni} \ln p_n{}^t \ln p_i{}^t + \sum g_{mn} \ln Q_m{}^t \ln p_n{}^t$$

$$+ \sum a_{mt} \ln Q_m{}^t \ln t + \sum b_{nt} \ln p_n{}^t \ln t + f_t \ln t + f_{tt}(\ln t)^2, \quad (3.6)$$

assuming constant returns to scale and competitive profit maximizing behavior, this index can be obtained by the use of the quadratic lemma.[13] The quadratic lemma yields the following identity:[14]

$$\frac{1}{2}[t^1 + t^0] = \ln \frac{p^1 x^1}{p^0 x^0} - \left[\frac{1}{2}\sum_{n=1}^{N} \left\{\frac{p_n{}^1 x_n{}^1}{p^1 x^1} + \frac{p_n{}^0 x_n{}^0}{p^0 x^0}\right\} \ln \frac{p_n{}^t}{p_n{}^0}\right]$$

$$- \left[\frac{1}{2}\sum_{m=1}^{M} \left\{\frac{P_{qm}{}^1 Q_m{}^1}{P_q{}^1 Q^1} + \frac{P_{qm}{}^0 Q_m{}^0}{P_q{}^0 q^0}\right\} \ln \frac{Q_m{}^1}{Q_m{}^0}\right], \quad (3.7)$$

where $t = \partial \ln C(\mathbf{Q}^t, \mathbf{p}^t, t)/\partial t$ for $t = 0, 1$, is the period t impact of technological change on cost and $\mathbf{p_q} = (p_{q1}, p_{q2}, \ldots, p_{qm})$ is a vector of output prices and is different from p_n. The right-hand side of equation (3.7) can be calculated only provided that data on prices and quantities for periods 0 and 1 are available.

NONPARAMETRIC APPROACH

The nonparametric method contrasts sharply with both the econometric and Divisia approaches in the sense that it doesn't involve any approximation at all. The name "nonparametric" is quite descriptive since no parameter estimation is involved. The essence of the approach lies in recognizing the distinction between period specific production functions. Using the above notations, let us suppose that $Q^t \geq 0$ is the amount of output produced by a firm during period t and $\mathbf{x}^t = (x_1^t, x_2^t, \ldots, x_n^t) \geq \mathbf{0}_N$ is the vector of inputs used in the production process during period t for $t = 1, 2, \ldots, n$. Suppose that for each period t, the firm's production function $f^t(\mathbf{x})$ is continuous, non-decreasing, and concave for $\mathbf{x} \geq \mathbf{0}_N$. Assuming that there is no technical progress, the period specific production function f^t are such that $f^t(\mathbf{x}) \geq f^r(\mathbf{x})$ for all $\mathbf{x} \geq \mathbf{0}_N$ if $t > r$; that is, the maximal output that can be produced by the input vector $\mathbf{x}$ during period, t, $f^t(\mathbf{x})$, is equal to or greater than the maximal output that can be produced by the same input vector $\mathbf{x}$ during a prior period $f^r(\mathbf{x})$. There are a number of tests that study the consistency of such production functions, f^t, with available firm data.[15] Successful application of these tests yield a sequence of estimated production functions, which can in turn be used to measure shifts in a firm's production function over time.

The existence of different approaches raises the question of how to choose among them. The choice involves analysis of the comparative advantages and disadvantages of these methods. Both the econometric and index number approaches involve an approximation error, part of which emanates from the lack of an appropriate data set. Dependence on market data for prices and quantities does not allow a complete determination of the true production possibility set because many relevant variables remain excluded. These approximations, therefore, seem reasonable only when placed in the context of limited data availability. The primary advantage of econometric approach is that it generates estimators for the underlying true production function f^t. However, estimation of a production or cost function, equations (3.1) or (3.2), necessitates the assumption that all systematic explanatory factors have been properly accounted for, which defies the rationale behind the concept of TFP as a residual measure. Given that our state of knowledge of production systems, the macro aspect in particular, does not permit complete specification of all systematic explanatory variables and full characterization of the nature of technological change, aggregate production functions produce estimates of parameters that may have dubious economic implications. The difficulty inherent in the precise economic meaning of statistical estimates of aggregate production function parameters is further aggravated by the fact that, in most macro production studies, time is very often used as a proxy for technological change. The conceptual equating of technological change to a shift in the production function over time does not imply that it can be estimated by using a time index. Time as a technical change variable portrays smooth and monotonous rates of change in the impact of technological progress on output. It invariably excludes the cycles inherent to the diffusion of innovations. At the micro level, adequate specification of the technological change variable requires detailed engineering knowledge of the innovation process. Such knowledge is rarely available at a firm level, much less at an industry or macroeconomic level.

In addition to the problem of an appropriate proxy for technological change, suitable econometric specification of the technological structure requires a precise distinction between embodied and disembodied technological change, as well as between scale-related and scale-independent technological change. Lack of precise characterization of technology can impair the economic and statistical validity of parameters and the reliability of empirical findings. Untangling of factors defining embodied and disembodied technology is a complex task, even at the micro level of production. Constrained by the complexity involved, economists often assume technology to be of the disembodied form, which limits the accuracy of their findings and interpretations.

An important advantage of the index number method derives from the fact that it allows for embodied effects. However, such allowance is made only through changes in input prices that in turn cause changes in the weights assigned for aggregation. The basic idea involved is that an enhancement in input quality would increase price by raising the average and marginal products associated with its use. This does not adequately account for the effects of technological change. Yet, in the case of the index number method, the adverse effects of imperfect specifications are likely to be smaller than in econometric estimations, since there is no reliance on statistical estimation techniques. Thus, the absence of the use of statistical estimation techniques defines a major relative advantage of the index number method.

Although the index number approach appears to offer a less sophisticated but potentially more reliable method for measuring technological change, it has certain disadvantages. The major disadvantage of the standard index number approach is the necessity to assume *a priori* the existence of constant returns to scale and competitive markets. In the case of the Divisia index, in particular, the main disadvantage is that it does not provide a unique formula for the shift in technology, since there are many ways of approximating continuous time derivatives by discrete differences. The exact index number method, on the other hand, is constrained by its form-specific character, and the assumption of a specific functional form of an underlying cost function is its major shortcoming.

Compared to econometric and index number methods, the biggest advantage of the nonparametric approach is that it does not require any restrictive assumptions regarding the functional form of a firm or industry production function. In spite of this advantage, the method is not generally used because (1) its validity rests on the assumption of continuous technological progress over time (it does not work if there is technological regress) and (2) it involves comparatively far more complex computation procedures.

In summary, each method has its advantages and disadvantages. No single method can be perceived as the right or best method. In the context of their applications, the appropriate choice depends on the specific purpose of the study. For example, if one is interested in finding out the structure of input relationships, the complementarity and substitutability between them, or the bias in technological change, the econometric method provides most advantages. Alternatively, if the objective is to decompose total factor productivity growth and identify different sources of this growth, the index number method would appear to be the proper choice. A majority of the studies in the productivity literature are directed toward identifying various interrelationships among production structure, technology bias, and productivity performance. Accordingly, the econometric approach is widely used.

TFP, TECHNOLOGICAL CHANGE, AND PRODUCTION FUNCTION

Regardless of the methodological differences in their derivation, all TFP measures depend, in an essential way, on an underlying aggregate production function. The concept of an aggregate production function defines the very basis of each of these measures. A number of problems with TFP measurement, thus, arise from such dependence. First, the concept of the production function is based on certain stringent assumptions and raises issues that are complex in nature.[16] Second, ignoring some of the thorny questions and assuming the existence of an aggregate production function, the exact specification and estimation of such a function becomes crucial for defining any TFP measure. Finally, given the estimates of the parameters of a production function, one has to deal with the problems of interpreting the nature of a productivity measure and/or a relevant form of technological change. The nature and form of technological change, in turn, becomes critical in the interpretation of TFP measures.

NATURE OF TECHNOLOGICAL CHANGE

Technological change has generally been considered as a measure of shift in a production function. There are a number of ways in which such a shift takes place. Conventional literature makes a distinction between embodied and disembodied technological change. Technological change is called disembodied if, independent of any changes in the factor inputs, the isoquant contours of a production function shift inward toward the origin as time progresses. This implies that, with time, the same desired level of output can be produced with less utilization of factor inputs. Thus, even if the inputs of capital, labor, and materials remain completely fixed in supply, the maximum output that can be produced increases over time as a result of disembodied technological change. This increase is attributed to improvements in techniques and/or organizational behavior that enhance the productivity of old inputs. Although there are situations when such technological change does take place (learning by doing for example), the hypothesis that technological change occurs in this disembodied fashion has been questioned. Casual observation indeed suggests that many inventions or improvements in techniques can be introduced only by building new capital equipment or improved design, by the introduction of new labor with enhanced skill, or by developing sophisticated material inputs. Technological change of this sort, where new capital or new skills or new materials define the essential source of improvements in techniques is called embodied technological change; it is built into or embodied in new capital equipment, trained labor, or newly developed materials. A simple mathematical representation of each of these two types of technological change would help clear understanding.

Disembodied Technological Change

A traditional neoclassical production function having n inputs and exhibiting disembodied technological change has the following general form:

$$Q = f(x_1, x_2, \ldots, x_n; t). \tag{3.8}$$

It is assumed that f has continuous second partial derivatives with respect to all the variables. It is also assumed that $f(x_1, x_2, \ldots, x_n; t)$ has the usual neoclassical properties regarding marginal productivity of factor inputs. Making the assumption that technology progresses over time, we have

$$f_t = \frac{\partial f}{\partial t} > 0 \tag{3.9}$$

for any given t, where $f_t > 0$ implies positive shifts in the production function. This states that output increases with time while all inputs are held constant, which is what is known as disembodied technological change. Disembodied technological change may be exemplified by factor augmentation. Assuming for convenience that the production function of equation (3.8) contains only two inputs, capital (K) and labor (L), factor augmenting can be represented as

$$Q = f(K, L; t) = g[b(t)K, a(t)L], \tag{3.10}$$

where a and b are functions of time alone and g is homogeneous of degree one. The terms b(t)K and a(t)L are often identified as effective capital and effective labor, respectively. Defining the ratio of effective capital to effective labor as

$$Z = \frac{b(t)K}{a(t)L}, \tag{3.11}$$

equation (3.10) may be written in the following form:

$$\frac{Q}{a(t)L} = g\left[\frac{b(t)K}{a(t)L}, 1\right]; \qquad g = (Z, 1) = g(Z). \tag{3.12}$$

Technological change is said to be purely labor augmenting if $Db(t) = 0$ and $Da(t) > 0$, whereas it is purely capital augmenting if $Da(t) = 0$, and $Db(t) > 0$.

Within the disembodied category, technological change may be biased or unbiased. There are various indices for defining biases. The index most commonly used is based on the change in relative factor shares. With the two inputs of capital and labor, this index (I) is defined as

$$1 = \frac{p_K K}{p_L L}\left[\frac{\partial(p_L L/p_K K)}{\partial t}\right]_Z, \tag{3.13}$$

where the association of Z with the second term implies that the partial derivatives with respect to time are taken along the specified path in Z. Once a specific path in Z is designated, equation (3.13) measures the percentage change in the ratio of relative shares and provides the following classifications:

1. Technological change is neutral if and only if relative shares remain unchanged and $I = 0$ for movements along a specified path.
2. Technological change is labor saving if the relative share of labor falls along a specified path; that is, technological change is labor saving if and only if $I < 0$. It is labor using if the relative share moves in the opposite direction.
3. Similarly, technological change is capital saving, if capital share falls along a specified path; that is, if and only if $I > 0$.

These definitions are not path independent; on the contrary, a specified path is essential. So far no consensus has emerged regarding the specification of a path. Accordingly, different authors have suggested different paths. Three commonly discussed paths, defined by the constancy of different ratios, are (1) capital/output ratio, (2) capital/labor ratio, and (3) labor/output ratio. Three different concepts of neutral technological change derive from the constancy of these three ratios. Technological change is Harrod neutral if and only if $I = 0$ for path 1; it is Hicks neutral if and only if $I = 0$ for path 2; and it is Solow neutral if and only if $I = 0$ for path 3. These three cases correspond to (1) pure labor augmentation, (2) equal labor and capital augmentation, and (3) pure capital augmentation. Thus, any type of neutral technological change is a special case of factor augmenting technological change.

Embodied Technological Change

When technological change is embodied in factor inputs, biases in technological change do not depend on changes in relative shares. Instead, they depend on (1) elasticities of substitution between factor inputs, σ, and (2) differential rates of growth of input embodiments. Embodiment means that the new inputs are more efficient than the old ones because of technological advances. Mathematical representation of this concept requires a production function as the starting point. Assuming that production function is represented by equation (3.10), the direction of technological change can be determined by observing the nature of the ratio a(t)/b(t). If a(t)/b(t) is constant, technological change is Hicks neutral; it is Harrod neutral with b(t) constant; and is Solow neutral with a(t) constant. Biases in embodied technological change, B(t), can be defined as[17]

$$B(t) = \left[\frac{Da(t)}{a(t)} - \frac{Db(t)}{b(t)} \right]\left(1 - \frac{1}{\sigma}\right) \tag{3.14}$$

where a and b are coefficients of factor augmentation and functions of time, D represents the derivative with respect to time, and σ is elasticity of substitution.

The problem in measuring embodied technological change lies in distinguishing it from (1) augmentation effect and (2) corrections for quality of input effect. The augmentation effect expresses the productivity increase of an input due to technological advance; it is equivalent to a specific increase in its quantity. Although the augmentation effect may at times be seen as the obvious consequence of embodiment effect, the two are quite distinct.[18] Similarly, quality improvements in an input can be expressed as equivalent to the embodiment effect.[19]

AGGREGATE PRODUCTION FUNCTION

The concept of an aggregate production function rests on strict assumptions about the properties of inputs and outputs. One of the stringent assumptions is that a firm operates at the production possibility frontier, which implies that a firm makes an efficient use of technology and inputs. This condition is rarely satisfied in the real world. The empirical problem associated with this, and other equally stringent assumptions, is obvious since real-world production systems are not efficient. Variations in the degrees of inefficiency among micro production systems affect a broadly defined measure of productivity and hence that of technological change. The problem becomes particularly acute at the macro-level, where the assumption that all or most agents in an economy are, or even can be, motivated to produce efficiently becomes all the more stringent. In addition, there are other problems arising out of the relationship between productivity measures and production functions. Three relevant problems are (1) separability, (2) distinction between value added and gross output concepts, and (3) aggregation of inputs and outputs.

Separability

Most theoretical and applied productivity analyses are based on the assumption of separability, which implies that the production possibility sets can be represented by a separable transformation surface defined by an equality between aggregate levels of inputs and outputs. These transformation surfaces are obtained by their own aggregate functions. Consider a production system completely defined by an implicit multi-input, multi-output production function F:

$$F(\mathbf{Q}, \mathbf{x}) = 0, \qquad (3.15)$$

where $\mathbf{Q} = (q_1, q_2, \ldots, q_m)$ and $\mathbf{x} = (x_1, x_2, \ldots, x_n)$ are vectors of output and input, respectively. Mathematically, the separability assumption implies that equation (3.15) can be specified as

$$g(\mathbf{Q}) = f(\mathbf{x}), \qquad (3.16)$$

where g and f are aggregate functions. Since most production processes, particularly at an aggregate level, do not in general exhibit independence of input and output substitution rates along the efficiency frontiers, this assumption is restrictive from the point of view of economic theory and reality. In a complex technology, changes in the input-possibilities functions are likely to affect the output-possibilities functions. Accordingly, recent research is attempting to develop an analytical framework that avoids separability assumption.[20]

Value Added and Gross Output

The measure of output generally used in the production function is one of real value added. For an economy, real value added is defined as the aggregate volume of all final goods and services net of all intermediate goods. A traditionally defined national net product adjusted for price changes usually serves as a proxy for a real value added concept. For industries and companies, the price adjusted value of goods and services purchased from outside the system are subtracted from the gross output to obtain real value added. The relationship of real value added to the production function inclusive of all inputs is not straightforward. Since real value added (VA) is defined as the difference between separately deflated gross output (Q) and intermediate material inputs (M), the use of value added in aggregate productivity studies as a measure of output implicitly assumes that the underlying production function is additive and separable; being of the form Q = VA + M. Although the use of a value added measure of output in aggregate productivity analysis is no doubt convenient from the point of view of macro-data availability, its validity rests only on certain restrictive assumptions regarding production technology.[21] This validity requires prices of outputs and inputs to vary in strict proportions. Apart from their restrictiveness, value added productivity measures, by excluding intermediate materials from both input and output aggregates, fail to capture their full impact of these elements on productivity. For example, value added based productivity measures distort changes in productivity growth related to the substitution of capital for imported intermediate goods.

Accordingly, gross output may be more appropriate for productivity studies.[22] At a firm level, readily accessible data on gross output facilitates its use in empirical studies. At an industry level, data facilitating separation between intermediate materials purchased within the industry and intermediate goods purchased from outside the industry needs to be obtained for gross output computation. At the economy level, the choice between a gross output measure inclusive of all intermediate commodities and a value added measure exclusive of these rests on the specific objective of study. For the purpose of assessing the productivity of the national production network, a gross output measure is preferable. On the other hand, if national economic welfare implications of productivity changes are to be analyzed, the choice of value added based measure of TFP may be suitable.

Input Aggregation

Traditional production theory rests on the assumption that homogeneous aggregates of different factor inputs exist. However, the concepts of aggregate labor and capital have been subjects of major controversy in economic literature. Labor and capital are aggregates of elements that are basically heterogeneous with divergent characteristics; they differ in their productive qualities, nature of growth, and mobilities. These heterogeneous properties are both a cause and a consequence of technological change in an economy.

Most of the controversy on aggregation has emerged from the problem of aggregating, or grouping, different types of capital goods. The neoclassical approach is based on the assumption of a competitive economy where market for capital goods is independent of both relative prices and income distribution. The necessary and sufficient conditions for grouping different types of capital are[23] (1) the rate of substitution between capital goods of different types must be independent of the quantity of labor used with them and (2) the marginal rate of substitution between any two types of capital goods must be constant; that is, these different types of capital goods are perfect substitutes. These conditions ensure malleability characteristics of capital goods in neoclassical production function.

There is a school of thought that argues that it is impossible to construct an index of the quantity of capital.[24] Capital is essentially a value concept; it is affected by changes in relative factor prices, such as interest rates and wage rates. Independence of capital from all these prices is feasible only in a simplified economy where there is only one type of capital good and no technological change. An extension of this argument suggests that technological change involves complementarity between different types of machines, or capital goods. They are, therefore, not perfect substitutes as required by neoclassical aggregation theorems. This notion of capital as a value concept in turn leads to the debate on double switching, which states that the relative price frontier is not a straight line so that the same method of production can be the most profitable at more than one rate of profit. If this is true, measurement of capital in physical units, as assumed by neoclassical theory, is ruled out. Without this assumption, the concept of factor intensity becomes meaningless and the neoclassical production function is not definable.

Apart from conceptual difficulties, measurement problems of aggregate capital input abound. There is currently, however, a consensus among applied researchers on the following points: (1) disaggregation of capital goods in terms of plant, equipment, and tools is acceptable, (2) imputation of flows of capital services rather than stocks of capital is appropriate (it conforms with other inputs and outputs as flows of goods and services), and (3) capital inputs need be adjusted for degree of utilization and depreciation whenever such data are available. There is, on the other hand, little agreement as to how to (1) make different vintage prices comparable, (2) handle intertemporal effects of capital on output, and (3) separate changes in quantities of capital services from those in quality, particularly for the purpose of construction of aggregate TFP measures. Since estimation of capital services requires imputation of non-market transactions, and there exists no unique method for such imputation, variations in capital input estimations are quite large between different studies.[25] These differences, in turn, have a significant effect on TFP measures and estimates.[26] Interpretation of TFP measures for economic efficiency or welfare needs to recognize the problems arising from capital estimation procedures.

FORMS OF AGGREGATE PRODUCTION FUNCTION

The magnitude and stability of all TFP measures depend on how accurately a production function is specified and estimated. In principle, if (1) all the explanatory inputs are included and properly measured and (2) the function governing their interaction is precisely specified, then the TFP measures should be zero. These are serious ifs that are seldom satisfied in the real world. In spite of the deviation of reality from theory, empirical research on the production function became popular since early 1930s following the estimation of a simple Cobb-Douglas function.[27] The essence of this approach is to specify an aggregate neoclassical production function relating output to aggregate inputs of capital and labor services. This specification implied serious separability restrictions.[28] In spite of its restrictiveness, however, this production function framework has proved useful for a variety of applications. In addition to the Cobb-Douglas function, the constant elasticity of substitution (CES) production function received much attention in the empirical literature. In spite of its advantage over the Cobb-Douglas, the CES function has also many shortcomings. The form of this function is not flexible enough to adequately identify sources of TFP growth, which has led to the development of generalized production functions; however, the CES provides a good starting point for such generalized forms.

CES Production Function

The two-factor CES production function has all the usual properties of a neoclassical production function. It includes Cobb-Douglas and Leontief functions as special cases. It has been derived from the empirical relation

$$\ln \frac{Q}{L} = a_0 + a_1 \ln \left(\frac{p_l}{p_q} \right) + u_0, \qquad (3.17)$$

where p_l is the price of labor, and p_q of output; u_0 is a random stochastic term; and a_1 is the estimate of elasticity of substitution. This relationship assumes competitive profit maximization behavior, independence of (Q/L) from capital intensity (K/L), no measurement error in the variables, and no adjustment lag between (Q/L) and (p_l/p_q). The usual CES production function derived from equation (3.17) may be written as

$$Q = \gamma \left[\delta K^{-\rho} + (1 - \delta) L^{-\rho} \right]^{\mu/\rho} \qquad (3.18)$$

where γ, δ, ρ, and μ are, respectively, the parameters of efficiency, distribution, substitution, and degrees of returns to scale. From equation (3.17), average labor productivity depends on capital intensity, (K/L), and the magnitudes of σ, δ, ρ, and μ. The elasticity of substitution, σ, is equal to $1/(1 + \rho)$; K and L are measured in physical units.

Empirical evidence indicates that the parameters of a CES production function are highly sensitive to slight changes in data and measurement of variables. The point estimates of the most important parameter, σ, vary considerably with changes in data sets, types of industries, and levels of aggregation. Furthermore, they are sensitive to cyclical fluctuations of demand. The only tentative conclusion is that most of the time series estimates of σ are below unity, while cross section estimates are generally higher than the time-series estimates and are close to unity. The evidence on the estimates of other parameters, γ, δ, and μ is also mixed. Estimates of γ vary widely, depending on the time period used and the assumption regarding returns to scale. The estimates of μ are generally greater than unity in time series and about unity in cross section estimates. Regardless of the type of data set used, these estimates are sensitive to rates of utilization of inputs and the level of demand. The instability and inconsistencies of these estimates are attributable to the restrictive nature of the CES function. It does not permit more than two factors in addition to interaction between them. Within the boundary of a two-factor production function, attempts to remove these restrictive features have resulted in the formation of yet another function, known as variable elasticity of substitution (VES) production function.

VES Production Function

The concept of the VES production function defines a significant step toward amendment of the standard two-factor CES function. VES stands for variable elasticity of substitution in comparison with CES where it is constant. In the CES function, elasticity of substitution, σ, is assumed to be invariant with respect to changes in factor proportions, skill mix, and returns to scale. The significance of the VES production function lies in the fact that variations in σ are accepted. The extent of variations in σ in relation to capital intensity, in particular, is tested by fitting the relation

$$\ln \frac{Q}{L} = a_0 + a_1 \ln \frac{P_l}{P_q} + a_2 \ln \frac{K}{L} + u_1, \qquad (3.19)$$

where u_1 is a random error term. If $a_2 \neq 0$, condition (3.19) implies the following VES production function:

$$q = [\beta_0 k^{-\rho} + \beta_1 k^{-m\rho}]^{-1/\rho}, \qquad (3.20)$$

where $q = Q/L$; $k = K/L$; and β_0, β_1, m, and ρ are parameters. These parameters are related to the parameters in equation (3.19) in the following way:

$$\beta_0 = \frac{1 - a_1}{(1 - a_1 - a_2)(a_0)^{1/a_1}},$$

$$\beta_1 = \frac{-C(1 - a_1)}{a_1(a_0)^{1/a_1}},$$

$C = $ A constant of integration,

$$m = \frac{a_2}{(1 - a_1)}, \quad \text{and}$$

$$\rho = \frac{1 - a_1}{a_1}.$$

The variable elasticity of substitution, σ_v,[29] for this function is defined as

$$\sigma_v = \frac{1}{(1 + \rho - m\rho/S_K)}, \qquad (3.21)$$

where S_K is the share of capital. Relation (3.20) includes the Leontief, Cobb-Douglas, and the CES production functions as special cases. If $\rho = 0$, the function reduces to the Cobb-Douglas function; if $m = 0$, it changes to the CES function. Since both m and S_K are positive, the relationship between σ_v and σ depends on the magnitude of ρ. If $\rho \geq 0$, $\sigma_v \geq \sigma$; on the other hand if $\rho < 0$, $\sigma_v < \sigma$.[30]

Duality-Based Production Functions

The VES function, similar to the CES, is confined to two inputs. Attempts to include more than two inputs have led to formulations of multifactor analogs of the conventional two-factor functional forms. Such formulations had serious deficiencies. For example, when three or more inputs are included in a CES function, strict assumptions about partial elasticities of substitution, σ_{ij}, are required for estimation purposes.[31] All pairs of partial elasticities of different classes of inputs must either have the same constant value or be unity for all subsets of inputs. Studies have shown that such an assumption is equivalent to strong separability restrictions and is based on concepts of aggregate indices of capital and labor.[32]

The severe limitations of the conventional functional forms have motivated substantial research toward the development of new forms that do not require *a priori* separability restrictions. An important outcome of such research is the formulation and estimation of aggregate production functions by exploiting the duality relation between cost and production function. The significance of such an approach lies in the fact that functions formulated by using a duality relation can estimate second-order parameters, such as elasticity of substitution, with reasonable efficiency. By establishing a unique correspondence between production and cost functions, duality permits one to estimate technological change by examining either of the two functions. This simplifies the task. Cost functions are easier to formulate and estimate than generalized production functions.[33] Also, they permit arbitrary degrees of substitutability between pairs of factors in an n-factor production process.[34] Finally, the link between short- and long-run cost relationships can be used to integrate short- and long-run production functions. These features are useful in the estimation of the behavior of factor productivity.

Two specific forms of duality-based production functions have been developed. One of these is known as a "generalized Leontief production function."[35] This is a quadratic form in an arbitrary number of inputs. It reduces to the Leontief function as a special case. The second form is called the "transcendental logarithmic production function," translog for short.[36] Derived through the Taylor series expansion, this form has both linear and quadratic terms with an arbitrary number of inputs. It reduces to CES and multi-input Cobb-Douglas forms under specific conditions. Our analysis in this study is based on this form.

NOTES

1. On the basis of real product per unit of labor, U.S. productivity grew by 3.5 percent in the first two decades after World War II. During 1966–1973, it slowed to 2.1 percent per year and over 1973–1983, to 1.1 percent. Similarly, total factor productivity had a slowdown of 2 percentage points; from 2.8 percent to 0.8 percent. As a result, increases in standards of living and real wages per worker have slowed down.

2. Western European nations had formed productivity centers by the early 1950s. The Japanese productivity movement started in 1953 and its productivity center was established in 1955. Various countries in South America and Africa had also established productivity centers by the 1960s. No specialized productivity agency was established in the United States until 1970, when the National Commission on Productivity was created

in June. In 1975 this commission was replaced by the National Center for Productivity and Quality of Working Life.

3. Fabricant (1983) distinguishes between economic efficiency and economic welfare.

4. Morrison and Diewert (1985) discuss this issue.

5. Among researchers who have contributed to the process of development of this measure, the prominent ones are Kendrick (1961, 1980), Solow (1957), Fabricant (1983), Denison (1978), and Christensen and Jorgenson (1969).

6. Jorgenson and Nishimiza (1978) suggest this interpretation.

7. Tinbergen (1942) originally and Solow (1957) proposed this interpretation.

8. This interpretation of technological change was proposed and formalized by Solow (1957). However, as Diwan (1968d) points out, it depends on a strict assumption about constant returns to scale. Diwan (1965, 1966) found that returns to scale in U.S. manufactures were of the order of 1.3; much higher than the assumed value of 1. Diwan and Gujerati (1968) and Diwan and Leonardson (1986) also supported earlier findings about economies of scale.

9. Binswanger (1974b) estimated a translog cost function. Berndt and Khaled (1979) used a generalized Box-Cox functional form for the cost function, which has translog and other functional forms as special cases.

10. The "exact index number approach" has also been discussed, for example in Diewert (1978).

11. Hulten (1973); Caves, Christensen, and Swanson (1980); Denny, Fuss and Waverman (1981); and Felemban (1989) have extended this approach to the case of multiple products.

12. Diewert (1980) makes a strong case for limiting the forms of production function to those that are flexible. He terms index numbers that are exact for flexible functions "superlative."

13. The quadratic lemma holds because the function of equation (3.6) is quadratic in the logarithm of output, input prices, and t.

14. Detailed steps involved in deriving this identity are given in Diewert (1980).

15. Diewert and Parkan (1979) have developed some of these tests.

16. Some of these issues are discussed as "capital controversies" dealing with the meaning and existence of aggregate capital and the aggregate production function. Harcourt (1969) summarizes these controversies, which question the very existence of an aggregate production function, in detail.

17. Diwan (1970) develops a measure for bias from a VES function.

18. Embodiment of technological change in capital through its impact on the marginal product of labor can be considered as a labor augmenting case of technological change. This point is discussed in Nadiri (1970).

19. There is a subtle distinction between the skill content of an individual worker and that of a group of workers. Productivity changes due to compositional changes in the labor force at a point of time are not a part of the embodiment effect; whereas improvements due to increased skills of the labor force are part of it.

20. Christensen, Jorgenson and Lau (1973) and Diewert (1976) have introduced a flexible form of the production function that does not need the constraint of separability of inputs.

21. Diewert (1978) elaborates this issue.

22. Denny and Fuss (1977) have developed a test for separability and effectiveness of value added measures in models of production function. Nadiri and Schankerman (1981) test separability empirically.

23. These are discussed in Nadiri (1970).

24. Robinson (1955) and Kaldor (1967) have been the chief proponents of this school. It was Robinson (1956) that started the debate on aggregate capital and production function that are now discussed as "capital controversies."

25. The two most common methods of capital measurement are those used by Denison (1962).

26. Christensen and Jorgenson (1970) and Hulten (1979) used the same macro data set and different capital measurement procedures. They obtained different TFP results.

27. It all started with Cobb and Douglas (1928). Diwan (1968a) discusses the problems of estimating the Cobb-Douglas function.

28. Such specification became the subject of intense criticism beginning in 1947 when Leontief established that the validity of such a function rests on stringent separability restrictions.

29. Diwan (1970) distinguishes σ_v from σ. The term σ_v has variations because of its relationship with input shares. However, input shares can also be expressed in prices so that variations can come from other sources as well.

30. Diwan (1970) found $\sigma_v > \sigma$ for U.S. manufacturing. Diwan (1970) and Hildebrand and Liu (1965) have shown that m $\neq$ 1, and technical change is non-neutral in the Hicksian sense. An interesting extension of the VES function has been made by Diwan and Kallianpur (1985, 1986) in their attempt to study the impact of biotechnology in agricultural productivity.

31. McFadden (1963) and Uzawa (1962) prove these theorems.

32. Berndt and Christensen (1973a) discuss this equivalence.

33. The sociology of the professionals involved in analyzing and estimating productivity indices believes in the cost function rather than the production function although cost functions are derived from the dual of production functions and are identical in theory.

34. This characteristic adds an artistry to estimates of substitution and complementarity and measures of productivity. In art, it is difficult to distinguish between the observer and the observed.

35. This has been developed by Diewert (1971).

36. It is derived in Christensen, Jorgenson, and Lau (1973).

4

The Translog Function

INTRODUCTION

Over the past decade, a number of variations of the translog function have been used. Indeed, the translog function has opened up a whole new frontier in productivity analysis by permitting researchers to shed light on a number of questions: (1) what factors are responsible for interindustry differences in productivity levels? (2) how do industries differ in terms of substitution possibilities among different inputs? (3) what are the different sources of growth in productivity? and (4) what explains international differences in levels of productivity and growth rates of technological change? These questions are crucial for defining policy measures that promote productivity advance and help other important economic goals. Our interest here lies in tracing the wide range of possibilities associated with the usage of translog and productivity measurement.

The simplest available methodology under the econometric approach consists of estimation of a cost function along with the relevant share equations. The cost function assumes homogeneity in prices. The share equations are derived from the conditions of producer equilibrium and Shephard's lemma.[1] In its most general form, a translog cost function may be written as:

$$C = C_o + a_q'Q + a_i'P + 1/2Q'a_{qq}Q + 1/2P'a_{ij}P + Q'a_{qi}P, \quad (4.1)$$

where all variables C, Q, and P are in logarithms. The variable C is a scalar and refers to total cost. The terms Q and P are column vectors of outputs and input prices, respectively. The term C_o is a scalar and basically a constant; a_q' and a_i' are row vectors; and a_{qq}, a_{ij}, and a_{qi} are matrices of coefficients. The order of these vectors and matrices is defined by the order of Q and P. Equation (4.1) is a multiproduct cost function that takes into consideration all sorts of interactions both within and between output quantities and various input prices. Economic theory places a number of constraints on this general form through the requirement for convexity of the production function. If one assumes constant returns to scale and a single output,[2] the cost function (4.1) reduces to

$$C^u = C_o + a_i'P + 1/2\ P'\ a_{ij}\ P,\qquad\qquad(4.2)$$

where C^u refers to unit cost as against C, which is total cost. It is generally assumed that conditions of symmetry, homogeneity, and homotheticity hold. These conditions imply

$$a_{ij} = a_{ji}\qquad a_i'\ I^c = 1,\qquad a_{ij}\ I^c = 0,\qquad\qquad(4.3)$$

where I^c is a column vector of 1s. Using Shephard's lemma, we can get share equations from the cost function. For the function (4.2) these are given by

$$S = a_i + a_{ij}P,\qquad\qquad(4.4)$$

where S is a column vector of input shares. In view of the restrictions in equation (4.3), the order of S is one less than that of P. One of the share equations is redundant.

This methodology has been extended to develop models of cost and production structure in multi-product industries by taking account of disaggregated output levels. Another extension involves combining translog with less flexible production processes and limited substitution possibilities. In view of the short-run restriction on a production process imposed by fixity of inputs, the translog function has been modified to allow for partial equilibrium analysis within a static framework. Such partial equilibrium analysis helps to distinguish between short- and long-run substitution between input pairs. Finally, to trace the adjustment path of inputs over the long run, the translog function has further been modified to allow for disequilibrium, which enables a distinction between short, intermediate, and long-run effects in productivity development.

ECONOMETRIC APPLICATIONS

An empirical framework has been developed by combining a three-factor translog production function with its value share equations to investigate the permissibility of aggregating diverse inputs in U.S. manufacturing for 1928–1968.[3] It also allows one to test the existence of agregate indices of equipment and structure in U.S. manufacturing and assess possibilities of substitution between them. The empirical results obtained on the basis of this methodology suggest that the degree of substitution varies between pairs of factors. Equipment and structures are more substitutable for each other than for labor. Hypotheses regarding separability between, (1) equipment and labor and (2) structure and labor were refuted by these results. It appears that while equipment and structure can be defined in terms of a consistent aggregate index, no consistent aggregate index exists for equipment and labor or for structures and labor.

Exactly similar methodology involving five input factors was used to estimate elasticities of derived demand and of substitution for the U.S. agricultural sector.[4] The forms of the cost function and share equations are equivalent to those defined in equations (4.2) and (4.4). While assuming constant returns to scale for greater simplicity in estimation, the method allowed the possibility of non-neutral technological change. The agricultural production function was found to be not separable between any input groups. In regard to input substitution, there is complementarity between labor-fertilizer and machinery-fertilizer pairs. On the other hand, land is substitutable for all inputs of production; this substitutability is most significant for fertilizers.[5]

Another application relates to the U.S. industrial sector. The authors designed a four-factor translog model for studying the production structure of the Bell System at the aggregate level, with research and development expenditure as an additional input, additional to the traditional inputs of labor, capital, and materials.[6] This study refers to some specific questions: (1) what are the patterns of substitution among factors inputs, especially between research and development and other traditional inputs? (2) what is the impact of technological change on the production structure? and (3) what is the impact of scale economies on the rate of growth of total factor productivity? The estimated coefficients of elasticity of substitution suggest substitutability between all traditional inputs; research and development is substitutable for capital and material, but complementary to labor. In studying the impact of scale economies, the study designed a supplementary decomposition procedure, the results of which indicate that scale economies accounted for between 60 to 70 percent of productivity growth in the Bell System over the entire postwar period.

The debate over energy price shocks and their possible impact on U.S. manufacturing production has stimulated numerous studies to investigate substitution possibilities between energy and non-energy inputs. One study characterized the technology of U.S. manufacturing by a four-factor translog model restricted with constant returns to scale and Hick's neutrality.[7] Estimated coefficients of elasticities of substitution in this study show substitutability between labor and energy and complementarity between capital and energy. These results have important implications for energy conservation policy. Other studies on the issue of the energy/non-energy input relationship show improvement by disaggregating energy inputs into several subtypes and modeling production with a non-homothetic structure,[8] and with a non-neutral technology.[9]

Use of the simple translog cost function has also gained popularity in international comparisons of production structure and productivity growth.[10] One study estimated a four-factor translog cost function together with the derived share equations to analyze multi-factor and labor productivity growth in the aggregate manufacturing sectors in Japan and the United States.[11] Sources of growth in output and productivity for each of the two countries were identified, and the study concluded that (1) the remarkable record of labor productivity growth in Japan is attributable in large part to the growth of capital stock and (2) an appropriate framework for studying productivity growth in an aggregate economy is gross output instead of value added based analysis, which requires assumptions about aggregation.

EXTENSIONS

A new variation of the translog function, the CES-translog function, has also been used in the productivity literature. As the name suggests, this function includes both the CES and the translog as special cases. It is compatible with a wider range of substitution possibilities than either of the two functions individually. This function takes the form[12]

$$\ln C(Q,\mathbf{p},t) = a_0 + a_q \ln Q + a_{qq}(\ln Q)^2 + a_t t + \frac{1}{2}a_{tt}t^2$$

$$+ \ln [\sum a_i p_i^{(1-S)}]^{1/(1-S)} + \frac{1}{2}\sum\sum a_{ij}\ln p_i \ln p_j$$

$$+ \sum a_{iq}\ln Q \ln p_i + \sum a_{it}t\ln p_i + a_{tq}t\ln Q. \qquad (4.5)$$

By Shephard's lemma, the input demand functions are given by

$$S_i = [a_i p_i^{(1-S)}/\sum a_j p_j^{(1-S)}] + \sum a_{ij}\ln p_j + a_{iq}\ln Q + a_{it}t, \qquad (4.6)$$

where S_i denotes the share of the ith factor in total cost. When all the a_{ij}, a_{iq}, a_{it}, a_{qq}, a_{tq}, a_{tt}, and a_t are zero, the function reduces to the CES. When s approaches 1, it reduces to the translog. A homothetic structure of production with Hick's neutral technological change is assumed with the following restrictions imposed on the cost function of equation (4.5):

$$\sum a_i = 0, \qquad a_{ij} = a_{ji} \quad \text{for all } i \neq j; \qquad \sum a_{ij} = 0; \qquad \sum a_{ji} = 0;$$
$$\sum a_{iq} = 0; \qquad a_{qq} = 0; \qquad \sum a_{it} = 0. \qquad (4.7)$$

Equations (4.5) and (4.6) were estimated using eight different samples of varying sizes and variables. The CES-translog was found to be a significant improvement over both the CES and the translog in a majority of cases. Two other studies support the conclusion about the performance of the CES-translog function.[13]

The simple translog has often been extended for modeling cost and production in multi-product industries. The first attempt in estimating a multi-product cost function was taken while studying the structure of cost and production in U.S. railroad services.[14] Defining freight and passenger services as two distinct outputs and labor, material, structure, equipment, and energy as inputs, U.S. railroad services were modeled with a cost function similar to the form of equation (4.1) utilizing cross-section data. Four different models were estimated: (1) an unrestricted model, (2) a model with homogeneity in prices and output, (3) a model with separability between inputs and outputs imposed, and (4) a Cobb-Douglas model. The unrestricted model was chosen. With the estimated coefficients, marginal cost and scale economies for different outputs were computed at the firm level. In addition, elasticities of substitution between pairs of inputs were also computed for characterizing the production structure of the U.S. railroad industry. A comparison of results for restricted and unrestricted cost function shows that *a priori* restrictions of homogeneity and separability lead to substantial errors in the estimation of marginal costs and scale economies. In a later study, cost elasticities with respect to output and factor prices for individual railroads were also computed.[15] Also constructed were industry average cost elasticities as weighted averages of individual railroad elasticities. These average elasticities were used as weights for combining rates of growth of outputs and inputs.[16]

All empirical translog models discussed so far have been constructed on the basis of an assumption of full equilibrium. Recognition of the fact that capital structure in certain production processes often remains fixed during a particular model year has inspired researchers to develop models with partial equilibrium in variable inputs. In the productivity literature, such models are called translog variable cost (TVC) models.[17] The TVC function with one fixed factor takes the following general form:

$$\ln CV = a_0 + \sum a_i \ln p_i + \frac{1}{2}\sum\sum a_{ij} \ln p_i \ln p_j + a_q \ln Q + \frac{1}{2}a_{qq}(\ln Q)^2$$

$$+ \sum a_{iq}\ln p_i \ln Q + a_K \ln K + \frac{1}{2}a_{KK}(\ln K)^2$$

$$+ \sum a_{iK}\ln p_i \ln K + a_{qK}\ln Q \ln K + a_T T + \frac{1}{2}a_{TT}T^2$$

$$+ \sum a_{iT}T \ln p_i + a_{Tq}T \ln Q + a_{TK}T \ln K. \qquad (4.8)$$

Homogeneity in prices and scale are ensured by the following restrictions:

$$\Sigma a_i = 1; \quad \Sigma a_{ij} = \Sigma a_{ji} = \Sigma a_{iq} = \Sigma a_{iK} = \Sigma a_{iT} = 0. \qquad (4.9)$$

Constant returns to scale require three additional restrictions:

$$a_q + a_K = 1; \quad a_{iq} + a_{iK} = 0; \quad \text{and } a_{Tq} + a_{TK} = 0. \qquad (4.10)$$

Share equations for variable factors are constructed by using Shephard's lemma as in the case of total cost function:

$$\frac{\partial \ln \text{CV}}{\partial \ln p_i} = a_i + \sum a_{ij} \ln p_j + a_{iT} T + a_{iq} \ln Q + a_{iK} \ln K. \tag{4.11}$$

Equations (4.8) and (4.11) are estimated jointly for deriving elasticities of substitution and nature of technological change.

Satisfactory results from TVC estimation were obtained in studying substitution possibilities in U.S. agriculture.[18] This estimation procedure has been used for studying the impact of technological change on optimal input-mix in specific manufacturing industries.[19] The production process in the U.S. auto industry was modeled with the TVC to analyze the impact of variable worker attitude on demand for the fixed factor, capital.[20] The significance of modeling production process with TVC instead of total cost (TC) function lies in the scope it provides for distinguishing between short- and long-run responses of inputs to changes in prices and output. By assuming full equilibrium adjustment in all the inputs, TC fails to allow for this distinction. However, one cannot define a long-run adjustment path for inputs by simply modeling and estimating TVC. In the final analysis, the TVC is limited by comparative static equilibrium. What is needed is a dynamic disequilibrium model.

DYNAMIC DISEQUILIBRIUM MODELS

The above discussion on empirical cost function models with associated factor demand equations provides the necessary background for grouping models under two different categories: (1) static and (2) dynamic. The models discussed so far belong to the former category. The basic characteristics distinguishing this group is that a static model considers the interrelationships among variable inputs, produced output, and fixed input on the basis of instantaneous adjustment. As such, it fails to distinguish between short- and long-run behavior of fixed inputs and consequently their effects on productivity growth. In contrast, dynamic models allow for quasi-fixed inputs and incorporate an endogenous adjustment process—investment path—toward desired levels of growth in the inputs. Such incorporation helps in the assessment of the impact of short-run input fixity and the speed of input adjustment on productivity growth.[21]

One such study is concerned with productivity performance in the electrical machinary industry in the United States and Japan.[22] The specific features of this methodology include (1) the normal *a priori* assumption of constant returns to scale was discarded in light of a fairly high growth rate of output in the electrical machinery industry both in the United States and in Japan. Returns to scale was estimated from the data. (2) In order to distinguish between short-run disequilibrium and long-run optimum, some factors of production were allowed to be quasi-fixed. Accordingly, an explicit account of the internal adjustment cost was included in the model. The quasi-fixed factors are assumed to satisfy separability conditions. (3) Technology in this model is defined by an exogenously determined time trend. Beginning with an analytical production function, homogeneous of degree r, with labor and material as variable factors and stocks of capital and R&D as the quasi-fixed factors, the duality theory is used to describe the production technology by the following normalized cost function:

$$
\begin{aligned}
G(W_t, X_{t-1}, \Delta X_t, Q_t, T_t) = & \left[a_0 + a_w W_t + \frac{1}{2} a_{ww} W_t^2 + a_{wt} T_t\right](Q_t)^{1/r} \\
& + a_K K_{t-1} \\
& + a_R R_{t-1} + a_{Kt} K_{t-1} T + a_{Rt} R_{t-1} T + a_K \Delta K_t \\
& + a'_R \Delta R_t \\
& + a'_{Kt} \Delta K_t T + a'_{Rt} \Delta R_t T \\
& + \frac{1}{2} a_{KK}(K_{t-1}^2/Q_t^{1/r}) + \frac{1}{2} a_{RR}(R_{t-1}^2/Q_t^{1/r}) \\
& + a_{KR}(K_{t-1} R_{t-1}/Q_t^{1/r}) + \frac{1}{2} a'_{KK}(\Delta K_t^2/Q_t^{1/r}) \\
& + \frac{1}{2} a'_{RR}(\Delta R_t^2/Q_t^{1/r}) + a'_{KR}(\Delta K_t \Delta R_t/Q_t^{1/r}) \\
& + a_{wK} W_t K_{t-1} + a_{wR} W_t R_{t-1} + a'_{wK} W_t \Delta K_t \\
& + a'_{wR} W_t \Delta R_t + a''_{KK} K_{t-1} \Delta K_t + a''_{RR} R_{t-1} \Delta R_t \\
& + a''_{KR} K_{t-1} \Delta R_t + a'_{RK} R_{t-1} \Delta K_t,
\end{aligned} \tag{4.12}
$$

where Q_t is gross output; W_t denotes the real wage rate; the prices of material is the numeraire, $X_t = [K_t, R_t]$, the vector of quasi-fixed inputs—capital and research and development; ΔX_t refers to internal adjustment cost of the quasi-fixed factors; T_t is the exogenous technology index; and a_{ij}s are parameters.

This functional form of a normalized cost function[23] is viewed as a second-order approximation to a general normalized cost function corresponding to a homogeneous technology. Also assumed were zero marginal adjustment cost under steady state, separability in quasi-fixed factors, and adjustment costs with the following restrictions:

$$
a_{wK} = a_{wR} = a'_{KK} = a'_{RR} = a'_{KR} = a'_{RK} = 0, \quad \text{and} \quad a_{KR} = 0. \tag{4.13}
$$

With the cost function, equation (4.12), and the restrictions of (4.13), an optimization problem was defined on the basis of the assumption that in each period t, for given initial stocks of K_{t-1} and R_{t-1}, the firm derives an optimal input path such that the present value of the future cost stream is minimized.[24] Choice of the quasi-fixed inputs in period t are therefore dependent on this optimal solution. The optimization problem for any period t with respect to the quasi-fixed factors is stated as

$$\min \Sigma \{[G(t + t) + Q_t^R I^R_{t+t}](1 - u_t) + Q_t^K I^K_{t+t}\}(1 + r_t)^{-t} \quad (4.14)$$

where $G(t + t) = G(W_t, K_{t+t-1}, R_{t+t-1}, \Delta K_{t+t}, \Delta R_{t+t}, Q_t)$; $I^K_{t+t} = K_{t+t} - (1 - d_K)K_{t+t-1}$; and $I^R_{t+t} = R_{t+t} - (1 - d_R)R_{t+t-1}$. The solution to this optimization problem provides the dynamic factor demand equations for the quasi-fixed factors K_t and R_t. The firm's demand equations for the variable factors are derived directly from the cost function, equation (4.12), through Shephard's lemma. Using time series data for the period 1967–1980, two sets of factor demand equations were estimated. The results show that although industries in both the United States and Japan are characterized by increasing returns to scale, the scale coefficient for Japanese industries is much higher and explains its substantial influence on productivity growth.

Another study is concerned with the aggregate manufacturing sector in the United States, Japan, and Germany.[25] Production structure is described by a cost function, basically same as equation (4.12). There are a few distinctions: (1) quasi-fixed factors are assumed to be non-separable and hence $a_{KR} \neq 0$ in the model, (2) adjustment costs of the factors are separable, and (3) technological change is the outcome of R&D expenditures and is treated endogenously. R&D represents an endogenously determined index of technological change instead of the conventional time trend T.[26] Factor demand equations derived from their cost function are estimated for studying differential input responses to changes in prices and output and rates of return on inputs among the countries. The results suggest that the speed of adjustment for capital is higher than that for R&D, rates of return for capital and R&D are similar across countries, and rate of return on R&D is higher than that for capital.

EMPIRICAL APPLICATIONS OF INDEX NUMBER METHOD

In addition to econometric estimation of production and cost functions, a particular variation of the index number method has also been used.[27] The index number method has been used for comparing aggregate economic growth in the United States and Japan, both at aggregated and disaggregated levels. The core of the method consists of forming indices of output, input, and technology. It includes three specific steps: (1) The starting point is a simple translog cost function (4.2) with an additional dummy variable. Inclusion of a dummy variable, D, results in the following functional form:

$$\ln Q = a_0 + a_K \ln K + a_L \ln L + a_D D + a_T T + \frac{1}{2} a_{KK} (\ln K)^2$$

$$+ a_{KL}\ln K \ln L + a_{KD}D \ln K + a_{KT}T \ln K$$

$$+ \frac{1}{2}a_{LL}(\ln L)^2 + a_{LD}D \ln L + a_{LT}T \ln L$$

$$+ \frac{1}{2}a_{DD}D^2 + a_{DT}DT + \frac{1}{2}a_{TT}T^2, \tag{4.15}$$

where Q is output, K is capital, L is labor, and T is time trend. Shares of capital and labor in the value of output is defined in the usual manner:

$$S_K = p_K K/p_q Q; \qquad S_L = p_L L/p_q Q, \tag{4.16}$$

where p_q = price of output, p_K = price of capital, and p_L = price of labor. Differences in technology between two countries, S_D, is defined as the log-arithmic differences in levels of output between the countries, holding capital, labor, and time constant; that is,

$$S_D = \frac{\partial \ln Q}{\partial D}. \tag{4.17}$$

An analogous definition of the rate of technical change, S_T, is the growth of output with respect to time; holding capital, labor, and country dummy variable constant, that is,

$$S_T = \frac{\partial \ln Q}{\partial T}. \tag{4.18}$$

(2) The second step consists of defining each of the aggregate output Q, capital input K, and labor input L as a function of their respective components. This step involves the formation of "translog indices" of output and inputs. The relationship between the aggregate output and its individual components is defined as

$$\ln Q = a_1 \ln Q_1 + a_2 \ln Q_2 + \ldots + a_M \ln Q_m$$

$$+ \frac{1}{2}a_{11}(\ln Q_1)^2 + \frac{1}{2} a_{12}(\ln Q_1 \ln Q_2)$$

$$+ \ldots + \frac{1}{2}a_{mm}(\ln Q_m)^2. \tag{4.19}$$

Value shares of individual outputs (S_{Qi}) are correspondingly expressed as

$$S_{Qi} = a_i + a_{1i}\ln Q_1 + \cdots + a_{mi}\ln Q_m, \qquad i = (1,2,\cdots m). \tag{4.20}$$

These value shares are used as weights in computing differences in aggregate output levels between two countries at a point of time, and for the same country between two different points of time. Specifically, differences between logarithms of aggregate output for the two countries is expressed as a weighted average of differences between logarithms of individual outputs with weights given by average value shares; that is,

$$\ln Q(US) - \ln Q(Japan) = \Sigma\ S_{Qi}[\ln Q_i(US) - \ln Q_i(Japan)], \quad (4.21)$$

where $S_{Qi} = 1/2[S_{Qi}(US) - S_{Qi}(Japan)]$. Similarly, for any given country at two discrete points of time, the difference between successive logarithms of aggregate output is expressed as a weighted average of difference between logarithms of individual outputs with weights given by average value shares:

$$\ln Q(T) - \ln Q(T - 1) = \Sigma\ S_{Qi}[\ln Q_i(T) - \ln Q_i(T - 1)], \quad (4.22)$$

where $S_{Qi} = 1/2[S_{Qi}(T) - S_{Qi}(T - 1)]$. Equations (4.21) and (4.22) are the translog indices of output.

Defining aggregate capital and labor functions in terms of their individual components, the differences between logarithms of aggregate inputs for the two countries is computed following the same rule as described in equation (4.21). Thus,

$$\ln K(US) - \ln K(Japan) = \Sigma\ S_{Ki}[\ln K_i(US) - \ln K_i(Japan)],$$
$$i = (1, 2, \cdots n)$$
$$\ln L(US) - \ln L(Japan) = \Sigma\ S_{Li}[\ln L_i(US) - \ln L_i(Japan)];$$
$$i = (1, 2, \ldots , n), \quad (4.23)$$

where $S_{Ki} = 1/2[S_{Ki}(US) - S_{Ki}(Japan)]$ and $S_{Li} = 1/2[S_{Li}(US) - S_{Li}(Japan)]$. Again, for a given country at two discrete points of time, the difference between successive logarithms is expressed as

$$\ln K(T) - \ln K(T - 1) = \Sigma\ S_{Ki}[\ln K_i(T) - \ln K_i(T - 1)]$$
$$\ln L(T) - \ln L(T - 1) = \Sigma\ S_{Li}[\ln L_i(T) - \ln L_i(T - 1)], \quad (4.24)$$

where $S_{Ki} = 1/2[S_{Ki}(T) - S_{Ki}(T - 1)]$ and $S_{Li} = 1/2[S_{Li}(T) - S_{Li}(T - 1)]$. Equations (4.19) and (4.20) are known as translog indices of capital and labor.

(3) The third and final step consists of defining translog indices of difference in technology and technological change. The technology index is constructed as a difference between logarithms of output for the two countries less a weighted average of the differences between logarithms of capital and labor inputs for these countries with weights given by average value shares. Thus,

$\ln Q(US) - \ln Q(Japan) = S_K[\ln K(US) - \ln K(Japan)]$
$+ S_L[\ln L(US) - \ln L(Japan) + S_D, \text{ where}$

$$S_K = \frac{1}{2}[S_K(US) - S_K(Japan)],$$

$$S_L = \frac{1}{2}[S_L(US) - S_L(Japan)], \quad \text{and}$$

$$S_D = \frac{1}{2}[S_D(US) - S_D(Japan)]. \tag{4.25}$$

Similarly, the average difference in technological change is expressed as the difference between successive logarithms of capital and labor inputs with weights given by average value shares, namely

$$\ln Q(T) - \ln Q(T-1) = S_K[\ln K(T) - \ln K(T-1)] + S_L[\ln L(T)$$
$$- \ln L(T-1)] + S_T$$

where

$$S_K = \frac{1}{2}[S_K(T) - S_K(T-1)],$$

$$S_L = \frac{1}{2}[S_L(T) - S_L(T-1)], \quad \text{and}$$

$$S_T = \frac{1}{2}[S_T(T) - S_T(T-1)]. \tag{4.26}$$

All these indices were computed from data at the two-digit manufacturing industry level in a study for assessing the role of technology gap and capital intensity in explaining differential rates of growth of output between the United States and Japan.[28] The results show a closing of the technology gap between the United States and Japan. However, a substantial gap between U.S. and Japanese capital intensity of production was observed. These findings suggest that the differences between U.S. and Japanese output were due to differences in capital intensity of production between the two countries, and not because of differences in levels of technology between them.

This index number framework was extended to incorporate intermediate inputs in a later study.[29] Such incorporation helped perform a disaggregated analysis of differences in the pattern of production at the industrial sectors levels. The findings provide additional information on the process of catching up the technology gap by the Japanese economy. It suggests that in almost all industries in Japan, growth rates of capital and intermediate inputs were high. The capital growth rate in Japan was twice the U.S. rate. The average annual growth rates of productivity in Japan were also higher than those in the United States. With some exceptions, Japanese manufacturing industries that have not closed the productivity gap with the United States belong to either light consumer or investment goods industries.

The index number method has also been used to estimate comparative growth rates of productivity in the automobile industry.[30] The index numbers, derived from a translog cost function rather than a production function, indicate average cost differences between inputs. These cost differences were further decomposed into differences in factor prices and total factor productivity growth. The results suggest that a substantial proportion of the cost advantage is attributable to superior productivity performance by the Japanese automobile industry.

The impact of changes in terms of trade on productivity growth has also been studied. Defining productivity as the aggregate output (Q) to aggregate input (X) ratio, the standard practice of computing changes in productivity is to take the difference $\partial \ln Q/\partial t - \partial \ln X/\partial t$. This modification of the total change in Q accomplished by subtracting $\partial \ln X/\partial t$ accounts for only a portion of the total change in productivity for an open economy, where terms of trade play a significant role in explaining productivity change.[31] This fact is taken into consideration by distinguishing between domestic and foreign products and incorporating the distinction in the model. The production function, therefore, includes three distinct product classes: (1) products sold to domestic purchasers and the government sector, Q_d with prices p_d; (2) products sold to foreign purchasers, or exports, Q_E with prices p_E; and (3) products purchased from foreign countries, or imports, Q_M with prices p_M. The impact of foreign trade is represented by the extent of export production and import use in relation to domestic production. Allowing for explicit inclusion of three different product classes, the production function takes the following disaggregated form:

$$Q = f(p_D, p_E, p_M, \mathbf{X}, t), \tag{4.27}$$

where Q = total output, $\mathbf{X}$ = vector of domestic inputs, and t = time trend. Then,

$$\frac{dQ}{dt} = \sum_D \frac{\partial f}{\partial p_D} * \frac{\partial p_D}{\partial t} + \sum_E \frac{\partial f}{\partial p_E} * \frac{\partial p_E}{\partial t} + \sum_M \frac{\partial f}{\partial p_M} * \frac{\partial p_M}{\partial t}$$
$$+ \sum_j \frac{\partial f}{\partial X_j} * \frac{\partial X_j}{\partial t} + \frac{\partial f}{\partial t}. \tag{4.28}$$

Using Hotelling's lemma, dividing both sides by Q, and using D as an operator to denote the time derivative, equation (4.28) can be written as

$$\frac{DQ}{Q} = \sum_D \frac{Q_D}{Q} * \frac{p_D}{p_D} * Dp_D + \sum_E \frac{Q_x}{Q} * \frac{P_x}{P_x} * Dp_x$$

$$+ \sum_M \frac{Q_M}{Q} * \frac{P_M}{P_M} * Dp_M + \sum_j \frac{P_j}{Q} * \frac{X_j}{X_j} * DX_j + \frac{\partial f}{\partial t} * \frac{1}{Q}. \tag{4.29}$$

In contrast to traditional measurement, equation (4.29) distributes total change in output between changes in total factor productivity and changes in terms of trade. The standard measure of productivity, equals $\partial f / \partial t * 1/Q$ only. It neglects the impact of terms of trade completely. Let the standard measure be denoted by ln R^t, and to extend this measure and take account of terms of trade impact, define a new component ln A^t. Then,

$$\ln R^t + \ln A^t = \frac{\partial f}{\partial t} * \frac{1}{Q} + \sum_E \frac{Q_x}{Q} * \frac{p_x}{p_x} * Dp_x$$

$$+ \sum_M \frac{Q_M}{Q} * \frac{p_M}{p_M} * Dp_M$$

$$= W^t. \tag{4.30}$$

Here, A_t represents international trade impact, W^t, on the other hand, captures changes in both productivity and terms of trade. Formation of R^t and A^t indices are dependent on the component indices defined on the basis of a translog production function.

Utilizing time series price and quantity data all the indices were computed for the U.S. and Japan.[32] The results show an overall downward trend in productivity growth for both countries. The average rate of productivity growth for Japan, however, was higher than for the U.S. throughout the sample period.

CONCLUDING REMARKS

The discussion of the different dimensions of productivity studies shows that considerable progress has been made in formulating and developing concepts and measurement of productivity growth based on a translog function. Some conclusions may be summarized as follows:

1. The formulation of more general forms of the production function via the duality concept has helped examine different aspects of production—input relationships, economies of scale, and technological changes—and assess their impacts on productivity growth.

2. With simple modifications these functions can help distinguish between short- and long-run production conditions, and study the significance of input adjustments in explaining productivity growth.

3. The formulation of these functions has enabled comparative studies on productivity growth. By identifying relative areas of strength in different countries such studies can make useful contributions toward the formulation of economic policy.

In spite of these extensions, the basic translog cost model remains necessary, robust, and valuable. It provides both quantitative information on, and interpretation of, different coefficients that relate to important economic concepts and variables.

NOTES

1. Cost functions have become relatively more common in the literature. However, production functions can also be obtained from these very conditions. In fact, arguments developed in terms of production functions and cost functions are then derived from duality conditions.

2. These assumptions are generally made in applied literature.

3. Berndt and Christensen (1973a) developed this framework.

4. Binswanger (1974a) provides details of this study.

5. Evidence on such substitution is also found in Diwan and Kallianpur (1985). The methodology in their study, however, is based on a VES production function.

6. Nadiri and Schankerman (1981).

7. Berndt and Wood (1975).

8. Fuss (1977) and Pindyck (1979) assume Hicks neutral technological change.

9. Denny, Fuss, and Waverman (1979) and Felemban (1989) use non-neutral technology in their analysis.

10. The significance of such studies in the context of the weakening of competitive strength of U.S. manufacturing needs no elaboration.

11. Norsworthy and Malmquist (1983).

12. Pollack, Sickles, and Wales (1984) introduced and estimated this form for the first time.

13. Andrikopoulos, Brox, and Carvalho (1986) and Brox, Carvalho, and Lusetti (1988) followed similar estimation procedures in studying input substitution for the Canadian manufacturing sector. Unlike Pollack et al. (1984), both these studies modeled non-homothetic production structure. Brox, Carvalho, and Lusetti, estimated non-homothetic production structure with non-neutral technological change utilizing time series data.

14. Among prominent efforts in this direction are those by Brown, Caves, and Christensen (1979) and Caves, Christensen, and Swanson (1981).

15. Caves, Christensen, and Swanson (1981).

16. The estimates indicate that the average railroad productivity grew at the rate of 1.5 percent per year during 1951–1974.

17. Initiated by Brown and Christensen (1982), the TVC function has been estimated by Levy, Bowes, and Jondrow (1983) and Norsworthy and Zabala (1985).

18. Brown and Christensen (1982).

19. Levy et al. (1983).

20. Norsworthy and Zabala (1985).

21. Nadiri and Prucha (1985) and Mohnen, Nadiri, and Prucha (1986) are among the prominent efforts in modeling dynamic production processes with an endogenous adjustment path.

22. Nadiri and Prucha (1985).

23. It was first proposed by Denny, Fuss, and Waverman (1981) and Morrison and Berndt (1981).

24. The optimization problem is a standard dynamic programming problem. Nadiri and Prucha (1985) provide detailed derivation and results.

25. Mohnen, Nadiri, and Prucha (1986) use time series data from 1965–1966 to 1977–1978.

26. If R&D is used as a technology index the time trend T has to be dropped from the model. Inclusion of a time trend t, along with R&D, introduces interaction between the two variables and consequently leads to difficulties of interpretation of the coefficients associated with those interactions.

27. Only a few studies are based on this method, namely, Jorgenson and Nishimizu (1978); Jorgenson, Nishimizu, and Kuroda (1985a); Fuss and Waverman (1985); and Diewert and Morrison (1985).

28. Jorgenson and Nishimizu (1978) studied these differences for 1952–1974.

29. Jorgenson, Nishimizu, and Kuroda (1985a) extended their earlier study to facilitate a better understanding of these findings at the macro level of aggregate eeconomic growth between the United States and Japan.

30. Fuss and Waverman (1985) have used this method for the period 1970–1980.

31. See Diewert and Morrison (1985).

32. Diewert and Morrison (1985) computed these indices for 1967–1982.

5

Toward a Theoretical Model

INTRODUCTION

We have already mentioned in chapter 3 that the development of flexible functional forms by taking recourse to duality theory defines a major breakthrough in the theory of production. The applications described in chapter 4 show that these formulations represent the current edge of the econometric-theoretical frontier. Their usage has allowed researchers to seek additional information on productivity growth, technological change, and input relationships. They have resulted in an increased attempt to establish large data sets that can exploit the potentials of the production function approach.

The emergence of these various flexible forms, however, is not free from problems. The similarity in their characteristics gives rise to a serious problem of choice. The question of choice is critical because alternative functional specifications may yield differing values of estimates of critical parameters, such as elasticity of substitution and technological change. Also, results furnished by statistical hypotheses tests depend on the particular functional form chosen. Differentiation among existing flexible forms is rather difficult. Each flexible form can be interpreted as a second-order differentiable function of the variables involved. Choice is made on the criteria of number of parameters, ease of estimation, and appropriate stochastic specification.[1]

The flexible functional form that merits particular attention for our study is the transcendental logarithmic (TLOG) form, popularly known as the translog function.[2] This form is compatible with the national aggregate data series on selected three-digit manufacturing industries prepared for this study. The TLOG also allows for estimation of parameters that help isolate the significance of different aspects of production, such as input growth and technological change.

A comprehensive understanding of the TLOG function defines the purpose of this chapter. Starting with an overview of the duality theory, which provides the basis of current econometric modeling of production processes, the nature of the translog function has been outlined with special emphasis on the role of its parameters in explaining its different properties. The objectives of different parameter restrictions imposed during the estimation procedure followed in this study are defined in the chapter.

DUALITY AND CHOICE OF FUNCTION

In order to estimate the underlying technology, one can examine either the production function or the associated cost function.[3] Recent work in duality theory has established a unique correspondence between the production and cost functions. All information about the underlying technology is contained in both the functions, given that the functions fulfill certain basic conditions.[4] The choice between the functions is then a matter of statistical convenience and analytical purpose.

In most empirical work, the cost function, instead of the production function, is chosen for three specific reasons. First, the cost function portrays the optimal minimum solution of total cost given input prices and the level of output. In contrast, the production function expresses maximum output in terms of quantities of factor inputs. Because of their larger variations, factor prices are treated as exogenous in both cost and production functions. Whether input levels can also be considered as exogenous is a debatable issue. The input variables are liable to be highly multi-collinear in production function estimation. There is usually little *a priori* multi-collinearity among factor prices.[5] An important statistical issue in the context of production and cost functions is whether the levels of output on which input decisions are based should be considered exogenous or endogenous. Although it is reasonable to consider output as endogenous, except in cases of regulated industries, this endogeneity often gives rise to complications in a study of production structure that represents disaggregated output levels.[6]

The second reason for preferring the cost function over the production function in general is that the former yields direct estimation of the various Allen elasticities of substitution. These parameters are key to describing the pattern and degree of substitutability and complementarity among the factors of production, an important point that needs elaboration.

For an n-factor production function with the general form

$$Q = \mathbf{f}(x_1, x_2, \ldots, x_n), \tag{5.1}$$

let $\mathbf{f}$ be the bordered Hessian matrix; $f_i = \partial Q / \partial x_i$, the marginal products; and $f_{ij} = \partial^2 Q / \partial x_i \partial x_j$, the second-order derivatives. Allen partial elasticities of substitution are then defined as follows:

$$\sigma_{ij} = [\Sigma \; x_i f_i / x_i x_j](f^{-1})_{ij}, \tag{5.2}$$

where $(f^{-1})_{ij}$ is the ijth element of $\mathbf{f}^{-1}$. If estimates of the coefficients of a particular functional form of equation (5.1) are available, the bordered Hessian can be computed, inverted, and the σ's found according to equation (5.2) for specific input levels. The inversion of a matrix of estimates inflates estimation errors. Since inversion of a matrix is a nonlinear transformation, econometric properties of σ_{ij} cannot be found even if such properties of the production function parameters are known.

Given cost minimization, there exists a dual minimum cost function corresponding to equation (5.1). The general form of such a function is

$$C = g \, (Q, \, p_1, \, p_2, \, \ldots, \, p_n), \tag{5.3}$$

where p_i's, with $i = 1, 2, \ldots, n$, are factor prices and C is total cost. The function is homogeneous of degree one in prices. Shephard's lemma implies[7]

$$\partial C / \partial p_i = x_i. \tag{5.4}$$

Equation (5.4) enables estimation of σ_{ij} directly from the parameters of the cost function, since

$$\sigma_{ij} = [\Sigma \; p_i x_i / x_i x_j] * (\partial^2 C / \partial p_i \partial p_j) \tag{5.5}$$

Avoidance of matrix inversion procedure improves the statistical precision of the computed elasticities of substitution for cost functions.

The third advantage of the cost function over the production function is that duality theory can be exploited without imposing any restrictions on the returns to scale in the underlying technology. For example, using Shephard's lemma, one can derive a set of cost-share equations from the cost function itself. Joint estimation of the cost function and share equations increases degrees of freedom and enhances the statistical precision of the estimates. The cost shares are constrained by definition to add to unity, but this does not impose any restriction on the underlying technology concerning the degree of returns to scale. On the other hand, the use of the production function together with the first-order conditions for profit maximization implies a set of value-share equations. When the value shares are constrained to add to unity, and are estimated jointly with the production function, constant returns to scale is implicitly assumed.

MODELING OF PRODUCTION STRUCTURE

Of all the duality-based flexible form functions, we have chosen the translog specification of the cost function in modeling the production structure of U.S. high-technology industry. The economy in the number of parameters used and the relative ease of computation and interpretation have been the deciding factors.

The translog can be viewed as a second-order logarithmic approximation to an arbitrary twice-differentiable transformation surface. In its general form, the translog imposes no *a priori* restrictions on the production structure. Consequently, it allows the testing of various restrictions—such as, homogeneity, Hicks neutrality of technical change, homotheticity, and unitary elasticities of substitution. It also allows assessment of the sensitivity of parameters to these restrictions.

Assuming that the cost of production is minimized under competitive factor markets, the general form of an aggregate cost function is given by equation (5.3). This general form may be extended to include a technology variable as

$$C = g(Q, \mathbf{P}, T), \qquad (5.6)$$

where C is total cost, $\mathbf{P}$ is a vector of n-factor prices, Q is level of output, and T is an index of the level of technology external to the firm or the industry concerned. Assuming all the variables to be in natural logarithms, the translog approximation to the general form, equation (5.6) can be written in the following matrix form:[8]

$$C = C_0 + a_q Q + a_T T + \mathbf{a}_i' \mathbf{P} + 1/2 a_{qq} Q^2 + 1/2\, a_{TT} T^2 + 1/2 \mathbf{P}' \mathbf{a}_{ij} \mathbf{P} +$$
$$\mathbf{a}_{iq}' QP + \mathbf{a}_{iT}' TP, \qquad (5.7)$$

where C_0, a_q, a_T, a_{qq}, and a_{TT} are scalars; $\mathbf{a}_i$, $\mathbf{a}_{iq}$, and $\mathbf{a}_{iT}$ are vectors of coefficients; $\mathbf{a}_{ij}$ is a matrix of coefficients; and $i,j = 1, 2, \ldots , n$ index the n different inputs.[9] The coefficients a_i for $i = 1, 2, \ldots , n$ in vector $\mathbf{a}_i$ are generally interpreted as average value shares of respective inputs in total cost. The coefficients a_{ij}s in matrix $\mathbf{a}_{ij}$, on the other hand, are known as share elasticities indicating the response of cost shares of inputs to proportional changes in their prices. All the variables in equation (5.7) are defined around some expansion point. In empirical terms this means that the variables are normalized around some point; for example, the sample mean. Normalization is a common procedure and is crucial to the interpretation of the coefficients and the time path of the translog parameters.[10]

A set of cost share equations associated with the translog cost function (5.7) is implied by the duality theory. Shephard's lemma helps obtain the derived demand for any input, x_i, through partial differentiation of the cost function with respect to the price of the input. Partial differentiation of equation (5.7) with respect to different elements in vector $\mathbf{P}$, yields a set of cost share equations as

$$S = a_i + a_{ij} \mathbf{P} + a_{iq}' Q + a_{iT}' T, \qquad (5.8)$$

where S is an $(n,1)$ vector of input shares. Equation (5.8) indicates that the coefficients in the share equations are a subset of those in the cost function. The concavity property of the translog, which follows from non-decreasing returns with respect to input prices, ensures that share elements S_i in vector S are non-negative.

HOMOGENEITY IN FACTOR PRICES

To be a well behaved function the cost function (5.7) must be linearly homogeneous in factor prices at (1) all values of factor prices and (2) the level of technology. This implies the following set of restrictions:

$$\begin{aligned}
a_i' I^c &= 1 \\
a_{iT}' I^c &= 0 \\
a_{iq}' I^c &= 0 \\
a_{ij} I^c &= \mathbf{0} \\
I^{c'} a_{ij} &= \mathbf{0},
\end{aligned} \qquad (5.9)$$

where I^c is a column vector of 1s.

It is important to note that homogeneity of degree one in input prices is not equivalent to homogeneity of degree one in input quantities. As such, the restrictions in equation (5.9) do not by themselves imply constant returns to scale. The latter specification regarding returns to scale requires an additional set of restrictions,[11] namely

$$\begin{aligned}
a_q &= 1, \\
a_{qq} &= 0, \\
a_{iq} &= \mathbf{0},
\end{aligned} \qquad (5.10)$$

where $\mathbf{0}$ is a null vector.

Two points are worth noting at this stage with reference to the set of restrictions (5.9). First, the restrictions imply that $I^{c'} S = 1$. Hence, only $(n - 1)$ of the n share equations in (5.8) are linearly independent. Second, since the translog is viewed as a quadratic approximation, the cross partial derivatives of the cost function must be equal to one another. This implies that the derivatives are independent of the order of the variables chosen. The matrix a_{ij} is therefore symmetric so that

$$a_{ij} = a_{ji}, \qquad \text{for } i \neq j \qquad (5.11)$$

where a_{ij} is the ijth coefficient in the matrix a_{ij}.

With estimated values of the coefficients in the a_{ij} matrix given and elements of vector S known, all the partial elasticities of substitution between pairs of factor inputs can be estimated. Partial elasticity of substitution between factors i and j, σ_{ij}, and the output compensated own and cross price elasticities of factor demand ξ_{ii} and ξ_{ij} are computed as[12]

$$\sigma_{ij} = (a_{ij}/S_iS_j) + 1, \text{ for } i \neq j$$
$$\sigma_{ii} = (a_{ii} + S_i^2 - S_i)/S_i^2,$$
$$\xi_{ii} = (a_{ii}/S_i) + S_i - 1,$$
$$\xi_{ij} = (a_{ij}/S_i) + S_j, \quad \text{ for } i \neq j. \tag{5.12}$$

As is apparent from equations (5.12), elasticity of substitution and price elasticity of demand are related to one another by the rule $\xi_{ij} = S_j{}^* \sigma_{ij}$. The symmetric property of the elasticities of substitution, which refers to the equality between σ_{ij} and σ_{ji}, follows automatically from the symmetry condition (5.11). The special case of a unitary elasticity of substitution between factors i and j holds if

$$a_{ij} = 0, \quad \text{for } i,j = 1, 2, \ldots, n,; i \neq j \tag{5.13}$$

thus reducing to a Cobb-Douglas function.

HICKS NEUTRALITY

The formulation of the cost function in equation (5.7) allows for both neutral and biased technological change. A measure of rate of growth of total cost using the translog cost function provides two different sets of parameters referring to two different sources of technological change. This is an important advantage of the translog over other functional forms. Most of the conventional forms of production and cost functions fail to distinguish between neutral and non-neutral change in technology.

Neutral technological change acts as a pure shift of the cost function over time while leaving the factor shares unchanged. It is represented by the parameters a_T and a_{TT} in equation (5.7). The parameter a_T measures the average rate of technological change holding the level of output and input prices constant. The parameter a_{TT}, on the other hand, defines the rate of acceleration in the average rate of technological change.[13] For a cost function, while a negative value of a_{TT} defines the rate of technological change as accelerating, a positive value shows its trend is decelerating. If the rate of technological change is independent of the level of technology, and if the technology is linear, the value of a_{TT} is zero.

In contrast to neutral technological change, biased technological change represents shifts in the level of technology that alter the equilibrium factor shares, holding the level of output and factor prices constant. The magnitude of such shifts is described by the parameters a_{iT}. Technological change is said to be ith factor saving (i-using) if the cost share of the ith factor is lowered (raised) by growth in technology. In terms of values of parameters in the cost function (5.7), technology is ith factor saving or ith factor using depending on whether

$$a_{iT} < \quad \text{or} \quad > 0, \tag{5.14}$$

where a_{iT} is the ith element in the vector $\mathbf{a_{iT}}$. In the absence of any factor specific bias, technological change is neutral and consequently,

$$\mathbf{a_{iT}} = \mathbf{0}. \tag{5.15}$$

In view of the restrictions (5.9), there are only $n - 1$ independent parameter constraints in equation (5.15).

SEPARABILITY OF FACTOR INPUTS

The assumption of consistent aggregate indices of factor inputs is equivalent to the assumption of a separable production or cost function. Under separability, a cost function can be written as a sum of many subfunctions, each subfunction consisting of a specific group of factor prices. If a cost function can be written in this way, then the marginal rate of substitution between pairs of inputs belonging in one group is independent of the inputs belonging in a separate group. In general, inputs i and j are functionally separable from input k if the underlying cost function, equation (5.6), satisfies the following condition:

$$g_i g_{jk} - g_j g_{ik} = 0. \tag{5.16}$$

Differentiating equation (5.7) and substituting into equation (5.16), one finds that the translog function is separable if and only if,

$$S_i a_{jk} - S_j a_{ik} = 0, \tag{5.17}$$

where S_i and S_j are cost shares of inputs i and j, respectively, and a_{jk} and a_{ik} are coefficients of matrix $\mathbf{a_{ij}}$.[14] Since factor shares are always positive, separability conditions (5.17) imply that if $a_{jk} = 0$, a_{ik} is also equal to zero. If a_{jk} is not equal to zero but $a_{ik} = 0$, then the inputs i and j are not functionally separable from the input k.

Condition (5.17) can be equivalently written as

$$a_i a_{jk} - a_j a_{ik} = 0. \tag{5.18}$$

When a_{jk} is non-zero, we can divide equation (5.18) by this parameter and alternatively write the separability condition as

$$a_i / a_j = a_{ik} / a_{jk}. \tag{5.19}$$

Satisfaction of condition (5.19) simultaneously ensures fulfillment of certain equality restrictions on Allen partial elasticities of substitution between pairs of inputs. Accordingly, separability in the cost function can alternatively be expressed with restrictions imposed on the substitution elasticities. In terms of elasticities of substitution, condition (5.19) implies an important condition:[15]

$$\sigma_{ik} = \sigma_{jk}. \tag{5.20}$$

Thus, elasticities of substitution between any factor belonging to a separable group and another from outside this group are equal for all inputs within the separable group.

HOMOTHETICITY

Returns to scale and economies of scale differ from each other unless the production function is homothetic.[16] A cost function dual to its corresponding production function is homothetic if it can be written as a separable function of factor prices and output.[17] This implies that the optimal factor combination is independent of the scale of outputs so that the expansion path is linear. It is clear from the share equations (5.8) that separability between factor prices and output requires

$$\mathbf{a_{iq}} = \mathbf{0}. \tag{5.21}$$

In view of the translog homogeneity constraints (5.9), homotheticity therefore imposes additional $n - 1$ independent parameter restrictions.

In this context, the cost function is homogeneous in output if the partial derivative of C with respect to Q is constant. This is interpreted as elasticity of cost with respect to output and is widely used as a measure of economies of scale.[18] From cost function (5.7), partial derivative of C with respect to output Q yields

$$E_{CQ} = a_q + a_{qq}Q + \mathbf{a_{iq}}'P, \tag{5.22}$$

where E_{CQ} refers to elasticity of cost with respect to output. Homogeneity in output imposes the following set of restrictions:[19]

$$\begin{aligned} a_{qq} &= 0, \\ \mathbf{a_{iq}} &= \mathbf{0}. \end{aligned} \tag{5.23}$$

There are n independent restrictions in equations (5.23). A close scrutiny of the restrictions reveals that $n - 1$ of them are identical to the homotheticity constraints described in equation (5.21). Therefore, homogeneity in output imposes only one additional restriction that needs to be tested formally as a hypothesis conditional on the acceptance of homotheticity.

Another interesting point is that if equation (5.23) holds jointly with equation

(5.12), the restrictions required for unitary partial elasticities of substitution between pairs of inputs, then the cost function reflects a homogeneous technology. Such a technology is equivalent to Cobb-Douglas technology. Thus a joint satisfaction of equations (5.23) and (5.12) reduces the translog function to the Cobb-Douglas.

Most of these parameter restrictions are tested in this study analyzing the production structure of the U.S. high-tech sector. The estimation technique and the testing procedures underlying those results are outlined below.

ESTIMATION AND DESIGNING PROCEDURE

In analyzing the production structure of the U.S. high-technology sector in aggregate, a translog unit cost function with three factor inputs has been estimated in this study. The unit cost specification refers to the fact that C in equation (5.7) defines, for our purpose, cost per unit of output and not total costs. Consequently, the following restrictions apply to the general cost function:

$$a_q = 0,$$
$$a_{qq} = 0,$$
$$\mathbf{a_{iq} = 0}. \qquad (5.24)$$

The three specific productive inputs that the function incorporates are labor (L), capital (K), and intermediate materials (M). Later the function will be extended to four factors by disaggregating total labor input into skilled and unskilled labor in studying some specific questions regarding the input structure. The basic, and the extended, function includes research and development, R&D, in its stock concept as a measure of the index of technology. Inclusion of R&D as a stock concept makes an important departure from earlier empirical studies with the translog cost function. In most cases, a simple index of time is used as an indicator of the level of technology. Therefore, the term "technological change" in these studies refers to time-related shifts of the cost function. Because R&D expenditure is the basic input in the process of innovation and invention, defining stages of technological progress, we consider it a rational choice in defining a significant proxy for the level of technology. Accordingly, technological change in our study refers to shifts in the cost function arising out of growth in the stock of research and development. Whereas the average rate of technological change in this context reflects the effect of increased R&D on the growth of cost of production, the measures of biases in technological change express its influence on factor shares.

With the form of the translog cost function defined as above, formal testing procedures utilized in the study are limited to four models. All models are estimated after imposing the constraint of linear homogeneity in factor prices. The four models are defined as (1) a translog cost function with biased technological change, (2) a translog cost function with strict neutrality of technological change, (3) a translog cost function with separability of labor and capital from material input, and (4) a translog cost function that reduces to a Cobb-Douglas form when additional restraints concerning unitary elasticity of substitution are imposed.

A system of equations consisting of the cost function and n − 1 (n = K, L, M) of the share equations have been estimated jointly by the technique of seemingly unrelated regression. This technique is equivalent to a generalized least-squares technique.[20] Exploiting duality theory and estimating the cost share equations jointly with the cost function increases the statistical degrees of freedom since the cost share parameters are a subset of the cost function parameters. If one is interested only in the parameters of elasticity of substitution, an estimation of share equations alone is sufficient. The length of the time series set and the multicolinearity implied in time series data strongly favor a joint estimation procedure. Including the cost function along with the share equations is important for us because of our interest in technological change measures. The parameter estimates needed to evaluate the neutrality of technological change are unobtainable from the set of share equations. In addition to combining the cost function and the share equations, additive disturbance terms have been specified for each of the equations. The disturbances are assumed to have a joint normal distribution as required for formal testing, with contemporaneous correlation allowed across the equations.

The seemingly unrelated regression technique, in spite of its wide use, has some problems. The crucial one is that the parameter estimates are not invariant to the choice of the share equation to be deleted. A number of attempts have been made to attain invariance of the parameter estimates obtained from a system of equations. Although an argument has been made for a maximum likelihood procedure that ensures invariance of the estimates, it has been shown that iteration on the seemingly unrelated regression method yields maximum likelihood estimates when there is convergence of the residual covariance matrix.[21] This technique, in effect, is equivalent to a maximum likelihood method of estimation and produces estimates that are invariant to the choice of share equations to be estimated.

The iterative technique has been selected and applied on the set of equations identified for our purpose. Given that these are maximum likelihood estimates, various restrictions on the parameters can best be tested with the likelihood ratio test. To aid such test, a statistic λ has been defined as

$$\lambda = U - R, \tag{5.25}$$

where U and R are the log likelihood values under the unconstrained and constrained versions of model chosen. 2λ is distributed asymptotically as a chi-square variate with degrees of freedom equal to the number of independent restrictions being tested. Models in the study are either accepted or rejected on the basis of the chi-square test results. The accepted model is used to interpret rates and biases of technological change in U.S. high-tech industries on the one hand, and possibilities of substitution between high-tech inputs on the other.

NOTES

1. A comprehensive analysis on the question of choice of flexible forms is provided in Fuss, McFadden, and Mundlak (1978).

2. Derivation of this functional form and its properties are delineated in Christensen, Jorgensen and Lau (1973).

3. The major proponent of the duality theory is Hotelling (1932). This theory was further developed by Shephard (1953).

4. As explained by Diewert (1982), the conditions to be satisfied by a cost function in providing a dual counterpart for any production function are those of monotonicity, continuity, convexity, and homogeneity of prices.

5. The presence of multi-collinearity prevents proper inversion of the coefficient matrix in production function estimation. Matrix inversion, however, is an essential step in deriving estimates of elasticity of substitution. Such inversion can be avoided altogether in cost function estimation by obtaining input shares by simple differentiation of the cost function.

6. The exogenous property of output has motivated wide use of multi-output cost function for studying regulated industries.

7. Shephard (1953) showed that for any cost function that satisfies the basic conditions and is differentiable with respect to input prices, the vector of cost minimizing input quantities can be found by differentiating total cost with respect to the components of the corresponding input price vector.

8. This form is obtained through a Taylor series expansion restricted to the second term. Taylor series expansion of equation (5.6) is as follows:

$$C = C_0 + (\partial C/\partial Q)Q + \Sigma (\partial C/\partial p_i)\, p_i + (\partial C/\partial T)T + 1/2\, \Sigma\, \Sigma\, (\partial^2 C/\partial p_i\, \partial p_j)p_i p_j +$$
$$1/2(\partial^2 C/\partial Q^2)^*Q^2 + \Sigma (\partial^2 C/\partial p_i\, \partial Q)^*Qp_i + 1/2(\partial^2 C/\partial T^2)^*T^2 + \Sigma (\partial^2 C/\partial p_i\, \partial T) +$$
$$\text{remainder.} \qquad (1)$$

Neglecting the remainder and assuming that all the derivatives and cross derivatives are constant, equation (1) takes the following form:

$$C = C_0 + a_q Q + \Sigma\, a_i p_i + a_T T + 1/2\, \Sigma\, \Sigma\, a_{ij} p_i p_j + 1/2 a_{qq} Q^2 + \Sigma\, a_{iq} p_i Q +$$
$$1/2 a_{TT} T^2 + \Sigma\, a_{iT} p_i T, \qquad (2)$$

where $a_q = \partial C/\partial Q$, $a_i = \partial C/\partial p_i$, $a_T = \partial C/\partial T$, $a_{ij} = \partial C/\partial p_i \partial p_j$, $a_{qq} = \partial^2 C/\partial Q^2$, $a_{TT} = \partial^2 C/\partial T^2$, $a_{iq} = \partial^2 C/\partial p_i \partial Q$, and $a_{iT} = \partial^2 C/\partial p_i \partial T$.

9. Griliches and Ringstad (1971) have shown that by imposing appropriate restrictions on the translog parameters, the function can be converted to either CES or Cobb-Douglas production functions.

10. Further clarification of this point is available in Denny and Fuss (1977).

11. This set of restrictions becomes ineffective in the case of a unit cost function. For a unit cost function both homogeneity and constant returns to scale can be imposed by the set of equations in (5.9).

12. These formulae are derived in Uzawa (1962).

13. The parameter a_{TT} is generally interpreted as a term representing a second deriva-

tive of cost with respect to time. Its formal definition as the rate of acceleration of technological change is elaborated in Jorgenson et al. (1985a).

14. Detailed derivation of separability restrictions in translog cost functions are given in Berndt and Christensen (1973b).

15. The link between separability of factor inputs and elasticities of substitution between pairs of inputs was formalized by Berndt and Christensen (1973b).

16. A comprehensive discussion on this issue is provided in Hanock (1975).

17. This definition of homotheticity is found in Shephard (1970) and Denny and Fuss (1977).

18. Nadiri (1982) and Fuss and Waverman (1985) test scale economies by this concept.

19. With homogeneity of output imposed on the translog cost function, a_q becomes the crucial parameter indicating returns to scale. If $1/a_q$ is greater than unity, returns to scale is increasing. A less than or equal to unity value of the ratio refer to decreasing and constant returns to scale respectively.

20. Zellner (1962) contains a full description of the seemingly unrelated regression method.

21. Barten (1969) has shown the effectiveness of the maximum likelihood method for a system of equations. Kmenta and Gillbert (1968), on the other hand, argue in favor of an iterative Zellner method.

6

Data Description and Historical Trends

INTRODUCTION

One of the major problems encountered in studying the aggregate high-technology sector is the availability of data on various inputs outputs, and price indices. While a number of attempts have been made to define the high-tech sector and identify its components over the last decade, a formal procedure for collection and computation of a relevant data set on high technology as such is yet to be developed. We tried to fill this lacuna by preparing a time-series data set on high technology for the first time with information drawn from a variety of sources.

The development of the data set is strictly guided by the model of production, cost, and technological change. The set includes measures of total cost, total output, research and development stock, and quantities and prices of the inputs of labor, capital, and intermediate materials. Data on these variables are derived and constructed by integrating different series available from different sources. The major sources are the Census of Manufactures (CM), the Annual Survey of Manufactures (ASM), the Bureau of Labor Statistics (BLS), and the National Science Foundation (NSF). These sources all provide data on different variables at either four-digit or three-digit industry levels. To create a data set on high technology we followed a two-stage aggregation procedure in the construction of each variable. The first stage aggregates all four-digit level variables to a three-digit level. The second stage involves aggregating all three-digit level industries that define high technology (see Table 2.7) to form a time series at the aggregate high-technology level.

The annual time series data on aggregate high-technology variables in this study covers the period 1967–1982. We chose this specific time period for two reasons: (1) We traced the high-technology characteristics as far back as they remain comparable. Given the high growth rate of new technologies, the farther one goes back in time, industries become less comparable so we stopped at 1967. Another reason to begin with 1967 is that 1968 marks a major milestone in the growth of U.S. high-technology industries: the trade surplus in high technologies became larger than the trade surplus in total manufacturing for the first time in 1968. It has maintained this characteristics since. (2) For all the data sources referred to above, 1982 is the latest year for which the necessary details are available, some of which have not been collected since. Therefore 1982 forms the end of our time series.

CONCEPT AND MEASURE OF VARIABLES: TOTAL COST AND OUTPUT

The conventional measure of total cost followed in the productivity literature is based on national income accounting procedures, which suggest an equivalence of value of gross output and resource cost of production. Accordingly, total cost of production, C_t, for an industry is defined as the sum of gross outputs at current prices. The sum of gross output at current prices, $P_t Q_t$, in turn is equal to the sum of (1) value of shipments, and (2) changes in inventories. Or

$$C_t = \Sigma \ (p_{it} q_{it} + \Delta lnv_{it}), \qquad (6.1)$$

where q_{it} refers to the real shipment of the ith component of the output at time t, p_{it} refers to the price of the ith component of output at time t, and Δlnv_{it} denotes changes in inventories for the ith component of output at time t. Data on real shipments and inventories for the industries comprising the high-technology sector are obtained at the four-digit level from the Census of Manufacturing, 1982. Gross output figures in constant dollars, Q_t, on the other hand, are provided by the Division of Industry Productivity studies in BLS. Gross output in constant dollars, Q_t, provides the quantity measure of output. Our interest lies in the average, or per unit, cost instead of total cost. The series for unit cost, c_t, is derived by dividing C_t by Q_t. Mathematically,

$$c_t = C_t/Q_t. \qquad (6.2)$$

There is a general consensus regarding the measure of gross output in current dollars. There is, however, a question about a measure of constant dollar output. The constant dollar measure of output used in this study is based on 1972 prices.

A real output measure based on more recent prices involves a revision. The question is, how useful is an output measure based on a single year price?[1] It has been observed that a measure of real output based on the prices of a more recent year increases less than a measure based on prices of an earlier year. The logic is quite simple: The commodities contributing a major share of growth in output are the ones with smaller increases in prices, thus when real output is recalculated using more recent prices, commodities with larger growth percentages receive smaller weights. This leads to reduced growth in the aggregate measure. Changes in the prices and quantities of new technologies and particularly computers have been large enough to make the measurement of real output sensitive to the choice of price weights.[2] As such it is being argued by the Bureau of Economic Analysis (BEA) that a single measure is not appropriate for comparisons over all periods and for all analytical applications. While we recognize the significance of having a set of alternative measures of real output, each suited to a particular industry, we are convinced that differences arising from the use of two different measures will be marginal, especially in the case of an aggregate analysis. Because this is a study of aggregate high-technology instead of a particular component of it, our measure of real output based on a single year price maintains comparability and makes good sense.

QUANTITY AND PRICE OF LABOR

The price of labor in general is defined as the ratio between total wage bill and total number of workers or work hours in the industry concerned. The price of labor, P_L, is defined as V_L/L, where V_L is the value of labor expressed in terms of total wage bill paid out in a given year, and L is the total labor force estimated either in terms of the number of workers engaged or in terms of total work hours utilized in the production process.[3] Therefore, P_L requires information on V_L and L. The data on V_L or total wage bill have been collected from the CM and the ASM. The wage bill figures reported in these two sources are available at the four-digit level and are measured in current dollars. The total number of workers, equivalently called total employment and total work hours, however, is obtainable from the Division of Industry Productivity Studies in BLS, and is given at the three-digit industry level. We utilized this source to form a series on L for the three-digit industries belonging to the high-technology sector. A series on P_L has been developed by dividing total wage bill by the corresponding value for total work hour utilized for each three-digit industry.

Our study takes into account the distinction between two components of total workforce, skilled and unskilled labor. We defined production or blue collar workers as unskilled labor and the remaining non-production workers as skilled labor. Consequently, we developed data series on prices of these two categories of labor. As indicated by the CM, the terms for production worker and non-production worker have wider connotations and include a broad range of laborers. Specifically, production worker includes laborers engaged in fabricating, processing, assembling, storing and warehousing, and maintenance and repair. This category includes workers who perform operational aspects of a traditionally designed mass scale production process without being involved in any responsibilities for improving and changing it. These are the unskilled workers in common parlance. In contrast, non-production workers are responsible for innovative and developmental activities. Even though this category includes laborers engaged in financing and managing the production process, the major share of these workers is made up of professionals and employees with advanced scientific knowledge. These employees are expected to develop new managerial and scientific tools that will, in turn, enhance productivity of the labor force as a whole. These are the skilled workers.

Data on the production worker wage bill as well as hours of work for production workers at the four-digit industry level have been obtained from the CM and ASM. We aggregated these data at the three-digit industry level. The ratio between these two variables forms a series of production worker prices, P_U. Information on non-production workers is not directly available. We define non-production workers, or work hours, utilized in production process as a residual. The number of production worker hours has been subtracted from total number of work hours so as to arrive at a series on non-production work hours. Number of non-production workers is, similarly, given by the difference between total number of workers and number of production workers. A similar rule has been followed in deriving the wages of non-production workers. Total wage bill less production worker wages define wages for non-production worker.[4] In the final stage, a series on prices of non-production worker, P_N, is obtained by dividing annual wage bill figures by totals of work hours for each year.

Note that work hours instead of number of workers provides the measure for quantity of labor throughout our analysis of the U.S. high-technology sector. For our general interest, however, we also computed data on the number of workers both at the aggregate and disaggregate levels. In addition to prices and quantities of labor, our model also requires information on the annual value of the labor share, S_L, in the total cost of production. Share of any input is conventionally defined as a ratio of the cost of the particular input to the total cost of production. Based on this definition, the share of labor is derived by dividing the total wage bill in each year by the total cost of production figure; thus,

$$(S_L)_t = (V_L)_t/C_t. \qquad (6.3)$$

Shares of the disaggregated components of labor are also computed in an identical way. While S_U, share of production workers, is a ratio between the production worker wage and the total cost of production, S_N, share of non-production workers is the ratio between non-production worker wages and the total cost of production.

PRICE AND QUANTITY MEASURE OF MATERIAL INPUT

Similar to labor input, the price of material input is defined as value per unit of the input, and is expressed as a ratio between the total value of material and the quantity of material. Unfortunately, direct information on the quantity of material is not available from any source. Data provided by the CM and ASM relate to value of materials, V_M, which is a product of two terms, price and quantity of material; that is, $V_M = P_M * M$, where P_M refers to price of material and M to its quantity. In view of the non-availability of either M or P_M one has to unscramble the V_M estimate by developing independent estimates of either P_M or M. Virtually no information is available for M from any source. The only official source for P_M is the Manufacturing Industry Data Set Prepared by the Center for Economic Studies (CES) in the Bureau of the Census. This data set covers only part of our sample period. Material prices reported in this set are at the three-digit level and for the period 1958–1976. No information on material prices is available beyond 1976. Accordingly, we used the CES data set for developing material prices for high-technology industry for the period 1967–1972, and updated it by our own estimate beyond 1972.

For the period 1967–1972, material prices have been collected from the CES for only those three-digit industries listed in table 2.8. A weighted average of these annual prices defines the average material price for aggregate high-technology industry. The material price for aggregate high-technology industries, P_M (HT), at a particular time period is equal to a sum of weighted prices in the respective time period and is written as

$$P_M \text{ (HT)} = \Sigma_i W_i P_{Mi}, \qquad (6.4)$$

where $i = 1, \dots, 25$ refers to the 25 three-digit industries comprising the high-technology sector. The weights W_i are output weights, obtained as a proportion of the ith industry's output in the aggregate high-technology sector.

The construction of the material price data set for the period 1973–1982 is based on four steps. In step one, a set of 15 different commodity groups has been identified from the 1977 input-output table as intermediate inputs utilized by the three-digit industries in the high-tech sector. In step two, time series data on price indices for these selected commodity groups are obtained from annual issues of the Producer Price Index published by the BLS. Step three consists of a weighted aggregation of the price indices for these commodity groups, for each of the three-digit industries included in our list. The weights are obtained from the proportion of each commodity group in the total supply of materials in the three-digit industry.

These weighted price indices now define material price indices for the respective industries. Combining all the steps together, material price for the ith industry, P_{Mi}, is equal to a weighted sum of commodity price indices, $\Sigma_j W_{ij} P_j$, where $j = 1, \dots, 15$ refers to the commodity groups used by the industry as intermediate inputs and P_j denotes price of the jth commodity group. Because our interest is the aggregate high-technology industry instead of its individual component, we follow a fourth step to integrate these indices so as to arrive at the final series of material prices for high technology. Given material prices at the individual three-digit industry level, material prices for aggregate high-technology industry is a weighted index of the set of these prices. The weights in step four, unlike those in step three, refer to the share of each industry's output in the total high-technology sector.

Having obtained the $P_M(HT)$ series, we computed the ratio between V_M and P_M to develop a series on M, the quantity of materials. Material share, S_M, is derived by dividing the value of material by the total cost of production for each time period.

INDEX OF CAPITAL PRICE

Capital is conventionally used as a stock variable. The implicit notion is that annual investments are transformed into annual stocks through a perpetual inventory calculation. The distinction between gross and net capital stock is established with the help of a predefined depreciation rate.[5] Neither value of capital, V_K, nor its price, P_K, is available directly from data on capital stock. Assuming that the total cost of production is the sum of all individual cost components, one way to estimate value of capital, V_K, at any time period t, is to subtract cost of material and cost of labor pertaining to that period from the total cost of production in period t. In algebraic terms,

$$(V_K)_t = (C - V_L - V_M)_t. \tag{6.5}$$

With prior estimates of C, V_L, and V_M we can obtain a series on the value of capital in current dollars.

The concept of the price of capital, P_K, opens a wide range of issues, both conceptual and empirical. First, capital is an aggregated concept; there exists no market for it. There is a market for specific new and old capital goods but not for aggregate capital. Second, it is not clear whether capital stock, which is accumulated investment goods, or capital service is the relevant concept for production theory.[6] Furthermore, complications involved in computing its price prevents it from being a useful empirical tool. Assuming that the flow of capital services varies among different components of capital stock because of differences in the rate of depreciation, an appropriate measure for the capital service price can be developed only by taking account of all the following variables: prices of individual asset components, rates of return on assets, rates of depreciation, and effective tax rates. The rental price of a capital component, R_i, where i refers to the ith component of capital, may be expressed as

$$R_i = [(1 - uz - c)/(1 - u)] * (p_i r + p_i d + Dp_i), \tag{6.6}$$

where p_i is price of the ith asset component, r is the rate of return on the asset, d is the rate of depreciation, and Dp_i is the change in asset price. The user price includes a tax term in which u is the corporate tax rate, z is the present value of a dollar's worth of depreciation, and c is the effective rate of investment tax credit.[7] Data on all these variables are not readily available. We, therefore, followed a simple methodology in computing capital price. We collected data on net capital stock from the capital stock data base provided by the Office of Business Analysis (OBA) in the Department of Commerce. All these data are at the three-digit industry level. Following our aggregation method, we aggregated the three-digit level information construct to a time series on quantity of capital stock, Q_k, for the aggregate high-technology industry for each year. With capital stock available in value and quantity terms, the price of capital, P_k, is derived by the ratio of value (V_k) and quantity (Q_k). A series on capital share, S_K, was obtained by dividing value of capital by total cost of production in the aggregate high-technology industry.

STOCKS OF RESEARCH AND DEVELOPMENT

In the productivity literature, economists have often approached the contribution of research and development by constructing a research and development capital stock. The procedure applied is identical to the one used for determining the tangible capital stock. The annual gross R&D expenditure is first deflated and then added to the net value of the existing R&D stock. Studies utilizing such concepts of R&D report the R&D contribution in productivity growth to be in the range of 20 to 30 percent annually.[8] Other studies, which approach the R&D contribution by developing an indirect measure of effects of R&D on improved capital, report somewhat higher percentage contributions.[9] Although the formation of a R&D stock appears to be the preferred way of analyzing the effects of R&D on productivity growth, one needs to be aware of a wide range of issues before actually developing a series of the stock of R&D. Because the net increase in R&D stock is relevant, not the gross R&D expenditures, the issue of the depreciation of R&D stock gains importance. Selecting an appropriate rate of depreciation for the R&D stock presents major conceptual and empirical problems similar to those encountered in the context of physical capital. At the conceptual level, the depreciation of R&D capital can be defined either in terms of physical productive capacity of the stock or in terms of obsolescence reflected in the private rate of return, which makes it important to choose an appropriate concept of depreciation prior to the selection of its rate. Available studies suggest a general consensus that the productive stock concept of R&D capital is the relevant one for productivity analysis.[10] Thus, a slow depreciation of productive stock definition of R&D is preferred over a rapid obsolescence version of the stock. The rationale for slow depreciation lies in the fact that at both the micro and macro levels, only a small portion of society's total stock of R&D ceases to contribute to the production process over time.[11]

At an empirical level, important issues concern the choice of a proper shape of depreciation, including identifying both the pattern and the rate of depreciation. The pattern of depreciation can be chosen as geometric, hyperbolic, or "one-horse-shay," each offering a distinct time path of depreciation.[12] Studies in the productivity literature suggest a wide range of selection. The empirical choice of depreciation rate falls between 0 and 20 percent of the geometric rate.[13] Another potential problem relates to the selection of a R&D deflator. The GNP deflator is most commonly used. It is used by NSF to deflate R&D expenditures into real values. Its limitations, however, are widely recognized. Some argue that the prices of scientific inputs increase at a more rapid rate than an index that includes all the prices in the economy. The disparity between these two indices becomes particularly pronounced during years of shortage of economic resources. Moreover, as the role of high technology in the economy expands, the relative price of scientific resources is expected to increase. A number of studies attempt to develop alternative deflators for R&D expenditures,[14] all of which show a similar pattern of divergence between the R&D price index and the GNP deflator. The divergence is more significant at the disaggregated level where R&D prices are constructed for individual industries. In spite of its limitations, the GNP deflator continues to be commonly used for constructing the R&D stock.

Following convention, the R&D stock for this study is defined by the perpetual inventory method:

$$(R\&D)t = [(1 - d)(R\&D)_{t-1}] + (E_{RD})_t, \qquad (6.7)$$

where R&D refers to the stock of research and development, d is the depreciation rate, E_{RD} is the deflated value of R&D expenditure, and t is the time period. Thus, the current period R&D stock is obtained by adding deflated values of current expenditures on R&D to the net stock of the previous period.

The first step in constructing the R&D stock requires a benchmark of the R&D stock for 1967, the starting year in this study. We defined the benchmark for 1967 as four times the deflated value of R&D expenditures in 1969. The data on nominal R&D expenditure flow per year were collected at the three-digit level from Industry Bulletins published annually by NSF. We followed the conventional method of deflation to arrive at the constant dollar values of these nominal flows. Nominal R&D expenditures have been deflated by manufacturing GDP deflators published in monthly issues of the Survey of Current Business. For each three-digit industry, the deflated values of R&D expenditures have been added to the net value of R&D stock for each year. In conformity with other studies, a geometric depreciation rate of 20 percent was applied to estimate net values of R&D stocks. The final data set on R&D stocks was obtained by aggregating the real R&D stock figures for all the three-digit industries included in the aggregate high-technology industry.

Following the conventional method of normalization to the mean for each variable used in the analysis, we have developed, for the first time, a times series of all production-related variables for the aggregate U.S. high-technology sector for the period 1967–1982. These data, given in appendix tables A1 to A5, fill an important gap. There is much discussion in both popular and learned journals about high-tech industries and this study provides quantitative estimates for this sector for the first time.

TRENDS IN HIGH-TECHNOLOGY INPUTS AND OUTPUT

As shown in table 6.1, total output in the U.S. high-technology sector experienced wide variation during 1967–1982. The mean for the overall period is $163.38 billion with a maximum of $227.69 billion and a minimum of $119.93 billion. These variations indicate a cyclical trend in the growth of output in this sector. The peaks and troughs of these cycles are easily identified in graph 6.1. A close look at this graph reveals that cycles in the high-technology sector are close to those for the U.S. economy. The cause and effect relationship between the high-tech sector and the U.S. economy, however, is not clear. To study the characteristics of the high-tech sector during the cycles in more detail, the overall period has been divided into subperiods. The peak capacity years for the U.S. GNP of 1969, 1973, and 1979 have been used to separate the four subperiods— 1967–1969, 1969–1973, 1973–1979, and 1979–1982—which provide useful comparisons over two business cycles, 1969–1973 and 1973–1979, as well as the upswing of 1967–1969 and the downswing of 1979–1982.

Compared to total output, the aggregate measure of inputs in the U.S. high-technology sector shared much less variation during the overall period. As shown in table 6.1, while the standard deviation for capital is 17.44, that for materials and R&D stock are almost negligible—6.52 and 7.82, respectively. Although the average capital value for the chosen period is $74 billion, the maximum is $107.80 billion and the minimum $52.75 billion. In contrast, the gaps between maximum and minimum for both materials and R&D are narrower.[15] Looking at their growth path in graph 6.2, while material growth is cyclical in nature R&D shows a smooth trend. As shown in table 6.2, labor input measured in terms of both number of employees and work hours in the U.S. high-technology sector showed least variation. The gap between maximum and minimum values is negligible for both total labor and its disaggregated parts. The growth paths of different categories of labor are shown in graph 6.3; it is consistent with the growth path of output in graph 6.2. When labor is decomposed, cycles are evident for the employment of production workers. For the skilled labor, cycles are much less pronounced.

As shown in table 6.3, over the whole period, the average price index for output is 138.74 with a standard deviation of 34.60. The range for average price indices for inputs is wider; 121.64 for capital and 202.18 for skilled labor. The nature of variation in prices also differs widely among inputs. Whereas the capital price shows the least variation with a standard deviation of 27.59, the highest variation is observed in the price of non-production worker. The standard deviation for skilled labor is 107.21. As is evident from graph 6.4, prices of all inputs (excepting capital) show continuous increase. Skilled labor registers highest growth.

Table 6.4 gives information on input shares. The shares of all the inputs in the total cost of production remained more or less constant over the years with almost equal shares for capital and materials. Together, these two inputs define

80 percent of total cost of production. Labor contributes the rest.[16] The sum of the average shares of inputs is not different from unity.

Table 6.5 gives the high-technology shares of constant dollar output and employment in total manufacturing for selected years in the period 1967–1982. A comparison of gross output reveals that the high-tech sector forms about a quarter of the U.S. manufacturing sector. After a dip in the late 1960s and early 1970s the high-technology industries started growing at a rapid rate. The increase in shares of both output and employment suggests that this growth has been particularly high after 1978. Accordingly, it seems worthwhile to look into the growth rates of output and different inputs in the high-technology sector.

GROWTH RATES OF OUTPUT AND INPUTS IN HIGH TECHNOLOGY

The average annual growth rates of quantities of gross output and inputs in the high-technology sector are reported in table 6.6. The growth rates for the upswing and downswing phases of the business cycle 1967–1969 and 1979–1982, are not comparable with the two cycles 1969–1973 and 1973–1979. The cycles represented are peak to peak so that growth rates for these periods are over the business cycle. In contrast, the growth rates for the phases of a cycle are only for parts of the cycle. Specifically, 1967–1969 defines part of the cycle ending with a peak; 1979–1982 reflects the part of the cycle declining to a trough. One can, therefore, reasonably expect that the growth rates for 1967–1969 are biased upward and those for 1979–1982 downward. The growth rates for 1969–1973 were lower than those for 1973–1979, perhaps because of the supply shock in 1973 caused by a large increase in oil price. The real growth in the high-technology sector took place during the cycle after the first oil shock when output grew at the rate of virtually 6 percent per year. While all the inputs grew at a rapid rate, the most striking growth took place in employment. The average annual growth rate increased from −1.1 percent to about 3 percent per year. While increase in growth rate of capital was small, material growth rate increased by 3 percent. However, for the overall period, there was little growth in employment. Materials and capital grew by 6 and 4 percent per year, respectively, a rate higher than that of output. Output in the high-technology sector became more capital and material intensive over the years. This observation agrees with *a priori* notions about high-technology industries.

SOURCES OF OUTPUT GROWTH IN HIGH TECHNOLOGY

A better understanding of the growth rates requires identification of the sources of growth. A method of decomposing output growth into its contributing factors follows directly from the theory of cost and production. With capital, labor, and material as three aggregated inputs, a constant returns to scale production function with traditional neoclassical curvature properties may be written as

$$Q = Af(K, L, M), \tag{6.8}$$

where Q is gross output, K aggregate capital, L total labor, M materials in aggregate, and A an index of technology. A growth equation is derived by a logarithmic differentiation of equation (6.8) with respect to time. It is given as

$$DQ/Q = S_K (DK/K) + S_L (DL/L) + S_M (DM/M) + (DA/A), \tag{6.9}$$

where S_K, S_L, and S_M represent shares of capital, labor, and material, respectively, and D refers to the time derivatives.[17] Traditionally, DA/A is interpreted as total factor productivity or technological change and can be obtained by rearranging equation (6.9):

$$DA/A = DQ/Q - S_K (DK/K) - S_L (DL/L) - S_M (DM/M). \tag{6.10}$$

Thus, total factor productivity is growth in output minus growth in aggregate input, where growth in aggregate input is the share weighted growth of individual inputs. Since S_K, S_L, and S_M add up to unity, one can rewrite equation (6.10) as

$$DA/A = S_K (DQ/Q - DK/K) + S_L (DQ/Q - DL/L) \\ + S_M (DQ/Q - DM/M), \tag{6.11}$$

which indicates that total factor productivity is a share weighted average of the single factor productivity measures.

Equation (6.9) can easily be computed from time series data set on output and inputs of the U.S. high-technology sector.[18] Average growth rates of inputs for the subperiods are multiplied with mean cost shares to define the right-hand side components of the equation. The results are reported in table 6.7, which identifies the sources of output growth in the high-technology sector. During both the cycles, 1969–1973 and 1973–1979, the contributions of materials is overwhelming—89 and 67 percent, respectively. By comparison, the contribution of capital is less—57 and 25 percent, respectively. During the cycle of 1973–1979, materials and capital together explain most of output growth. Contributions of total factor productivity are not significant. It is in the upswing of 1967–1969 that total factor productivity plays the most significant role. Interestingly enough, during the downswing of 1979–1982, capital accounts for almost all the growth in output since none of the other factors is significant enough. This seems to be a building-of-capacity period for the high-technology industries. For the overall period, 1967–1982, the story is similar to that during the cycle of 1973–1979,

materials and capital explain all of the growth in output. Contributions of labor
and total factor productivity are negligible.

INPUT PRODUCTIVITY GROWTH IN HIGH TECHNOLOGY

Given the time series data set for gross output and inputs of capital, labor, and
intermediate materials, growth rates of different output-input ratios can be computed by rearranging equation (6.9). These output-input ratios are known as
factor productivities. Patterns of these factor productivities, labor productivity,
and material productivity, in particular, in the U.S. high-technology sector provide useful insights. Decomposition of labor productivity into its sources is of
general interest. In view of its large contribution to output growth, decomposition of material productivity growth is relevant for the high-technology sector.

Labor Productivity Growth

Labor productivity growth, $\partial(\ln Q - \ln L)/\partial t$, is defined as $(DQ/Q - DL/L)$.
A simple manipulation of equation (6.9) yields

$$(DQ/Q - DL/L) = (DA/A) + S_K(DK/K - DL/L) \\ + S_M(DM/M - DL/L). \qquad (6.12)$$

Equation (6.12) states that growth in labor productivity is the sum of total factor
productivity and the weighted growth rates of inputs relative to labor, where
weights are cost shares. Decomposition of labor productivity growth has been
quantified in table 6.8. In view of little growth in employment together with the
high growth rate of output, one would expect the labor productivity growth rate
to be significant, and this is precisely what the table reveals. Growth in labor
productivity has been significantly high all through the time period. For the
overall period, 1967–1982, this growth rate was 3.5 percent per year. The
growth rate in the upswing of 1967–1969 was around 4 percent. Over the cycle
1969–1973, labor productivity growth did not show much improvement beyond
this rate in spite of a significant fall in the rate of growth of employment; the
growth rate accelerated by only 0.26 percent. This low growth is explained by
the fall in the rate of growth of output. During the cycle, 1973–1979, the growth
rate decelerated to 2.7 percent per year and remained close to that in the downswing of 1979–1982. While the low growth rate in 1973–1979 is caused by high
growth rate in employment relative to output, as suggested in table 6.6, its low
growth during 1979–1982 is the result of a smaller output growth rate.

The major contributors to labor productivity growth rates are materials, for the
whole period 1967–1982; this contribution amounts to 73 percent. For the two
cycles, 1969–1973 and 1973–1979, the material contribution was approximately

75 and 100 percent, respectively. This contribution highlights the significance of materials in the growth of high-technology industries. As expected *a priori,* total factor productivity contributed 73 percent of growth during the upswing of 1967–1969; it was not significant in other periods. During the downswing of 1979–1982, capital explained almost 93 percent of growth in labor productivity. Capital has played a significant role in the downswing in explaining both output and labor productivity growth.

Material Productivity Growth

In comparing the growth rates of output and inputs in the high-technology sector, table 6.6 brings out the crucial fact that of all the inputs, materials has been growing at the fastest rate. Output in high-technology industries is becoming material intensive. To gain a competitive edge, it may be prudent to devise production processes that economize the use of materials. Improvements in material productivity or economizing material use is thus a profitable strategy. Derivation of material productivity growth follows easily.[19] Simple manipulation and rearrangement of equation (6.9) defines the components of material productivity growth as

$$(DQ/Q - DM/M) = DA/A + S_k(DK/K - DM/M)$$
$$+ S_L(DL/L - DM/M). \qquad (6.13)$$

Quantitative estimates of material productivity growth in U.S. high-technology industry and its contributing factors are listed in table 6.9. Based on prior observation of higher material productivity growth rate relative to output over the two cycles of 1969–1973 and 1973–1979, one would expect material productivity growth rates to be negative and the quantitative magnitudes reported in table 6.9 are in agreement with this expectation. The growth rate of material productivity is more or less equal for the two cycles; −3.5 percent per annum. For the overall period 1967–1982, it is approximately 3 percent per year. Whereas the annual average growth rate of materials is close to zero over the downswing of 1979–1982, it is more than 3 percent in the downswing of 1967–1969.

In regard to the sources of material productivity growth, major explanations for the negative growth rate for the period 1969–1973 are provided by labor (which explains 55 percent of the growth rate) and total factor productivity (which explains another 35 percent). During the business cycle of 1973–1979, capital and labor are the major contributing factors in material productivity growth; capital contributing about 55 percent and labor 40 percent. Total factor productivity plays a significant role only in the upswing part of 1967–1969, contributing 50 percent. On the other hand, capital is the major influencing factor during the downswing of 1979–1982. For the overall period, labor contributes 50 percent and total factor productivity another 30 percent.

PARTIAL AND TOTAL FACTOR PRODUCTIVITY

Partial factor productivity relates to a particular input, whereas total factor productivity takes into account all the inputs used in the production process. Tables 6.6 through 6.9 contain information on all the partial and total factor productivity measures relevant for the high-technology industries. Relevant information from these tables has been consolidated in table 6.10 to facilitate a comparative analysis.

As expected, all productivity measures grow at a high positive rate over the upswing of 1967–1969. Of all these growth rates, the highest rate is for labor productivity. Between the two cycles of 1969–1973 and 1973–1979, however, the nature of the change in productivity growth rate differs significantly among the inputs. For 1969–1973, labor productivity registers a positive and high growth rate. The rates of growth of both capital and material productivity reflect a sharp decline. Whereas the growth rate for capital productivity decreases from 2.38 to −0.69 percent, that for material productivity decreases from 3.20 to −3.40 percent; a fall of 3.07 and 6.60 percent, respectively. The productivity growth rate of all factors combined shows a significant decrease also. During the cycle 1973–1979 both labor and capital productivity reflect positive growth; however, growth rate of labor productivity is smaller than that for the earlier cycle. Material productivity decreases at the same rate. The productivity growth rate of all factors combined, though negative, shows an increase of 1.08 percent over the period 1969–1973. In the downswing of 1979–1982, capital productivity shows a large negative growth rate. While labor productivity maintains its growth rate, material productivity registers stagnation, which is an improvement over decline. For the overall period, 1967–1982, it is only labor productivity growth that plays a significant role.

CONCLUSION

This is the first study that provides a time series data set for the U.S. high-technology sector. By providing this data set, it defines, for the first time, the U.S. high-tech sector, historically. The high-tech sector forms more than one-fifth to one-fourth of the U.S. manufacturing sector and this proportion is increasing. We have developed this data set for the U.S. high-technology sector for the period 1967–1982. The year 1967 marks the beginning of a trade surplus in high-technology goods, whereas 1982 is the last year for which data, at the level of detail we have worked with, are available. Our data set quantifies the important concepts in production theory: output, capital, labor, materials, and research and development. We further divide labor into skilled and unskilled labor. Our data set provides data for both quantities and the prices of these variables and a times series of unit costs and cost shares of labor, capital, and materials. For R&D we quantify a stock concept. These data have been divided into four periods on the basis of GNP peaks in 1969, 1973, and 1979 to facilitate a comparative analysis of business cycles as well as the upswing and downswing phases of a cycle. These periods are (1) 1967–1969, representing an upswing; (2) 1969–1973, a business cycle; (3) 1973–1979, a business cycle; and (4) 1979–1982, reflecting a downswing phase.

Our findings are that the high-technology sector output conforms to the business cycle in the U.S. GNP. The mean value of this output, in terms of 1972 constant dollars, is $163 billion with a maximum of $228 billion. There is large variability in output over the years. By comparison, variability in inputs is low. The growth path of materials and total labor is cyclical, consistent with output cycles. Average employment during this period is 4 million workers with a maximum of 4.6. Although employment has not been growing, there are little cycles in skilled labor employment. The share of skilled labor in total labor is increasing so that in recent years it forms a larger part. Capital and materials each form 40 percent of costs, the remaining 20 percent being due to labor.

Output in this sector has been growing at an average 3 percent per year rate. Materials are growing at double this rate and capital at 4 percent per year, so that output is becoming capital and material intensive. Employment, on the other hand, is stagnant. The largest contribution to growth in output comes from materials and little from total factor productivity. Labor productivity has been growing at a faster rate of 3.5 percent per year. Here too, the major source contributing to this growth is materials. Material productivity, on the other hand, has been declining. These are general observations. The behavior over the two business cycles and their different phases is quite different. Total factor productivity played a major role in the 1967–1969 upswing. Part of the reason that total factor productivity does not contribute to growth may be that technological change is embodied in capital and labor.

Table 6.1
Output and Inputs in U.S. High Technology: 1967–1982 (Constant Billion Dollars)

	Output	Capital	Material	R&D
Mean	163.38	74.00	50.92	58.79
Standard Deviation	38.32	17.44	6.52	7.82
Maximum	227.69	107.80	59.47	74.03
Minimum	119.93	52.75	40.53	46.56

Source: Appendix table A2.

Table 6.2
Labor in U.S. High Technology: 1967–1982 (In Millions)

	Labor[1]	Hours[2]	Unskilled Labor	Unskilled Labor Hours[3]	Skilled Labor	Skilled Labor Hours[4]
Mean	4.07	8.55	2.19	4.35	1.85	4.17
Standard Deviation.	0.31	0.67	0.17	0.40	0.18	0.48
Maximum	4.60	9.63	2.41	4.99	2.26	5.13
Minimum	3.63	7.59	1.86	3.57	1.61	3.58

1. Aggregate measure of labor inclusive of production and non-production workers.

2. Hours of work performed by total labor.

3. Hours of work performed by production workers only.

4. Hours of work performed by non-production workers.

Source: Appendix table A3.

Table 6.3
Price Indices in U.S. High Technology: 1967–1982 (1967 = 100)

	Output	Capital	Total Labor	Unskilled Labor	Skilled Labor	Material
Mean	138.74	121.64	179.81	163.81	202.81	133.56
Standard Deviation	34.60	27.59	73.69	50.63	107.21	29.41
Maximum	207.34	177.86	319.25	256.78	434.20	195.54
Minimum	100.00	81.55	90.77	100.00	56.55	100.00

Source: Appendix table A4.

Table 6.4
Input Shares in U.S. High Technology

	Capital	Material	Unskilled Labor	Skilled Labor
Mean	0.40	0.39	0.13	0.10
Standard Deviation.	0.05	0.05	0.08	0.02
Maximum	0.49	0.44	0.42	0.13
Minimum	0.33	0.32	0.09	0.05

Source: Appendix table A5.

Table 6.5
Growing Importance of High Technology (High Tech as a Percentage of Total Manufacturing)

Year	Output	Employment
1967	20.3	21.0
1972	19.5	18.9
1978	20.3	20.4
1982	26.3	23.3

Source: Census of Manufactures, 1977, 1982, and Annual Survey of Manufactures, 1967–1982.

Table 6.6
Growth Rates of Output and Inputs in U.S. High Technology (In Percentages)

Period	Output	Labor	Capital	Material
1967-1969	5.47	1.55	3.09	2.28
1969-1973	3.08	-1.10	3.77	6.48
1973-1979	5.82	2.79	3.97	9.36
1979-1982	1.61	-1.17	5.83	1.58
Average Growth Rate for Overall Period				
1967-1982	3.38	-0.12	4.17	6.21

Notes: Output, capital, and materials are measured in 1972 dollars. Labor is measured by
total hours worked. Growth rate DQ/Q and DX/X, for X = L, K, and M are
measured as ln Q_t − ln Q_{t-1} and ln X_t − ln X_{t-1}, t refers to time period.

Source: Growth rates of output and inputs are computed from time series data in
appendix tables A2 and A3.

Table 6.7
Sources of Output Growth in U.S. High Technology

Period	Output Growth	Labor Contribution	Capital Contribution	Material Contribution	TFP
1967-1969	5.47	0.33	1.47	0.83	2.84
1969-1973	3.08	-0.14	1.67	2.77	-1.21
1973-1979	5.82	0.59	1.45	3.92	-0.13
1979-1982	1.61	-0.25	2.17	0.66	-0.97
Decomposition for Overall Period					
1967-82	3.38	-0.39	1.63	2.58	-0.82

Note: TFP stands for total factor productivity.

Source: Table 6.6.

Table 6.8
Decomposition of Labor Productivity Growth in U.S. High Technology (In Percentages)

Period	Labor Productivity Growth	Capital Contribution	Material Contribution	TFP
1967-1969	3.92	0.76	0.32	2.84
1969-1973	4.18	2.40	3.00	-1.22
1973-1979	2.69	0.41	2.76	-0.14
1979-1982	2.78	2.58	1.17	-0.97
1967-1982	3.50	1.73	2.56	-0.82

Source: Table 6.6.

Table 6.9
Decomposition of Material Productivity Growth in U.S. High Technology (In Percentages)

Period	Material Productivity Growth	Capital Contribution	Labor Contribution	TFP
1967-1969	3.20	0.60	-0.25	2.84
1969-1973	-3.40	-0.30	-1.89	-1.21
1973-1979	-3.54	-1.96	-1.44	-0.13
1979-1982	0.03	1.54	-0.54	-0.97
Decomposition for Overall Period				
1967-1982	-2.83	-0.57	-1.44	-0.82

Source: Table 6.6.

Table 6.10
Partial and Total Factor Productivity in U.S. High Technology (In Percentages)

Period	Capital	Labor	Material	TFP
1967-1969	2.38	3.92	3.20	2.84
1969-1973	-0.69	4.18	-3.40	-1.22
1973-1979	1.85	2.69	-3.54	-0.14
1979-1982	-4.22	2.78	0.03	-0.97
	Productivity Growth for Overall Period			
1967-1982	-0.78	3.50	-2.83	-0.82

Source: Tables 6.6 through 6.9.

Graph 6.1
Output in U.S. High-Tech Sector

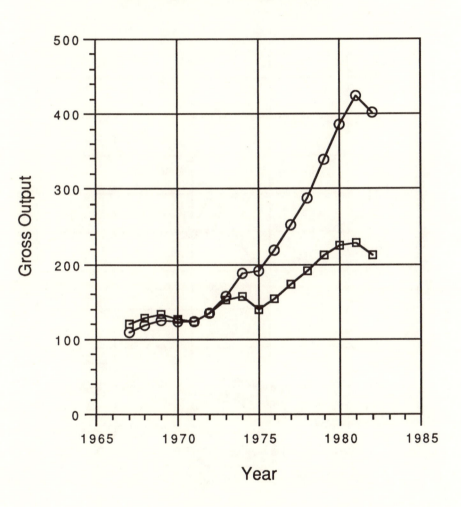

U.S. High Technology Sector

 1    2

Key: 1. Current Prices; 2. Constant Prices

Graph 6.2
U.S. High-Tech Sector: Output and Inputs

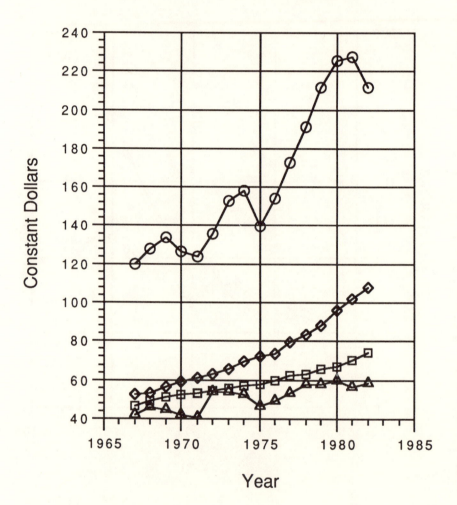

U.S. High Tech Sector Outputs & Inputs

 1   ▲ 2   ⊟ 3   ◆ 4

Key: 1. Output; 2. Materials; 3. R&D; 4. Capital

Graph 6.3
U.S. High-Tech Industry: Labor Input

U.S. High Tech Industry: Labor Input

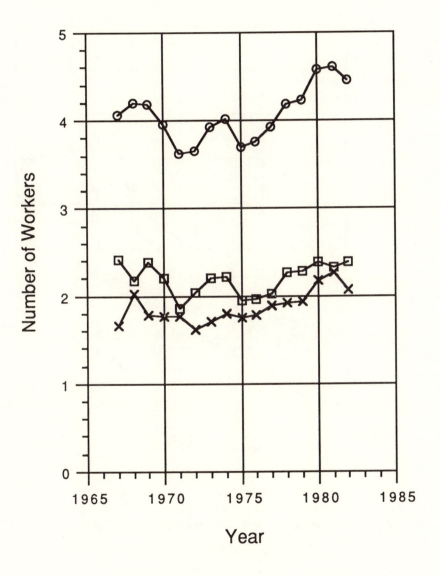

⊖ 1   ⊟ 2   ✳ 3

Key: 1. Total Labor; 2. Unskilled Labor; 3. Skilled Labor

Graph 6.4
U.S. High-Tech Industry: Input and Output Prices

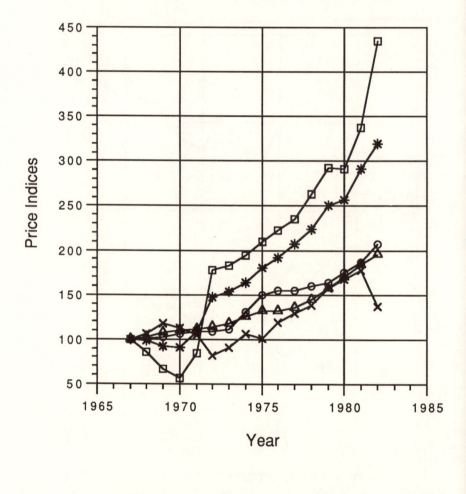

U.S. High Tech Industry: Input and Output Prices

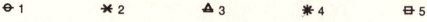

Key: 1. Output; 2. Capital; 3. Material; 4. Unskilled Labor; 5. Skilled Labor

NOTES

1. Young (1989) discusses the limitations of the present measure of real output.

2. Price sensitivity of real output measure has been studied by Denison (1989).

3. Choice of definition regarding quantity of labor, L, is guided by the availability of data for a particular industry. For example, while data on production worker hours are available from the CM for most of the industries at the four-digit level, those on total work hours are available only for selected three-digit industries from the Division of Industry Productivity Studies in the BLS. To compute price of aggregated labor at the four-digit level, one relies on number of worker measure of total labor.

4. Such residual measures of non-production worker is common.

5. The concept and choice of a depreciation rate is a controversial issue. Harper (1983) and others conceive depreciation as decay of physical capital, which proceeds at a slower rate. Terleckyj (1982a) and others consider it as obsolecence arising from a fall in rate of return. They assign it a higher rate. Pakes and Griliches (1984b) have even argued for a zero depreciation rate at early stages of capital. Hulten and Wykoff (1981a) provide a comprehensive and detailed study of depreciation of physical capital in the context of capital stock construction.

6. Kendrick (1961) discusses the issue of capital stock and distinctions of capital service as well as their effectiveness in production theory.

7. Harper (1983) provides a critical review of the rental, or user, price of capital.

8. Griliches (1980) and Terlekyj (1982b).

9. Scherer (1982).

10. Pakes and Schankerman (1984) and Terleckyj (1982b) offer a comprehensive analysis of the appropriate choice of an R&D stock depreciation rate.

11. Sveikauskas (1987) illustrates this issue with an effective example of research expenditures conducted on highly energy intensive methods of production in the late 1960s and early 1970s.

12. The geometric pattern of depreciation assumes a constant rate of depreciation over the years. The hyperbolic rate allows for different depreciation rates in different years, and for the possibility of slow depreciation in earlier years and more rapid depreciation in later years. The "one-horse-shay" pattern assumes that there is no depreciation at all; that is, the investment concerned retains its full potential throughout its lifetime.

13. Griliches (1980) assumes 0, 10, and 20 percent geometric rates of decay of R&D stock as alternative annual rates of depreciation. He then calculates R&D capital stock for each assumption. Terleckyj (1982a) and Griliches and Lichtenberg (1984) assume no depreciation. Nadiri (1985) chooses a 10 percent rate of geometric decay for his analysis of the U.S. machine-tool industry.

14. Griliches (1971) constructs a deflator specifically for technological expenditures and also points out the serious limitations of his attempt. Goldberg (1979) creates a deflator based on substantial input detail for 14 manufacturing industries. However, he points out that data for part of the study period was unreliable. Mansfield (1984) and Mansfield, Romeo, and Switzer (1983) study the R&D deflator for various manufacturing industries and find wide variations in their estimates.

15. The annual data for output and inputs for the period 1967–1982 are given in the appendix tables A1 to A3.

16. Detailed data for input prices and shares are given in the appendix tables A4 and A5.

17. Logarithmic differentiation of equation (6.8) yields,

$$\partial \ln Q/\partial t = (\partial \ln Q/\partial \ln K)(\partial \ln K/\partial t) + (\partial \ln Q/\partial \ln L)(\partial \ln L/\partial t)$$
$$+ (\partial \ln Q/\partial \ln M)(\partial \ln M/\partial t) + (\partial \ln Q/\partial \ln A)(\partial \ln A/\partial t).$$

The partial derivatives $\partial \ln Q/\partial \ln K$, $\partial \ln Q/\partial \ln L$, and $\partial \ln Q/\partial \ln M$ are output elasticities, which under competitive market conditions equal input cost shares. These cost shares are denoted as S_K, S_L, and S_M. Since $\partial \ln Q/\partial \ln A = 1$, $\partial \ln A/\partial t = (1/A)*(\partial A/\partial t)$, $\partial \ln Q/\partial t = DQ/Q$. Analogously for the inputs, $\partial \ln K/\partial t = DK/K$, $\partial \ln L/\partial t = DL/L$, and $\partial \ln M/\partial t = DM/M$.

18. Growth rate of output, DQ/Q, is obtained by the operation $(\ln Q_t - \ln Q_{t-1})$. A similar procedure is followed to compute the input growth rates, DK/K, DL/L, and M/M.

19. Subtraction of DM/M from the left-hand side and $(S_K + S_L + S_M)(DM/M)$ from the right-hand side of equation (6.9) and rearrangement yields

$$(DQ/Q - DM/M) = (DA/A) + S_K(DK/K - DM/M) + S_L(DL/L - DM/M).$$

7

Structure of Production and Technological Change

INTRODUCTION

In chapter 6 we developed a quantitative profile of the U.S. high-tech sector. We examined growth trends in output and inputs, and analyzed alternative measures of productivity. There are other aspects of production that need to be studied. A description and understanding of the production structure is helpful, even necessary, in the formulation of economic, and industrial, policy. Without such information, policy remains a matter of hypotheses and hunches. Not only does this information illuminate the relevance of existing and past policies, it also provides a basis for consensus building so that future policy can be developed from an agreement on common information. On the other hand, it is also true that quantitative information regarding a production structure is sensitive because it is obtained from second-order derivatives.

In this chapter we pursue three specific tasks: (1) To investigate and analyze empirically the production structure of the U.S. high-tech sector at an aggregate level. There are hardly a handful of empirical studies that provide quantitative analyses of the U.S. high-tech sector; particularly at the level of detail we are interested in.[1] A production structure is a large set. Some elements of this set are defined by a production and/or cost function that relates outputs with inputs, both individually and in the aggregate. Questions arise as to whether gross output or value added is an appropriate measure of output in such an analysis. Accordingly, relevant investigation involves testing hypotheses associated with value added approach to productivity analysis.[2] (2) To examine the relationships between factor inputs involved in a production process. Some of these relationships are expressed in patterns of substitution and complementarity. Although concepts of substitution and complementarity are deeply rooted in economic theory, their quantification and interpretation remain rather complex.[3] Our objective is to further explore this pattern by decomposing traditional labor input into skilled and unskilled workers that have *a priori* relevance to high-tech industry. (3) To analyze and quantify the impact of R&D as a technology index on the production structure of high-tech industry. Generally, shifts in production or cost functions have been defined as technological change and measured through a time trend variable. Issues here include not only the rate of technological change, or R&D-based shifts in production or cost functions, but also the extent to which it alters the optimal mix and level of different inputs that follow from factor bias of technological change.[4] These objectives are followed through an application of a translog model.

TRANSLOG COST FUNCTION

Various aspects of a translog cost function have already been discussed in chapters 4 and 5. The relevant portions of these aspects of a translog cost function are given below. Assuming competitive factor markets and using Shephard's lemma, a cost function is obtained as a dual of a production function.[5] A translog cost function in its general form may be written as[6]

$$C = C_o + a_q'Q + a_i'P + 1/2Q'a_{qq}Q + 1/2P'a_{ij}P + Q'a_{qi}P, \quad (7.1)$$

where the variables C, Q, and P are in logarithms. The variable C is a scalar referring to total cost; Q and P are, respectively, column vectors of output and input prices; C_o is a scalar and basically a constant; a_q' and a_i' are row vectors; and a_{qq}, a_{ij}, and a_{qi} are matrices of coefficients. The order of these vectors and matrices is defined by the order of Q and P. Equation (7.1) is a multi-product cost function, which takes into consideration all sorts of interactions both within and between output quantities and various input prices. Economic theory places a number of constraints on this general form through the requirement for convexity of the production function. If one assumes constant returns to scale and a single output, the cost function of equation (7.1) reduces to

$$C^u = C_o + a_i'P + 1/2\ P'a_{ij}P, \quad (7.2)$$

where C^u refers to unit cost, whereas C is total cost. It is generally assumed that conditions of symmetry, homogeneity, and homotheticity hold. These conditions imply that

$$a_{ij} = a_{ji}, \qquad a_i'I^c = 1, \qquad a_{ij}I^c = 0, \quad (7.3)$$

where I^c is a column vector of 1s. Using Shephard's lemma, we can get share equations from the cost function. For the function (7.2) these are given by

$$S = a_i + a_{ij}P, \tag{7.4}$$

where S is a column vector of input shares. In view of the restrictions in equation (7.3), the order of S is one less than that of P; that is, one of the share equations is redundant.

Given elements of the matrix a_{ij} and vector S, one can compute substitution elasticities, σ_{ij}, between various inputs.[7] Elasticities σ_{ij} are defined as

$$\sigma_{ii} = (a_{ii} + S_i^2 - S_i)/S_i^2, \quad \text{and} \quad \sigma_{ij} = 1 + (a_{ij}/S_iS_j), \quad i \neq j, \tag{7.5}$$

where a_{ij} and S_i are the elements of the above mentioned vectors and matrices. Economic theory gives meanings to the elasticities σ_{ij} and not to the coefficients a_{ij}.[8] In view of the convexity of the production function, elasticities of substitution, σ_{ii}, are negative by definition. Thus, $\sigma_{ii} < 0$. On the other hand, σ_{ij} are cross elasticities between inputs i and j. These can be both positive and negative. When $\sigma_{ij} < 0$ there is complementarity between factors i and j, whereas $\sigma_{ij} > 0$ refers to a relationship of substitution.

It is possible, and common, to add other variables to a translog cost function, such as T for time, which has commonly been used to analyze shifts due to time and thereby to represent various types of technological change. Translog cost function (7.2) can be generalized by augmenting various vectors and matrices to incorporate these additional shift variables. The augmented translog cost function may be written as

$$C^u = C_o + \begin{bmatrix} a_i' & b_i' \end{bmatrix} \begin{bmatrix} P \\ Z \end{bmatrix} + \frac{1}{2} \begin{bmatrix} P' & Z' \end{bmatrix} \begin{bmatrix} A_{11} & A_{12} \\ A_{21} & A_{22} \end{bmatrix} \begin{bmatrix} P \\ Z \end{bmatrix}, \tag{7.6}$$

where Z and Z', respectively, are column and row vectors of these additional variables. Vector a_i and matrix a_{ij} of equation (7.2) are now parts of the augmented matrices, $[a_i \; b_j]$ and A. Specifically, matrix a_{ij} of equation (7.2) refers to the partitioned matrix A_{11} of equation (7.6). The conditions of equation (7.3) do not relate to all parts of the augmented matrices but refer only to partitioned matrices because vector Z is composed of shift variables. Equation (7.6) can also be written in a different form:[9]

$$C^u = C_o + a'P + b'Z + 1/2 \, P'A_{11}P + 1/2 \, Z'A_{22}Z + P'A_{12}Z. \tag{7.7}$$

Since $S_i = \partial C/\partial P_i$, the share equations now are written as[10]

$$S = a + A_{11}P + A_{12}Z. \tag{7.8}$$

FORMULATION OF TRANSLOG FUNCTION
FOR HIGH TECHNOLOGY

Economic theory defines the cost function in terms of input prices. In this analysis variable output is defined as gross output and the production function is cast in terms of three inputs, namely capital (K), labor (L), and material (M). The costs are defined by the prices of these three inputs. Accordingly, row vector $\mathbf{P'}$ = $[P_K \; P_L \; P_M]$ has input prices as its various elements. In addition to price variables, we have defined two shift variables, namely, T for technology and D, a dummy variable. In the augmented version, equation (7.7) row vector $\mathbf{Z'}$ has two elements and is defined as $\mathbf{Z'}$ = $[T \quad D]$.

In this study, T refers to technology. In the literature on cost and production functions, T has generally been defined as a shift time variable that takes the values 1, 2, . . . , n, n being the number of observations in a times series data. Although researchers have commonly used the T variables thus, they have invariably expressed dissatisfaction with this proxy for a technology variable.[11] Our contention is that if T is to reflect technological influences, it should be based on a meaningful measure of technology. The literature on innovations, inventions, and diffusion argues in favor of a variable like R&D and patents.[12] Accordingly, we have defined T on the basis of the stock of R&D. Although R&D has its own problems and detractors,[13] we are persuaded that such a measure of technological change would catch most of the variations in changes in technology over time and that it is a major improvement in definition over the shift variable T measured by discrete time intervals. There is economic and empirical rationale for changes in R&D to reflect changes in technology. We identify this variable by R so that $\mathbf{Z'}$ = $[R \quad D]$.

The dummy variable D is obtained from a residual analysis of our preliminary studies. After we made various tests of hypotheses and looked at the graphs of residuals, we were convinced about the existence of shifts in our data. We, therefore, decided to introduce a dummy variable to reflect these shifts. After 1972, as a result perhaps of the energy price shock, our data suggested a clear shift. Accordingly, we have defined D as a variable such that its value is 0 for 1967–1972 and 1 for 1973–1982. Considering that this dummy variable coincides with energy shocks, there is a great temptation to interpret it as price of energy effect. Second thoughts, however, suggest that one would need much more information to analyze energy effects.[14]

Given the translog cost function (7.7) and definition of $\mathbf{P}$ and $\mathbf{Z}$ vectors, we can define the cost function for our analysis. The various vectors and matrices are specified as follows:

$$\mathbf{a}_i = \begin{bmatrix} a_K \\ a_L \\ a_M \end{bmatrix}; \qquad \mathbf{b}_i = \begin{bmatrix} b_R \\ b_D \end{bmatrix}; \qquad \mathbf{P} = \begin{bmatrix} P_K \\ P_L \\ P_M \end{bmatrix}; \qquad \mathbf{Z} = \begin{bmatrix} R \\ D \end{bmatrix}$$

$$\mathbf{A}_{11} = \begin{bmatrix} a_{KK} & a_{KL} & a_{KM} \\ a_{LK} & a_{LL} & a_{LM} \\ a_{MK} & a_{ML} & a_{MM} \end{bmatrix}; \mathbf{A}_{12} = \begin{bmatrix} a_{RK} & a_{DK} \\ a_{RL} & a_{DL} \\ a_{RM} & a_{DM} \end{bmatrix}; \mathbf{A}_{22} = \begin{bmatrix} a_{RR} & s_{RD} \\ a_{DR} & a_{DD} \end{bmatrix}. \quad (7.9)$$

Variables C, P_K, P_L, P_M, and R are based on time series data for the period 1967–1982 for the U.S. high-technology sector and are expressed in logarithms. They refer to unit total cost, price of capital, wage rate, material price, and stock value of R&D in constant 1972 dollars.

Matrix $\mathbf{A}_{11}$ is by definition a symmetric matrix, and therefore has only six independent elements that need to be estimated. In its triangular form, it may be written as

$$\mathbf{A}_{11} = \begin{bmatrix} a_{KK} & a_{KL} & a_{KM} \\ & a_{LL} & a_{LM} \\ & & a_{MM} \end{bmatrix} \quad (7.10)$$

We have thus 22 coefficients to estimate; namely C_o, $\mathbf{a} = 3$, $\mathbf{b} = 2$, $\mathbf{A}_{11} = 6$, $\mathbf{A}_{12} = 6$, and $\mathbf{A}_{22} = 4$.

In addition to the translog cost function above, we have share equations derived from the translog, given in equation (7.8). Because of three inputs, there are three share equations. However, because of the restrictions in equation (7.3) one of these three is redundant; we can have only two independent equations. Of these three equations, we decided to eliminate the capital share equation, S_K. Our implied assumption, therefore, is that labor and material share equations are independent. As a result of this elimination, vector $\mathbf{a}$ and matrices $\mathbf{A}_{11}$ and $\mathbf{A}_{12}$ all lose the top row in equation (7.9). These two equations are as follows:

$$\begin{bmatrix} S_L \\ S_M \end{bmatrix} = \begin{bmatrix} a_L \\ a_M \end{bmatrix} + \begin{bmatrix} a_{LK} & a_{LL} & a_{LM} \\ a_{MK} & a_{ML} & a_{MM} \end{bmatrix} \begin{bmatrix} P_K \\ P_L \\ P_M \end{bmatrix} + \begin{bmatrix} a_{RL} & a_{DL} \\ a_{RM} & a_{DM} \end{bmatrix} \begin{bmatrix} R \\ D \end{bmatrix} \quad (7.11)$$

The translog cost function defined by equations (7.7) and (7.9) and shares equations (7.11) can be estimated jointly as a simultaneous equation system.

DESIGN OF HYPOTHESIS TESTS

Before we estimate the translog cost function, we must ask what our maintained hypothesis is. The idea behind a maintained hypothesis is to make the underlying assumptions explicit.[15] The need to make some of the underlying assumptions explicit is all the more necessary in flexible form since they have a very large number of possibilities and hence assumptions. Although conventions in empirical analysis in productivity measurements suggest a particular form of cost or production function, there are a number of variations to these forms so that choice of criteria is essential to specify a particular form. There are two issues at this stage: (1) which and how many variations of the form to work with? and (2) what criteria to follow in choosing a particular form? Note that the translog cost function, equation (7.7), can be easily varied by the inclusion or exclusion of a variable from either of the vectors P and Z. Such an inclusion or exclusion involves imposing *a priori* restrictions on the elements of the coefficient vectors and matrices a, b, and A. There is no well-defined theory that deals with the issue of including or excluding a particular variable or imposing certain restrictions. On the other hand, there are some guiding principles that need to be followed. Since the objective here is to make explicit some of the underlying assumptions, relevant restrictions relate to matters of technological change, returns to scale, and separability. The criterion for the choice of one of these forms, and the set of forms on which choice has to be performed, is empirical. The majority of these functional forms are purely statistical in so far as they have been estimated from a data set. Statistical tests based on the log of likelihood of estimated functions provide a meaningful criterion about which there is a general consensus.

At this stage of our empirical investigation, we have not made any decision about a dummy variable. Variable D does not yet exist, so that it is excluded from vector Z in equation (7.9). The basic object of experimentation here is to choose a particular form and not to estimate coefficients for final analysis. We have worked with the following four different models based on different restrictions of the coefficients.

Model I: A translog form implying both neutral and non-neutral technological change. We assume that there is no acceleration or deceleration in the rate of technological change. This implies that the underlying cost function is given by equations (7.7) and (7.9) without the variable R^2 and its associated coefficients, so that $a_{RR} = 0.$[16]

Model II: A translog form implying only Hicksian neutral technological change. This model is more restrictive than Model I. Thus there are *additional* restrictions—specifically, $a_{RK} = a_{RL} = a_{RM} = 0$; that is, the first column of the matrix $A_{12} = 0.$[17]

Model III: In addition to Hicksian neutral technological change this model further assumes strong partial separability between capital and materials. The object of the separability condition is to test the statistical significance of the output measure. This relates to the distinction between gross and value added measures of output. The separability condition is in addition to that of neutral technological change so that Model III is more restrictive than Model II, and hence more than Model I. There are *further additional* restrictions on coefficients, $a_{KM} = a_{LM} = a_{MM} = 0$, which means that the last row of the matrix $A_{11} = 0$.

Model IV: This model assumes that the production function is Cobb-Douglas, and is the most restrictive assumption. The model is also historical because the Cobb-Douglas is one of the oldest and most widely used functions in empirical economics. Here the assumption is that equation (7.7) is a linear homogeneous function with a unitary elasticity of factor substitution between capital and labor and constant returns to scale. Note that this assumption follows from the separability assumption above. Since the Cobb-Douglas production function is defined in terms of value added, it does not make much sense for a gross value measure of output. The assumption of a Cobb-Douglas production function introduces more restrictions on the coefficients. It implies that A is a null matrix. Model IV implies that the remaining two rows of the matrix $A_{11} = 0$.

Having formalized the models, and their underlying assumptions, the next question is which of these models to choose. The objective is to choose one of these models that best fits the data. Our next step, therefore, is to decide about a sequence of comparing and testing these models. In view of the fact that these models have been defined in terms of progressively increasing restrictions, one sequence is obvious; it compares and tests Model I with Model II, Model II with Model III, and so on. This is a sequential testing design.[18] Another sequence simply compares and tests a model with the least restrictive one, namely Model I. Thus we can compare Model II with Model I, Model III with Model I, and so on. We have followed both these sequences, which are outlined in table 7.1.

These tests involve the estimation of the translog cost function, equation (7.7), to the time series data for the U.S. high-tech sector. We have estimated all four models by the seemingly unrelated regression method.[19] For purposes of this test we have estimated both translog cost and production functions.[20] Quantitative results of this estimation are given in the table 7.1. For purposes of comparing and testing different models, we need information on the log of likelihood. The log of likelihood and the estimates of the test statistic for different models are summarized in table 7.2. The test statistic is specified as $2[U - R]$, where U refers to the value of the log of likelihood of the estimate of the unrestricted equation, and R that of the restricted equation. This test statistic has a chi-square distribution. Given the value of this test statistic, it allows us to accept or reject the hypothesis whether or not we should choose one model in preference to the other. The hypothesis we are testing is: Compared to another, should a model be accepted or rejected on the basis of the value of the test statistic. The results of this test, to accept or reject a hypothesis, are also given in the last columns of table 7.2.

Basically, all these results suggest that none of the models is preferable to Model I. When compared with Model III, the test suggests that Model IV be chosen. However, when Model III is compared with Model I and/or Model II, the test statistic rejects the hypothesis of accepting Model III. The conclusion that these tests lead to is acceptance of the maintained hypothesis in Model I. Considering that Model I is also the least restrictive, it is consistent with *a priori* rationale. Acceptance of Model I and therefore implications of these tests are (1) technological change in high-tech industries is non-neutral, (2) gross output is a better approximation to the concept of output than value added,[21] and (3) the translog is a better approximation than the Cobb-Douglas.

EMPIRICAL RESULTS

We have tested four different models and found that Model I, defined by equation (7.7), provides the maintained hypothesis. The next step in our research involves estimating this translog cost function. At this stage we looked at the results of estimates referred to above and analyzed the residuals. Analysis of residuals suggested that there is a clear distinction between the two periods 1967–1972 and 1973–1982. To take this fact into consideration we define a dummy variable D such that it is 0 for the first period and 1 for the second.[22] It is thus a vector whose elements are 0 and 1. This is one of the variables in the matrix $\mathbf{Z}$. The various variables and coefficients in equation (7.7) are as defined in equation (7.9). In addition to the translog cost function equations (7.7) and (7.9), there are two share equations following from the translog of equation (7.7), which are defined in equation (7.11). We have thus 2 sets of equations, (7.7), and (7.11), made up of a translog cost function, labor share, and material share functions. However, we assumed that there are no square terms for either the dummy variable D or the technology variable R, neither did we include interaction terms between these two variables. This amounts to the assumption that $\mathbf{A}_{22}$ is a null matrix. The rationale for these assumptions are as follows: (1) It is difficult to interpret D-squared and the interaction term between D and R. Inclusion of these terms would simply be *pro forma* and mechanical. (2) Our maintained hypothesis did not include an R-squared term. Once again, it is difficult to interpret rate of change of neutral technological change once it is accepted that technological change is biased. We also assumed that the sum of the a_i coefficients is unity. This assumption is obvious. Assuming that these equations have random terms associated with them, these have been estimated for the 1967–1982 time series data for the U.S. high-tech sector described in chapter 6. We estimated these three equations simultaneously by the seemingly unrelated regression method.[23]

Empirical results for the U.S. high-tech sector of the estimation of equations (7.7) and (7.11) are given in table 7.3. Judging from statistical measures, estimates of R square are quite high; between 0.87 and 0.97. The standard errors of the estimated coefficients are quite low. Accordingly, these results are statistically acceptable. So far as the signs and magnitude of the coefficients are concerned, there are few *a priori* expectations. From theory-imposed restriction we know that the sum of coefficients a_i, i = K, L, M, must add to one. These coefficients do add to one; but this constraint was imposed in estimation so that it does not say much about the meaningfulness of these magnitudes. On the other hand, the magnitudes of these three coefficients do seem to be in the ball park.

The second *a priori* expectation is that $a_R < 0$. The estimate of this coefficient agrees with this expectation.

These are the first, and only, coefficients of a translog for the U.S. high-tech sector. There is, therefore, no particular expectation about the magnitudes of these coefficients. Also there are no comparable studies from which one can develop some idea about these magnitudes. The best one can do is to look at studies that are, although not strictly comparable, in somewhat close proximity. There is a similar estimation of a translog for a larger aggregate, namely, U.S. manufacturing.[24] There is another study that estimates a similar function for an individual three-digit industry; specifically, semiconductors.[25] It needs to be pointed out that comparison with such studies are at best tenuous because model specification, time period of analysis, econometric package, and method of estimation are all different. However, if we compare our estimates in table 7.3 with similar estimates for manufacturing and the semiconductor industry, our estimates are in the ball park. Thus from both statistical and *a priori* expectations, these results are acceptable.

INPUT SUBSTITUTION

One way to look at the coefficients is to estimate related economic elasticities for which there are *a priori* expectations. From translog coefficients it is possible to compute Allen partial elasticities of substitution between the three inputs, K, L, and M. Economic theory and convexity of the production function implies that own elasticities of substitution, σ_{ii}, are all negative. Cross elasticities, σ_{ij}, however, can be both negative and positive. There is thus *a priori* expectation about only own elasticities of substitution. Elasticities σ_{ii} and σ_{ij} are defined in terms of the coefficients of the translog cost function in equation (7.5). Using this formulation, we can compute the quantitative magnitudes of these elasticities.

The quantitative magnitudes of these elasticities are given in table 7.4, and have been taken from appendix table C1. Since these elasticities are estimated for each year, only mean values, the range, and the standard deviation are given in this table. In view of the low standard errors of the coefficients in table 7.3, the standard errors of these means are also quite low. Taking own elasticities first; we find that all these values are negative, which is expected *a priori*. This provides further confirmation about the significance of the statistical results in table 7.3. The range is not large. For capital, the range is around two times the minimum value while for both labor and materials it is much less. The standard deviation of the means are also low, suggesting that the mean values are stable. So far as the magnitudes of the elasticities are concerned, the estimates suggest that all these elasticities are greater than one. They are all elastic. They also compare well with estimates for semiconductor industry.[26] Interpreted at their face value, these magnitudes suggest that materials is the most elastic input and capital the least.

By comparison, there is much larger variability in cross elasticities. The range for capital-labor is much higher and so is its standard deviation. The cross elasticity between labor and capital is not significantly different from zero. The other two cross elasticities are significantly different both from zero and one. This may partly explain the rejection of the hypotheses about separability and the Cobb-Douglas. The range and standard deviations are quite low. All the cross elasticities are positive, which means that there is substitution between all the three inputs. Capital and labor are the closest substitutes.

Elasticities of factor substitution is still a complex concept, depending as it does on the second-order derivative of an n dimensional relationship. These elasticities, however, also relate to a less complex and comparatively simpler concept of demand elasticity for an input, ξ_{ij}. Demand elasticity of factor input follows from a demand-price relationship. Given certain assumptions, we can write these demand elasticities in terms of substitution elasticities.[27] These relations are:

$$\xi_{ij} = S_j \, \sigma_{ij}, \quad \text{and } \xi_{ii} = S_i \, \sigma_{ii}, \qquad i, j = K, L, M \qquad (7.12)$$

Since ξ_{ij} can be easily estimated, and there are some *a priori* expectations about them, they provide another test of the meaningfulness of the estimates of the translog cost function, equation (7.3). By virtue of being well-behaved demand functions, the expectation is that own price elasticities are negative. These estimated demand elasticities are presented in table 7.5, and are taken from appendix table C2. Once again, we have these estimates for all the years. In this table we have given mean values, the range, and standard deviation to provide information about their distributions.

As expected, mean values of own demand elasticities are all negative. They are statistically different from both zero and one. The fact that they are less than one implies that these demand functions are not elastic. The demand for materials is the most elastic, its estimate being -0.66, and for labor the least. The range of these elasticities is quite small so that the values are stable over time. Unlike substitution elasticities, cross elasticities of demand for inputs are not symmetric. These are also far more sensitive and thus more variable. Here again, all the cross elasticities are positive, implying a relationship of substitution. The range of these values is larger than for own price elasticities of demand. The values of these elasticities are generally low, and ξ_{KL} and ξ_{LK} are both not significantly different from zero. Over the period, some of the values are even negative, implying possibilities of a complementary relationship between capital and labor.

INPUT SUBSTITUTION OVER THE BUSINESS CYCLE

As explained in chapter 6, the period of analysis spans four business cycles.[28] These cyclical periods are the upswing of 1967–1969, business cycles of 1969–1973 and 1973–1979, and the downswing of 1979–1982. Since we have estimated substitution and other elasticities for each year of the period 1967–1982, we can estimate average elasticities for these four periods in order to compare the production structure over the business cycle. The data for various own and cross elasticities of input substitution is given in table 7.6.

All the three own elasticities are numerically greater than one. The own elasticity for labor, σ_{LL}, is the most stable, having more or less the same magnitude over the 1967–1969 upswing as over the 1979–1982 downswing in addition to during the two cycles of 1969–1973 and 1973–1979. On the other hand, own elasticity of material, σ_{MM}, is numerically the highest among all the own elasticities. It shows a declining trend. It is the highest during the upswing of 1967–1969, and is higher over the cycle 1969–1973 compared to 1973–1979. Own elasticity of capital, σ_{KK}, follows a pattern completely opposite to that of σ_{MM}. The trend is upward. It is lower during the upswing of 1967–1969 and higher in the downswing of 1979–1982, and is higher for the later cycle of 1973–1979 compared to the earlier one, 1969–1973. Thus all the three elasticities behave differently over the these cycles. Graph 7.1 brings out the highlights.

In the case of cross elasticities, σ_{KM}, is elastic, being greater than one, while σ_{LM}, is inelastic. Both these cross elasticities are stable over the cycle and its various phases. It is the capital-labor substitution elasticity, σ_{KL}, that reveals an interesting trend. Its value is falling over time. Graph 7.2 shows it vividly. For the upswing of 1967–1969, it is positive, implying substitution between capital and labor. Over the business cycle of 1969–1973, the substitutional character continues even though its magnitude falls. The estimates of σ_{KL} become negative after 1973. Over the 1973–1979 business cycle, this relationship takes an about turn and turns toward complementarity. This complementarity holds for the downswing of 1979–1982, which suggests that a major change has been taking place during the decade of the 1970s. It has been argued in popular as well as in professional writings that high-tech industry promotes a different relationship between labor and capital. Technologically sophisticated machines in high-tech industry require skilled labor. Skilled labor is not a substitute for but a complement to machines and capital in general. The evidence on this cross elasticity in table 7.6 is consistent with this view. It suggests that the composition of labor in high-tech industry has been changing during this period. One can postulate that there are two elements in the aggregate called labor; namely, (1) skilled workers and (2) unskilled workers. It would seem that there was a preponderance of unskilled work in the first part of this period, but a greater share of skilled work in the second period. This important finding requires further analysis to incorporate this distinction between skilled and unskilled work.

TRANSLOG COST FUNCTION WITH DISAGGREGATED LABOR

To analyze the implications of change in σ_{KL} from positive to negative we disaggregated the labor variable into two components: (1) skilled labor and (2) unskilled labor. Unskilled labor is defined as production workers and is denoted by U. In the economist's terms, production workers generally relate the concept of labor that is employed for factory work on an assembly line and is hired and fired on the spot unless they are protected by unions. For want of a better data source, skilled workers refer to non-production workers in the data on labor force.[29] This category is designated by N, and involves administrative and non-blue or white collar workers. Accordingly, P_U, P_N, S_U, and S_N, refer to the logarithms of wage rate of unskilled workers, salaries of skilled workers, share of production workers, and share of non-production workers in output, respectively. The observation following from changing sign of σ_{KL} implies that the production workers have a substitutional relationship with capital while non-production workers have complementarity relationship. Thus $\sigma_{KU} > 0$ and $\sigma_{KN} < 0$. This is the hypothesis to be tested.

To estimate σ_{KU} and σ_{KN} and test the hypotheses above, we need to reestimate translog cost function (7.7) and shares equations (7.11) after substituting the variables U and N for L. This substitution respecifies equations (7.9) and (7.11). Equation (7.9) becomes

$$
\mathbf{a}_i = \begin{bmatrix} a_K \\ a_U \\ a_N \\ a_M \end{bmatrix}; \qquad
\mathbf{b}_i = \begin{bmatrix} b_R \\ b_D \end{bmatrix}; \qquad
\mathbf{P} = \begin{bmatrix} P_K \\ P_U \\ P_N \\ P_M \end{bmatrix}; \qquad
\mathbf{Z} = \begin{bmatrix} R \\ D \end{bmatrix}
$$

$$
\mathbf{A}_{11} = \begin{bmatrix}
a_{KK} & a_{KU} & a_{KN} & a_{KM} \\
a_{UK} & a_{UU} & a_{UN} & a_{UM} \\
a_{NK} & a_{NU} & a_{NN} & a_{NM} \\
a_{MK} & a_{MU} & a_{MN} & a_{MM}
\end{bmatrix}; \quad
\mathbf{A}_{12} = \begin{bmatrix}
a_{RK} & a_{DK} \\
a_{RU} & a_{DU} \\
a_{RN} & a_{DN} \\
a_{RM} & a_{DM}
\end{bmatrix}; \quad
\mathbf{A}_{22} = \begin{bmatrix}
a_{RR} & a_{RD} \\
a_{DR} & a_{DD}
\end{bmatrix}.
$$

$$(7.13)$$

Similarly, share equations (7.11) become

$$
\begin{bmatrix} S_U \\ S_N \\ S_M \end{bmatrix} =
\begin{bmatrix} a_U \\ a_N \\ a_M \end{bmatrix} +
\begin{bmatrix}
a_{UK} & a_{UU} & a_{UN} & a_{UM} \\
a_{NK} & a_{NU} & a_{NN} & a_{NM} \\
a_{MK} & a_{ML} & a_{MN} & a_{MM}
\end{bmatrix}
\begin{bmatrix} P_K \\ P_U \\ P_N \\ P_M \end{bmatrix} +
\begin{bmatrix}
a_{RU} & a_{DU} \\
a_{RN} & a_{DN} \\
a_{RM} & a_{DM}
\end{bmatrix}
\begin{bmatrix} R \\ D \end{bmatrix}.
$$

$$(7.14)$$

Excepting this change, all other assumptions regarding the coefficients in the vectors and matrices remain the same; we still assume that there is no square term of technological change variable R, the cost function is homogenous, and separability conditions are satisfied. Since our interest is in focusing on labor disaggregation, we decided to eliminate the variable D for this case. Equation (7.7) specified by equations (7.13) and (7.14) define the system of simultaneous equations made up of the translog cost function and three related cost share equations; the capital-share equation has been eliminated. Coefficients of the translog can be estimated from these equations jointly. Our assumptions are that the elements of **a** sum to one, the elements of the rows of A_{11} sum to zero, A_{11} is symmetric, and A_{22} is a null matrix. Given the time series data, we have estimated these equations simultaneously by seemingly unrelated regression method, as before.

The results of estimating the system of equations and translog coefficients are given in table 7.7. The R-squares for all the four equations are high: 0.73 for material share equation, between 0.84 and 0.89 for the two components of labor share equation and 0.9 for the translog. Standard errors of the coefficients are quite low. The empirical results are thus statistically acceptable. We do have some *a priori* expectations about the coefficient from table 7.3. Interestingly, first-order coefficients a_i, i = K, U, N, and M, have the correct signs and the magnitudes are in the ball park. Comparing with table 7.3, the coefficient for capital has gone down while that of materials has gone up; more or less by the same amount. The coefficient of technical change, a_R, is negative as expected; however, its numerical value has gone down. This is perhaps as one should expect. Decomposing labor into skilled and unskilled should pick up some amount of technological change in the biased category reducing the neutral technological change in the process. There are few expectations about second-order coefficients; these are both sensitive and have larger variations. Taking this fact into consideration, the second-order coefficients, a_{ij}, when compared with table 7.3 are in the ball park. These results are acceptable on all these bases.

INPUT SUBSTITUTION ELASTICITIES
WITH DISAGGREGATED LABOR

We have estimated input substitution elasticities from table 7.7 using the relationship in equation (7.5). These are taken from appendix table C3 and are given in table 7.8.[30] Comparing these with similar elasticities in table 7.4 for aggregated labor, the own elasticities for capital and material have increased in magnitude, which implies that there is greater elasticity in the system. Also, the variability in terms of both standard deviation and range is much higher. Unskilled labor has a much higher level of own elasticity of substitution, particularly in comparison with skilled labor. These results conform to the general notions about the high-tech industry. Decomposition of labor into these two components provides acceptable results.

In terms of cross elasticities, the capital-material elasticity, σ_{KM}, remains close to one. There is an increase in the magnitude of σ_{UM} and σ_{NM} as compared with σ_{LM}. The effect of decomposing labor has been to make relationship between labor—skilled and unskilled—and material highly elastic. However, the most interesting result in this table relates to σ_{KU} and σ_{KN}; one being positive and the other negative. Thus there is substitution between capital and unskilled labor. As expected there is complementarity between capital and skilled labor.[31] This is exactly the hypothesis that we had set up from the results in table 7.5; the results in table 7.8 not only confirm the expectation from the results in table 7.5, they also sharpen the conclusions therein.

We also estimated price elasticities of demand for inputs from table 7.8, which are given in table 7.9. In view of the formula to estimate demand elasticities from substitution elasticities, it is not surprising that all estimates are in full conformity with our findings from substitution elasticities. The estimates of price elasticities of demand for the model with disaggregated labor are consistent with those of elasticities of substitution. All own price elasticities are in conformity with expectations about them and lie within a narrow range. Estimates of cross elasticities, once again, distinguish the relationship between capital and skilled labor from that between capital and unskilled labor. Although ξ_{KN} and ξ_{NK} are negative, implying complementarity between capital and skilled labor, ξ_{KU} and ξ_{UK} are positive.

Table 7.10 gives the estimates of the substitution elasticities for the U.S. high-tech sector over the business cycle. All the own elasticities are highly elastic with their magnitudes being greater than 1, and σ_{UU} as high as 8. The earlier conclusions about σ_{KK} and σ_{MM} still hold: σ_{KK} moves upward and σ_{MM} declines over time and over the two cycles. The rate of growth and of decline in these two, however, is now less. What is new here is that the stability of σ_{LL} gives way to a well-defined movement in σ_{UU} and σ_{NN}. Both gain elasticity as they move from the business cycle of 1969–1973 to that of 1973–1979. Both are low in the upswing of 1967–1969 and virtually one and a half times higher during the downswing of 1979–1982.

Although all the own elasticities are highly elastic, the majority of the cross elasticities are inelastic; σ_{UM} and σ_{NM} are the only elastic cross elasticities. There is a large decrease in the value of σ_{KU}. σ_{KN} and σ_{UM} are basically stable over the two business cycles and over the two phases of the business cycle. The major shifts are in σ_{KN} and σ_{MN}, with σ_{KN} comparatively high in the upswing of 1967–1969, low in the downswing of 1979–1982, and virtually half in 1973–1979; σ_{MN} follows a similar pattern.[32] The only difference between these two is that the latter is elastic and stays elastic over the whole period. The other interesting conclusion is that the elasticity of substitution between unskilled labor and all other inputs is stable over time; over the business cycles and over the two phases of the business cycle.

TECHNICAL CHANGE IN HIGH-TECH INDUSTRIES

Our analysis of technological change is quite different from the majority of other studies where an index of technology is defined by a dummy variable for time trend. A time trend variable implies that production and cost functions shift over time and these shifts are interpreted as expressions of technological change. Instead of a time trend index, we use an R&D stock as a variable for measuring technological change.[33] The logic of this formulation is that technological change takes place through shifts due to R&D expenditures. R&D is a recognized source of innovations and diffusion of technology and its stock, like a time trend variable, is able to catch shifts in production and cost functions. This formulation treats R&D as a half way construct between a variable like capital and a trend like time. The effects of technological change, therefore, are quantified through the coefficients of R.

In our analysis, we have assumed that technological change is linear so that there is no R-squared term. The estimated effects are related to changes in R alone. The translog cost function and the share equations that we have estimated both for aggregate and disaggregated labor contain the variable R and both the coefficients related to R as well as interaction terms of R with variables K, L, M, U, and N. There are thus two effects of technological change: (1) a direct effect given by a_R, and (2) an indirect effect through the coefficients of the interaction terms a_{Ri}, i = K, L, M, U, and N, which are the elements of the column in A_{12}. Direct effects are interpreted as neutral technological change and indirect as non-neutral technological change, a neutral technological change acts as a pure shift in the cost function, which leaves factor shares unchanged. Therefore, if the prices of capital, labor, and material are fixed, the minimum cost needed to produce a given output decreases over time. The decrease follows from improvements in techniques, learning by doing, and better quality management that enhances productivity of inputs. The parameter representing such technological change, a_R, therefore is expected to be negative. In contrast, biased technological change represents shifts in the level of technology that alter the equilibrium factor shares, holding factor prices constant. There is thus no *a priori* expectation regarding the sign of parameters defined by elements of the column in A_{12}. The condition $a_{Ri} < 0$ implies that the technological change is ith factor saving, and similarly $a_{Ri} > 0$ means that it is ith factor using.

The estimates of the coefficients of R in the two systems of equations, (1) using L as an aggregate labor input, and (2) decomposing labor into unskilled, U, and skilled workers, N, are given in table 7.11. Looking at the coefficient a_R, we find that it is -0.03 when an aggregate measure of labor is used, which implies that there is neutral technological change. However, when aggregate labor, L, is decomposed into U and N, the value of this estimate falls to half, -0.015.[34] Thus R&D expenditures do cause shifts in the cost function and reduce costs; however, the magnitudes of these cost reductions is not high. We have already tested the hypothesis that the data exhibit only neutral technological change by comparing Model I with Model II in table 7.2, and our statistical results rejected the hypothesis of only neutral technological change. This test supported the proposition that technological change is biased; a_{Ri}, i = K, L, M, is not zero. Table 7.11 confirms this proposition. We can also estimate the total value of the biased technological change. We define total biased technological change, BTC, as follows:

$$BTC = [(\partial C/\partial R)/\partial t] = \Sigma [a_{Ri}Dp_i/p_i]. \qquad (7.15)$$

The estimate of average BTC for aggregate labor works out to be −0.06 for the entire period 1969–1982. This is twice the value of neutral technological change, which is −0.03. BTC has been cost-increasing during the upswing of 1967– 1969 and the business cycle of 1973–1979, but cost reducing during the first business cycle of 1969–1973 and the downswing of 1979–1982. For the case where labor is an aggregate measure, we find that technological change is labor saving and capital and material using.[35] Capital using coefficient is 3 times that for materials. This conclusion changes, as it should, when labor is decomposed. In this case technical change is highly material using. It is capital, skilled and unskilled labor saving. As one would expect, the greatest savings are in unskilled labor. Part of the capital saving effect may also follow from the complementarity between capital and skilled labor.

DYNAMICS OF THE U.S. HIGH-TECH SECTOR

On the basis of results above, the following dynamics of the U.S. high-tech sector emerge. The U.S. high-tech sector is propelled by a high rate of technological change, which is improving the productivity of materials. Cost minimizing policies of production units incorporate such technological change by using relatively more material input. Increase in the quantity of materials has two effects on labor. First, it increases labor productivity. Second, in so far as material input substitutes for labor, it reduces employment of labor input. Since own elasticities of substitution of both labor and material are high, the second effect becomes magnified and the demand for materials is further strengthened. Increases in labor productivity and a decline in the employment of labor changes the composition of the labor input, which becomes obvious when we decompose labor between skilled and unskilled workers. In view of the much higher elasticities associated with decomposed labor, this dynamic process is further accelerated.

The change in composition of labor has two opposite effects on costs: (1) the decline in employment of labor input reduces total costs and (2) increases in productivity as well as complementarity of skilled workers with capital puts an upward pressure on the wage bill. The employment effect reduces cost while the price effects raise it—opposite effects are taking place to the cost of materials. Technological change and substitution with labor promotes increases in the quantity of materials used; increases in demand push material costs up. Thus, material input raises costs both from quantity and price. Capital is both a complement of skilled workers and a substitute for material input. However, neither of these effects are strong. The price and quantity effects of capital are determined not only from the nature of this production structure but also from macro economic policies.

The story, outlined above, suggests the following hypotheses about costs: (1) material costs are increasing, (2) it is not obvious if labor costs are decreasing or not, and (3) there is no clear signal about capital costs. However, if material costs are increasing, and labor costs are constant, capital costs must be decreasing proportionately. To test these hypotheses, we have decomposed changes in costs in terms of price and quantity. Writing input costs as $p_i x_i$, where p and x refer to price and quantity, respectively, and i stands for input, i = K, L, and M. We define

$$(Dc/c) = S'[(Dp/p) - (Dx/x)], \qquad (7.16)$$

where **S**, **p**, and **x** are vectors of shares, prices, and quantities with elements referring to the three inputs. Since our analysis has been in terms of logarithms, it needs to be pointed out that S, p, and x are defined in non-logarithmic terms. We measure **Dp/p** and **Dx/x** as $[\mathbf{P}_t - \mathbf{P}_{t-1}]$ and $[\mathbf{X}_t - \mathbf{X}_{t-1}]$, respectively, where capital letters **P** and **X** are measures in logarithms. Equation (7.16) provides a decomposition of costs in terms of price and quantity of inputs.

Estimate of this decomposition is given in table 7.12. For the period as a whole, the costs have grown at the rate of 7.5 percent per year. Costs due to the labor input have gone down, while wage costs have gone up. Material costs have grown both in terms of quantity and price. Proportionally, growth in material costs explain 57 percent of growth in total costs, while labor accounts for only 16 percent. During the upswing of 1967–1969, capital costs accounted for 77 percent of the rise in total costs. Since then its share has been continuously declining, and by the downswing of 1979–1982, capital costs accounted for 30 percent. By comparison, material costs have continuously increased to form a large part of the rise in total costs; the proportion grew from 29 percent in the upswing of 1967–1969 to virtually 50 percent in the downswing of 1979–1982.

CONCLUSION

We have designed tests in two different sequences to choose the maintained hypothesis. Among the four models tested, our test statistics accepts the least restrictive model of a translog function with non-neutral technological change. Accordingly, we estimate a translog cost function with three inputs, capital, labor, and material. We also had a semi-shift variable in stock of R&D as a proxy for technological change. In view of the clear data shifts after 1972, we designed a dummy variable that takes the value zero for 1969 to 1972 and one for 1973 onward. These two variables defined our augmented translog cost function. We estimated this function for the U.S. high-tech sector for the period 1967–1982, spanning two business cycles, one upswing and another downswing. Our results are acceptable both from statistical and *a priori* expectations.

Our findings are that own elasticities of input substitution are elastic. Own elasticity of materials, numerically, is the highest and that of capital the lowest. Own elasticities of materials and capital move opposite to each other over time. Substitution elasticity for materials falls over the period while that of capital rises. Cross elasticity for capital-labor switches sign over the period implying a change in the relationship from substitution to complementarity. To verify further this result, we decomposed the input labor into skilled and unskilled workers and reestimated the translog cost function, this time excluding the dummy variable. Over the period the share of skilled labor in total labor is increasing. Our estimates for disaggregated labor confirmed the above result. The own elasticities become more elastic. Cross elasticity between capital and skilled labor implies a relationship of complementarity, whereas the relationship between capital and unskilled labor is one of substitution.

Our empirical results confirm our hypothesis about non-neutral technological change. These imply embodied technological change. For the case of aggregate labor, neutral technological change has a coefficient of -0.03, implying a cost reduction of 3 percent per year. When labor is decomposed into skilled and unskilled labor, this number falls to -0.015; shifts in cost function reduce cost by much less. When we estimate the coefficient for biased technological change, we obtain the value as -0.06, implying that embodied technological change is reducing costs by 6 percent per year; twice the rate of neutral shifts in the cost function.

The costs of production have gone up by 7.5 percent per year. Whereas wage costs have gone up, costs due to labor input have gone down, implying reduction in employment. Growth in materials costs explain 57 percent of the growth in total cost, due to an increase in both the price and quantity of material input. Materials costs have grown over time, while capital costs have declined.

Table 7.1
Design of Hypothesis Test

Maintained Hypothesis	vs	Alternative Hypothesis	No.	Restrictions
				Parameter Restrictions
SEQUENCE A:				
Model I: Non-Neutral Technical Change	vs	Model II: Hicks Neutral Technical Change	2	$a_{ir} = 0; i = K, L, M$
Model II: Hicks Neutral Technical Change	vs	Model III: Strong Partial Separability	2	$a_{im} = 0; i = K, L, M$
Model III: Strong Partial Separability	vs	Model IV: Cobb Douglas	2	$a_{rr} = a_{ll} = 0$
SEQUENCE B:				
Model I	vs	Model II	2	$a_{ir} = 0$
Model I	vs	Model III	4	$a_{ir} = a_{im} = 0$
Model I	vs	Model IV	6	$a_{ir} = a_{im} = a_{rr} = a_{ll} = 0$

Table 7.2
Tests for Separability and Technological Change

Hypothesis	Log of Likelihood	Test Statistic U - R		Accept / Reject	
		A	B	A	B
COST FUNCTION					
Model I	116.20				
Model II	121.21	9.45	9.56	R	R
Model III	95.42	44.00	55.56	R	R
Model IV	95.86	5.12	60.60	A	R
PROD.FUNCTION					
Model I	115.73				
Model II	109.97	11.52	11.52	R	R
Model III	89.60	40.68	56.26	R	R
Model IV	83.68	20.16	44.10	R	R

Note: The test statistic is two times the difference of the logs of the likelihood function of unrestricted and restricted estimates. It has a chi-square distribution with degrees of freedom equal to the number of restrictions given in table 7.1.

Table 7.3
Translog Cost Function

Coefficient	Estimate	Standard Error
a_o	-0.13293	0.01047
a_K	0.41072	0.01414
a_L	0.24470	0.01072
a_M	0.34458	0.01071
a_R	-0.03153	0.00445
a_D	0.07003	0.01254
a_{KK}	0.03900	0.04000
a_{KL}	-0.08116	0.02928
a_{KM}	0.04215	0.03605
a_{LL}	0.10503	0.02497
a_{LM}	-0.01828	0.03605
a_{MM}	-0.01828	0.03019
a_{KR}	0.11614	0.03742
a_{LR}	-0.16133	0.02443
a_{MR}	0.04519	0.03014
a_{KD}	-0.04502	0.01414
a_{LD}	-0.02803	0.01114
a_{MD}	0.07305	0.01148

LOG OF LIKELIHOOD 157.49

Equation	D. W. Statistic	R-Squared
Total Cost Function	1.1749	0.9725
Labor Share Equation	1.4611	0.8699
Material Share Equation	1.7769	0.9823

Table 7.4
Substitution Elasticities

Elasticity	Mean	Standard Deviation	Minimum	Maximum
A: OWN				
σ_{KK}	-1.2908	0.25487	-1.6387	-0.0660
σ_{LL}	-1.3641	0.01905	-1.3803	-1.3100
σ_{MM}	-1.7505	0.36452	-2.3077	-1.3703
B: CROSS				
σ_{KL}	0.0358	0.10144	-0.09158	0.21747
σ_{KM}	1.2778	0.01291	1.26040	1.30410
σ_{LM}	0.7057	0.05067	0.59976	0.76394

Source: Table 7.3.

Table 7.5
Demand Elasticities

Elasticity	Mean	Standard Deviation	Minimum	Maximum
A: OWN				
ξ_{KK}	-0.50199	0.0346	-0.5486	-0.4272
ξ_{LL}	-0.29272	0.0231	-0.3322	-0.2498
ξ_{MM}	-0.66132	0.0514	-0.7375	-0.6021
B: CROSS				
ξ_{LK}	0.0178	0.0438	-0.0352	-0.0954
ξ_{KL}	0.0078	0.0219	-0.0178	0.0511
ξ_{MK}	0.5091	0.0693	0.4308	0.6252
ξ_{KM}	0.4940	0.0579	0.4056	0.5635
ξ_{ML}	0.1521	0.0220	0.1117	0.1937
ξ_{LM}	0.2746	0.0483	0.1920	0.3337

Source: Table 7.3.

Table 7.6
Substitution Elasticities over the Business Cycle

Elasticity	1967-1969	1969-1973	1973-1979	1979-1982
A: OWN				
σ_{KK}	-1.0234	-1.1595	-1.4212	-1.3541
σ_{LL}	-0.3642	-1.3469	-1.3704	-1.3707
σ_{MM}	-2.2198	-2.0200	-1.5312	-1.5514
B: CROSS				
σ_{KL}	0.1932	0.1114	-0.0311	-0.0592
σ_{KM}	1.2844	1.2835	1.2761	1.2689
σ_{LM}	0.6657	0.6761	0.7309	0.7145

Source: Table 7.3.

Table 7.7
Translog Cost Function, Disaggregated Labor

Coefficient	Estimate	Standard Error
a_0	-0.22226	0.00115
a_K	0.35484	0.00201
a_U	0.10299	0.00111
a_N	0.11515	0.00361
a_M	0.42702	0.00374
a_R	-0.01493	0.00590
a_{KK}	0.07700	0.03316
a_{KU}	-0.00372	0.01470
a_{KN}	-0.06386	0.01029
a_{KM}	-0.00942	0.03287
a_{UU}	-0.30800	0.01678
a_{UN}	-0.00250	0.00412
a_{UM}	0.03702	0.01372
a_{NN}	0.05286	0.00338
a_{NM}	0.01350	0.00939
a_{MM}	-0.04110	0.03865
a_{KR}	-0.06044	0.03320
a_{UR}	-0.13216	0.01383
a_{NR}	-0.09890	0.01111
a_{MR}	0.29150	0.03515

LOG OF LIKELIHOOD 192.66

Equation	D. W. Statistic	R-Squared
Total Cost Function	0.8770	0.9403
Prod. Worker Share	0.4939	0.8945
Non-Prod. Worker Share	0.4140	0.8498
Material Share	0.5629	0.7268

Table 7.8
Substitution Elasticities, Disaggregated Labor

Elasticity	Mean	Standard Deviation	Minimum	Maximum
A: OWN				
σ_{KK}	-1.8815	0.3960	-2.4391	-1.2344
σ_{UU}	-0.9866	2.2913	-13.7100	-6.4808
σ_{NN}	-2.9221	1.7626	-3.7295	-2.8285
σ_{MM}	-1.9099	0.4058	-2.5310	-1.4884
B: CROSS				
σ_{KU}	0.9177	0.9898	0.9452	0.9856
σ_{KN}	-0.6407	0.3977	-1.6651	-0.2097
σ_{KM}	0.9397	0.2856	0.9320	0.9418
σ_{UN}	0.7786	0.0623	0.4256	0.6260
σ_{UM}	1.8282	0.1125	1.5282	2.0024
σ_{NM}	1.3844	0.1933	1.1458	1.8684

Source: Table 7.7.

Table 7.9
Input Demand Elasticities, Disaggregated Labor

Elasticity	Mean	Standard Deviation	Minimum	Maximum
A: OWN				
ξ_{KK}	-0.4042	0.0284	-0.4352	-0.3509
ξ_{UU}	-0.7308	0.0590	-0.9023	-0.6590
ξ_{NN}	-1.1562	0.0631	-1.2975	-1.0661
ξ_{MM}	-0.3430	0.1673	-0.4729	-0.1850
B: CROSS				
ξ_{KU}	0.1006	0.0197	0.0799	0.1371
ξ_{UK}	0.3900	0.0561	0.2941	0.4666
ξ_{KN}	-0.0672	0.0080	-0.0807	-0.0490
ξ_{NK}	-0.3031	0.1835	-0.8205	-0.1335
ξ_{KM}	0.3868	0.0426	0.3001	0.4113
ξ_{MK}	0.3935	0.0497	0.3131	0.4641
ξ_{UN}	0.0774	0.0216	0.0300	0.1072
ξ_{NU}	0.0891	0.0152	0.0697	0.1178
ξ_{UM}	0.7104	0.0939	0.5786	0.8460
ξ_{MU}	0.2137	0.0301	0.1751	0.2595
ξ_{MN}	0.1348	0.0198	0.0907	0.1694
ξ_{NM}	0.5341	0.0302	0.4738	0.5588

Source: Table 7.7.

Table 7.10
Substitution Elasticities over the Business Cycle, Disaggregated Labor

Elasticity	1967-1969	1969-1973	1973-1979	1979-1982
A: OWN				
σ_{KK}	-1.4643	-1.6841	-2.0820	-1.9762
σ_{UU}	-7.6586	-8.3653	-11.2335	-11.3674
σ_{NN}	-2.4794	-2.6378	-3.7104	-3.3775
σ_{MM}	-2.4321	-2.2098	-1.6605	-1.6878
B: CROSS				
σ_{KU}	0.9414	0.9321	0.9049	0.9087
σ_{KN}	-0.8659	-0.9589	-0.5763	-0.3348
σ_{KM}	0.9364	0.9367	0.8038	0.9399
σ_{UN}	0.7630	0.7459	0.7830	0.8064
σ_{UM}	1.8016	1.8019	1.8493	1.8634
σ_{NM}	1.5509	1.5457	1.2993	1.2614

Source: Table 7.7.

Table 7.11
Technological Change, Translog Model

Coefficient	Aggregate Labor	Labor Disaggregated
a_R	-0.0315	-0.0149
a_{KR}	0.1161	-0.0604
a_{MR}	0.0452	0.2915
a_{LR}	-0.1613	------
a_{UR}	------	-0.1322
a_{NR}	------	-0.0980

Sources: Table 7.3 and Table 7.7.

Table 7.12
U.S. High-Tech Sector Input Contribution to Growth in Costs

Period	Costs (% Growth)	Contributions By					
		Labor		Material		Capital	
		Quantity	Price	Quantity	Price	Quantity	Price
1967-1969	6.74	0.33	-0.77	1.47	3.74	0.83	1.14
1969-1973	6.60	-0.14	2.44	1.67	-1.10	2.77	0.96
1973-1979	13.45	0.59	1.62	1.45	3.87	3.92	2.00
1979-1982	7.85	-0.25	1.83	2.17	0.23	0.66	3.21
1967-1982	7.49	-0.39	1.60	1.63	1.01	2.58	1.71

Source: Appendix Tables A1–A5.

Graph 7.1
Own Substitution Elasticities

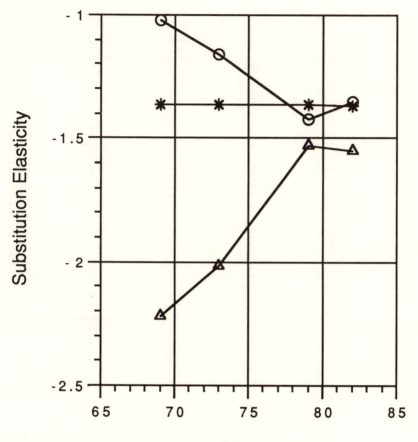

$\ominus$ 1 $\triangle$ 2 $*$ 3

Graph 7.2
Cross Elasticities of Substitution

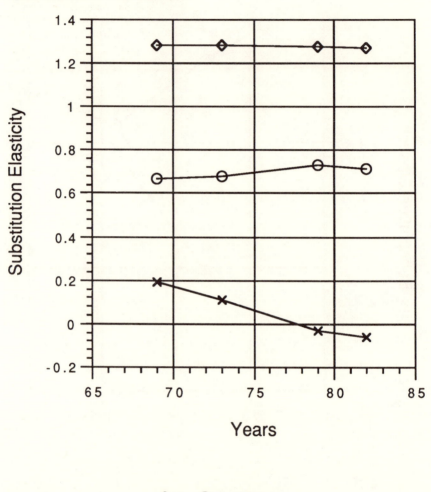

NOTES

1. This is evident from the discussion in earlier chapters; particularly in chapter 6, which presents a historical data base and trends on the U.S. high-tech sector.

2. This is a subsidiary issue that follows from the analytical approach taken here.

3. Concepts of substitution and complementarity were first defined in terms of demand analysis where they make intuitive sense, see Hicks (1946). Their extension to

production analysis is logical but not obvious. Complexity results from the importance and nature of technological change, which is an essential part of a production process.

4. Concepts of neutral and biased technological change follow from changes in the slope of an isoquant.

5. It needs to be emphasized that assumptions regarding competitive factor markets as well as Shephard's lemma are stringent indeed. These assumptions pose, perhaps, major limitations to neoclassical economics. Thurow (1984) points out other deficiencies and limitations of the price-auction models.

6. This is given in chapter 4, equation (4.1).

7. These elasticities are explained in chapter 5 on pages 93–94.

8. Binswanger (1974b) provides the derivation and meanings of substitution elasticities.

9. This follows from the symmetry of the large $\mathbf{A}$ matrix so that $\mathbf{A}_{12} = \mathbf{A}_{21}$, one being the transpose of the other. Therefore, $\mathbf{P}'\mathbf{A}_{12}\mathbf{Z} = \mathbf{Z}'\mathbf{A}_{21}\mathbf{P}$; again, one being the transpose of the other.

10. Since the meaning is obvious and unambiguous, we have removed the subscripts from the vector $\mathbf{a}$ and $\mathbf{b}$ in equations (7.6) and (7.7).

11. Beginning with Solow (1957), there has been a controversy as to whether T is a measure of technology or simply a catch all and a residual. This controversy has not been settled to date and there are exponents of both propositions.

12. Griliches (1984), Pavitt (1984), and Scherer (1980) discuss the relevance of R&D as a measure of technology and argue that patents and R&D are highly correlated.

13. It may be argued that some of the changes in the R&D stock reflect cost items. These may, therefore, generate a bias in the quantitative estimates. This is, however, a matter of fact and not of theory. At present there is little information about the nature of any potential bias.

14. Such interpretations have been made in the literature, particularly immediately after price energy shocks.

15. All empirical analysis requires a maintained hypothesis. Generally, a maintained hypothesis and the underlying assumptions are implicit. These assumptions are made explicit when quantitative estimates challenge a particular interpretation.

16. Without the variable D in $\mathbf{Z}$, matrix $\mathbf{A}_{22}$ reduces to the scalar a_{RR}. Model I thus implies that $\mathbf{A}_{22}$ is a null matrix.

17. Since the second row of this matrix does not exist, because of the non-existence of D, it implies that this is a null matrix.

18. These test procedures were designed by Berndt and Christensen (1973b) and modified by Denny and Fuss (1977). They have now been used in a number of studies.

19. Zellner (1962, 1963) provides details and an explanation of this methodology. We estimated it by a Shazam computer program on an IBM microcomputer.

20. Although there is a greater acceptance of cost functions in empirical literature, there is no theoretical rationale for the preference of one over the other.

21. This separability test agrees with Norsworthy and Malmquist (1983).

22. Such dummy variables have been used in a few other studies as well.

23. Once again, we estimated it by a Shazam computer program on an IBM microcomputer.

24. There are a number of such studies for U.S. manufacturing; for example, Jorgenson, Kuroda and Nishimizu (1985c).

25. The study we know of is Kallianpur and Jang (1987).

26. Kallianpur and Jang (1987) provide comparable estimates for capital and material elasticities for the semiconductor industry in the United States. Their estimates are $\sigma_{KK} = -1.3141$, and $\sigma_{MM} = -1.8443$. These magnitudes compare very favorably with those in table 7.4.

27. These are stringent conditions assuming perfect factor markets and well-behaved production functions. These stringest assumptions have been made in this analysis.

28. These cycles are defined in chapter 6, page 109. Business cycle is defined from peak to peak.

29. The data on the labor force distinguishes only between production and non-production workers. Non-production workers are more a residual and a somewhat gross category. Production workers are defined narrowly and refer to assembly type work.

30. These elasticities compare favorably with those for the semiconductor industry in Kallianpur and Jang (1987).

31. Kallianpur and Jang (1987) also get a similar result for the semiconductor industry.

32. Nadiri and Prucha (1985) and Jorgenson and Kuroda (1985b) use R&D expenditures as an index of technology.

33. The estimated value of this coefficient for the semiconductor industry in Kallianpur and Jang (1987) is -0.019.

34. Note that the sum of the elements of the column in A_{12} is designed to add to zero.

35. This result seems to be consistent with large layoffs of production workers in major industries like automobile and steel. There are counterparts in other industries as well. On the other hand, employment in industries employing skilled labor have maintained growth.

8

Capital-Labor Complementarity in High Technology

INTRODUCTION

Our empirical analysis suggests that the high-tech sector differs significantly from the manufacturing sector. Although at present the high-tech sector forms a small proportion of the manufacturing sector, the dynamics of the new techno-economic paradigm ensure that this proportion will continue to grow since the growth rate of the high-tech sector is higher than that of the manufacturing sector. There is now a growing consensus about the importance of the high-tech sector in the United States, reflected in an increase in debate and discussion about high-tech industries.[1] The captains of industry, senior executives of private corporations, and senior government officials now regularly discuss what the United States has to do to catch up in the high-tech sector and maintain its lead in some industries such as fast computers and aerospace. There is a consensus on the following two propositions:

1. The United States is losing its competitive edge in the global market.
2. The United States has to promote the high-tech sector to regain its competitive strength.

To promote the competitiveness of U.S. high-tech industries a number of studies have been commissioned and a number of commissions set up. In 1984, The Committee for Economic Development published *Strategy for U.S. Industrial Competitiveness,* and the following year, in 1985, the President's Commission on Industrial Competitiveness produced two volumes of its report, entitled, *Global Competition: The New Reality.* Private business groups got into the act and produced two reports in two years. Business Roundtable came out with its report, *American Excellence in a World Economy* and the Council on Competitiveness published *America's Competitive Crisis: Confronting the New Reality*. Governor Mario Cuomo of New York has been interested in the strength of the New York State economy, which is linked to the U.S. economy. He set up a Commission on Trade and Competitiveness, which produced *The Cuomo Commission Report* in 1988. During this period the Massachusetts Institute of Technology (MIT) set up a commission on industrial productivity, which issued its report in 1989 entitled, *Made in America*.[2]

Although all these reports deal basically with policy issues, there is as yet no consensus on what particular policies should be adopted. Opinions range from the extreme of *laissez-faire* to that of a meaningfully targeted industrial policy. The only consensus seems to be that something has to be done; the policy of *status quo* is not a viable option. These studies deal with the whole gamut of economy and industry and develop policies at various levels, based on diverse perspectives. These developed policies have similarities and differences arising from underlying assumptions about the U.S. industrial culture.[3]

HIGH TECHNOLOGY AND POLICY ISSUES

The above studies deal with the future of American industry and economy. Interestingly, some of the bases of these policies are consistent with the conclusions from our empirical studies in this book. The major policy oriented conclusions of our empirical studies deal with technology and inputs. As we have argued, high technology is the essential part in the emerging new technology regimes. We have defined the high-tech sector of the U.S. economy. In our view, it will be the strategic sector of the U.S. economy of the future. In view of the fact that the statistical dimensions of this sector in relation to the U.S. economy is small, some argue that this is not a strategic sector.[4] This argument suffers from the fallacy of small ratios and is akin to the question, does manufacturing matter? It is not the size of the sector that matters; instead it is dynamics. The fact that manufacturing matters has been well articulated, and precisely because it is essential and dynamic.[5] The high-tech sector is all the more important because it forms the dynamo of U.S. manufacturing and of the economy.

Our empirical study of the U.S. high-tech sector shows that it is radically different from the aggregate manufacturing sector to which it belongs. Some of the important policy oriented conclusions are: (1) Capital and labor are complements, which follows from the finding that σ_{KL} changes its sign from positive to negative after 1973, and also from the findings that $\sigma_{KN} < 0$ and $\sigma_{KU} > 0$. This goes against the general presumption of capital-labor substitution in private enterprise economies, where it is generally assumed that an efficient production process substitutes capital for labor.[6] In this sense, this conclusion is quite radical. Its policy implications are many, some even drastic. First, it implies that labor is an asset and not a cost. Second, it implies cooperation between labor and capital. Third, it implies that labor is not a variable factor; instead, like capital, labor is a fixed or quasi-fixed factor. (2) The nature of technological change in the U.S. high-tech sector is embodied, which follows from the finding that the biased technological change is higher than the neutral technological change; the coefficient values being -0.06 and -0.03, respectively. Thus, both inputs and outputs are affected by innovative activity. The rates of innovative activities and embodiment in different inputs are, however, different in view of the different values of a_{Ri}, $i = K, L,$ and M. How such embodiment takes place is a matter of R&D and related policy. (3) Materials are an important source of productivity and costs. Our results suggest that materials form 50 percent of the growth rate in total costs over the entire period, this proportion has been growing over the period. Once again this conclusion goes against the general perception that wage costs are the largest costs. Materials are an aggregate and a residual factor in the production function. In the final analysis, materials for one production process are the products and processes of another; they are the intermediate products. Policy issues here take us to questions of output, productivity, and innovations in general, following from the structure and growth of an economy as a whole. We take up the relevant policy issues implied by the conclusions from our empirical evidence in this chapter and in chapter 9.

CAPITAL-LABOR COMPLEMENTARITY AND PRODUCTION THEORY

One of the major conclusions of this study is that capital and skilled labor are complements while capital substitutes for unskilled labor in high-tech industries. The conclusion regarding capital-labor complementarity has far reaching implications in terms of both theory and policy. Neoclassical theory of production is based on the idea that capital and labor are substitutes. The neoclassical production function has convex isoquants in the labor-capital-output space, with the convexity of the isoquants following from the substitution relationship. Profit maximization or output maximization, subject to a neoclassical production function, requires this condition of convexity. Stability of the growth path also depends, essentially, on this convexity and factor substitution.[7] Marginal productivity cannot be defined without reference to other factors. Substitution between factors allows the expression of marginal products of capital and labor to be expressed only in terms of output and the particular factor. With complementarity, or without substitution, expression for marginal productivity loses its elegance and depends on other factors as well. The equivalence of marginal productivity with factor price, then, does not follow from algebra. Theories and policies based on this equivalence require revisions. The assumption of factor complementarity creates discontinuities in a production function. The Leontief isoquants have a sharp discontinuity and there is only one corner point solution. Even a single point of discontinuity causes major difficulties in the analysis. The fact of complementarity between factors gives rise to more than one point of discontinuity. Once there are kinks in a function, calculus and resulting marginal analysis is no longer applicable.[8] The impact of these discontinuities may be similar to the effects that oligopoly has in the analysis of the market. To date, there is no consensus among economic theorists as to how to deal with complementarity. Analyzing implications of factor complementarity forces theorists to deal with economic reality; something they tend to avoid in view of the complications and messiness it involves.[9] The fact of capital-labor complementarity not only changes the isoquants, it also affects the labor market. In turn, this involves changes in the theory of labor markets, where there are already different schools of thought. The neoclassical approach treats labor like any other commodity so that the wage rate is determined by well-behaved supply and demand functions that define a labor market. As a result, one obtains flexible wage rates. In Keynesian economics, these supply and demand functions are not well behaved. There is, instead, a rigidity in the wage market. Capital-labor complementarity explains and further adds to such rigidity.[10]

At another level, capital-labor complementarity implies a number of theoretical propositions: first that labor is an asset. Labor's association with capital leads to increases in productivity—both capital productivity and labor productivity. Because labor is an asset, it is, like capital, a stock and not a flow variable. Therefore, one can think in terms of improving the quality of labor over time. The assumption that labor quality can be improved implies that it is a heterogenous factor. This relates to theories of learning by doing and of human capital. Treating labor purely as a homogeneous variable, as is assumed in some theories, misses an important part of reality. Second, it is implied that economic agents, whose responsibility it is to combine capital and labor to generate output, have the wherewithal to recognize that labor is an asset and a complement of capital. This implication deals with the nature and structure of management decision making. Certain management structures are based on the assumption that labor is a variable in large supply, which can be easily replaced and substituted by capital, as and when needed. Other structures that consider labor to be an asset seek to make continuous investment for its improvement. Such management values labor highly, and follows policies to retain it, since the replacement costs are high. Third, capital is an asset that needs upgrading *along with* labor. It has generally been assumed that new capital becomes more productive by replacing and substituting for labor. The fact of capital-labor complementarity questions this assumption, suggesting instead that improvements in capital need to incorporate those new innovations that make labor more productive without replacing it. All this involves different theoretical formulations as well as different attitudes to both labor and capital. In view of our findings, such theoretical formulations are particularly pertinent to the U.S. high-tech industry.

IS LABOR AN ASSET OR A COST?

Our finding is that capital is a substitute for unskilled labor while skilled labor is a complement of capital. If capital can substitute for labor, then labor is a cost that capital investment can reduce. This has been the general perception about labor. It is particularly relevant to a technological regime exemplified by mass production techniques. If, on the other hand, labor cannot be substituted but is instead a complement of capital so that capital investment improves with investment in labor, then labor is an asset to be taken care of. Our finding is that in high-technology industries, more and more labor is complementary to capital. For the development of the U.S. high-tech sector, therefore, labor has to be treated as an asset. Treating labor as an asset instead of a cost means a major departure from existing theory and practice. In order to analyze the various implications of the proposition, that labor is an asset, it is useful, even necessary, to start *ab initio*.

The objective of employing labor is to produce an output. Generally labor is joined together with capital or tools. Labor is embodied in a person, as opposed to a technique, which is contained in a machine. A person, however, is more than an embodiment of labor alone. A person has (1) physical abilities, (2) intelligence potential, and (3) emotional capacities. Our analysis is based on the recognition of all these three bundles of qualities of a person embodied in labor. The idea that capital is a substitute for labor refers only to a person's physical abilities. The conventional wisdom has been that such labor is a cheaper way of obtaining mechanical and physical energy. In this perspective, labor is viewed as a body or a limb, not unlike a mechanical contraption that moves as fast as is possible on a given assembly line. When improvements in capital take place that perform these mechanical tasks, labor is replaced or substituted and costs are reduced. Such labor is acquired in a market that assumes that a person embodying this labor would automatically produce the desired number of body or limb movements for a given wage rate. This concept of labor, that relates only to the physical abilities of a person, is designated by unskilled labor. Development of such unskilled labor is not relevant to the progress of the U.S. high-tech sector.

If labor is considered not only as the embodiment of physical abilities but also as having intelligence potential, its relationship with capital changes. An attempt to take into consideration some amount of intelligence potential is made by theories of learning by doing and human capital. Learning by doing theories[11] involve a wide range of learning from acquiring skills by doing repetitive tasks to hands on experiences and engineering. Similarly, theories of human capital[12] deal with a wide spectrum of knowledge and training obtained by a person, prior to and/or while working with a machine to produce an output. The key issue here is that labor combines physical abilities with a certain level of a person's intelligence potential; for example, labor is an aggregated bundle of qualities (1) and (2). The basic questions here are how to develop this intelligence potential, and once developed, how to use it in the production process. High-tech industry involves a rapid rate of technical change so that the labor involved has to keep abreast with changing techniques. Accordingly, these issues are particularly appropriate for high-tech industries. The progress of high-tech industries require, in an essential way, promotion of intelligence development in labor. Once this is recognized, labor is no more a cost; it has become an asset. To some extent the concept of human capital lends respectability to labor since some amount of capital has been embodied in a human person.

Physical abilities transform labor energy into work. Intelligence potential, when realized, makes this effort larger by providing the necessary skills that can complement machines and tools. Both physical ability and intelligence potential define the level of possibilities, determining the maximum effort and work that can be put out by labor. How much effort is actually made, and how much work is produced, depends on the state of mind of a person—quality bundle (3). What we have called emotional capacities defines a person's state of mind. Emotional capacities and state of mind are determined by motivational factors. In neo-classical economics, marginal productivity theory determines wage rate. Thus, wage rate is the monetary value of the output produced by labor at the margin. This formulation assumes that individual productivity is measurable yet it assumes away any motivation issues. Not only are these assumption heroic, they are also unrealistic.[13] Motivation is, perhaps, one of the most important subjects in a production process,[14] and it depends on a host of factors: perceptions by a worker about work and self image, the institutional framework in which one works, and general social matrix of an economy defining how and what work is valued. For the U.S. high-technology industries, acquisition and availability of skills is important. However, it is only a necessary condition. Since high-tech industries operate in an international context where markets are global and competitiveness is the name of the game, motivation provides the sufficient condition for international competitiveness.

There is a consensus, although implied, on the following propositions that: (1) high-tech industries have the necessary dynamics for maintaining growth in the U.S. economy, (2) high-tech industries are international and are affected by competitiveness at the international level, (3) the growing part of labor input in U.S. high-tech industries is skilled labor, and (4) skilled labor is complementary with capital so that this labor is an asset and not a cost. It follows that promotion of the U.S. high-tech sector is necessary, which, in turn, requires policies that improve skill formation and increase worker motivation. We discuss the policies and factors that support the twin objectives of skill formation and motivation promotion in the following.

SKILL FORMATION

As high tech becomes a larger part of manufacturing in the United States, a large proportion of the U.S. labor force will move from unskilled to skilled. For such a change, skills must be imparted to an increasingly large labor force. Not only do high-tech industries require greater skills, they also involve changing types and levels of skills over time as technology keeps on changing continuously; something intrinsic to the new technology regimes. What is needed is not only imparting of particular skills to the labor force but developing a base within it such that it is able to appreciate, understand, and incorporate continuous changes emanating from a fast rate of technical change. Given the nature of high technology and the emerging techno-economic paradigm, skill formation involves two different types of facilities that encourage and realize intelligence potential: (1) Education, considered in its broadest sense, develops intelligence so that a person can deal with, and contribute to, technical change. (2) Training, again in a broad sense, instills specialized and particular skills that relate to a category of machines and tools.

Policies and institutions that promote education and training are very different. At some places and times they connect while at other times and places they diverge and may even be inimical to each other. The object of meaningful policy, most helpful to high technology, is to ensure that policies not only promote education and training individually but that they also blend so as to develop synergies. These synergies help ensure a self-perpetuating growth process. Coordination of different, and differing, policies is therefore equally important. We will look at policies for education and training, one by one.

Education

Education provides a base that encourages the growth in intelligence and the realization of its potential. It is, therefore, important to a production system where processes are based on rational principles.[15] In the case of high-tech industries where technology, and change therein, is an essential feature, education is a necessity. The most relevant part of education in this area is that of logical reasoning and the search for new paradigms and relationships, best typified by science and mathematics. For high technologies, general education is necessary and curricula in science and mathematics all the more so. Such education is relevant at all levels, from high school to college and beyond.

The U.S. educational system in the 1950s was the pace setter for the world. The majority of the schools were public and of good quality. It was generally felt that education is a source of equalizing opportunity. Over the past 40 years, however, both the nature and quality of education has changed, some think for the worse.[16] Americans are talking of "A Nation at Risk"[17] basically from the lack of educational opportunities with an alarmingly high, and growing, drop out rate particularly in inner cities. Schooling at the high school level, in urban areas, does not provide useful education. Many high school graduates cannot even read the diploma they receive. Comparisons made with other industrialized countries show that students in U.S. high schools lag behind in virtually all the three Rs, and are especially weak in science and mathematics. This is particularly serious for high-tech industries since science and mathematics form the very basis of the new technologies. The average school year in other countries is longer and educational requirements and achievements higher. Teachers, in the U.S. schools, are poorly paid. There is a growing shortage of science and math teachers because few students with science degrees join the teaching profession.

Currently, college enrollments in science and math are declining because fewer students learn these subjects in schools. There is too much emphasis on bureaucratic procedures and too little on actual teaching.[18] Every year a larger share of the educational expenditure is allotted to administration. Communities that pay for education are revolting at additional taxes for school budgets. In view of federal budget deficits, severe cuts in social programs, growing deficits among state budgets, and tax revolt at county and school district levels, high school education in the U.S. is in serious decline; it is in crisis in core cities. There have been a number of studies, commissions, and reports on how to improve the quality of education. There is no dearth of ideas; there is, in fact, a good deal of awareness about the problem judging from the amount of discussion in the press and political campaigns.[19] The solution involves nothing less than reordering priorities. This is an area where action can be taken by governments at various levels: school district, county, state, and federal. Considering that a high school education is a necessity for anyone entering the labor force in manufacturing, this situation provides a grim future for the capacity of the U.S. firms to compete internationally; the implications for the U.S. high-tech sector are all the more serious.

Moving from high school to college level—the United States has some of the best universities and colleges in the world, and attracts students and faculty from all over the globe. Lately, however, some shortcomings at the university level of education are emerging as well.[20] Universities are supposed to educate not only the workers, technicians, and engineers but also the employers and managers. We assume universities are capable of setting the right priorities and introducing changes in technology and workplace environment, but their ability to adequately fulfill this function is being questioned. Part of the reason that universities, and particularly liberal education therein, are in crisis is that they have begun taking a participatory role in society.[21] This is especially true of the business schools. In the past decade, the business schools have been severely criticized for their rationalist approach based on unrealistic economic text book rules.[22] The basic difficulty with the business schools' curriculum has been that it provides no understanding of the idea that labor is an asset. On the contrary, it places all the emphasis on financial returns, which distorts priorities, promotes short-term profitability, and encourages confrontations. There is now an ongoing debate about the relevance of business schools to the nature of manufacturing productivity in the United States. This debate is going to continue and will have impact in the mid-1990s.

The most relevant part of college education for high-tech industries deals with science and engineering. The United States has some of the finest science and engineering colleges, and there was a growth in these universities and in student enrollments in science and engineering schools during the 1950s. By the 1980s, however, this growth has actually turned to a slight decline; particularly in terms of numbers of students enrolled and numbers of degrees awarded in science and engineering. The graduate schools in these universities now mostly depend on student enrollment from other parts of the world. In addition, there is not enough recognition of the impact of changes in technology and nature of international competitiveness. The MIT Commission on Industrial Productivity has argued that curriculum in the engineering schools needs to take into account the changing nature of the manufacturing industries. They have suggested an emphasis on hands on experience as well as a better appreciation of the international dimension.[23] This has particular relevance to the U.S. high-tech sector.

The promotion of the U.S. high-tech sector requires a major policy change in education. Priorities and policies of education at the high school level need to be radically changed to encourage more study in mathematics and science, which involves encouraging science and engineering curricula at the college and university level and raising salaries for teachers of mathematics and science. The curriculum in science and engineering needs to deal with more manufacturing concerns on the one hand, and with international dimensions on the other. This international dimension involves not only understanding foreign languages but also the whole gamut of foreign cultures. These changes are both necessary and expansive; there are no short cuts.

Training

The other source of skill formation is training. Whereas education provides a base that enables realization of intelligence potential, training infuses specific skills in the use of a machine or set of tools. Part of the reason that labor becomes a complement to capital follows from this specific skill to work with a machine so that both labor and machine become more productive. Skills are acquired both in educational institutions where "how to" instead of "why" type courses are taught and in work places where learning is by doing. Although it is not necessary to have a high school diploma for learning some trades, it is considered desirable. The United States is endowed with a structure of community colleges that provide excellent training in various technically related areas. The cost of getting training in these colleges is cheap and the quality of training is considered quite good. Since high technology experiences rapid and continuous technological change, however, the training of beginning workers is not the only issue. These colleges also provide retraining to workers whose skills needs change and who find that technology at their work place is changing faster than they can handle with existing skills.

However, this training is not enough. It has to be supplemented with on-the-job training, the lack of which is one of the deficiencies of the U.S. business system. The U.S. firm believes that (1) a worker acquires skills outside the firm and (2) the firm can obtain these skills in the labor market. In the real-world labor market, on the other hand, what is available is labor with a potential that can be realized with training—training that has to be on the job. Although trained labor does not exist in the market, employers still behave as if it does, with the result that only minimal on-the-job training is provided. Firms do not provide adequate resources for training partly because of a miscomprehension of the real nature of the labor market, and partly because of the fear that the trained worker will leave the firm to seek higher wages with a competitor. In the final analysis, training is a public good with a free ride clause so that no private employer finds it profitable to provide. This is similar to the case of a "prisoner's dilemma." Strategies that seem economic for an individual turn out to be uneconomic for the public, which in turn make them uneconomic for the individual as well. In the end both the individual and the society suffer. Firms also suffer because they are stuck with less skilled workers and higher costs. The end result is that a worker acquires training depending on his/her circumstances, opportunities, abilities, and interests. The real cost of training is borne by lapses in the quality of products and processes and it shows up in consumer distrust, lack of sales growth, a fall in the market share, and a decline in competitiveness. This is especially pertinent for the U.S. high-tech industries which face international competition.

What is needed here is a cooperative effort by the employers where they pool their resources to provide training to the entering work force as well retraining of those that have to learn new and changing technologies. For this to be practical requires that managers and employers place a realistic, and desired, priority on training, which implies a certain level of respect for a worker; a paradigm change that considers workers assets instead of costs. Advancement of this idea will need the freeing of financial and other resources for training. The initial costs would be large since such an institutional framework does not exist at present. However, given the size of the U.S. manufacturing industry, setting up a structure of training institutes should not be too difficult or unmanageable a task.

We offer a specific suggestion: management needs to set up a special fund for the training and retraining of workers. For it to be meaningful and to be taken seriously, this fund would have to be at a level sufficient to provide meaningful training to a majority of willing workers. The objective of this training fund would not be to provide rewards for good behavior, as is done in some firms, but to provide genuine training to a sizable part of the labor force. Unless management and labor perceived that anyone could obtain the necessary training, and that there were sufficient funds as well as resources to provide it, such a training fund could not achieve its goal. A good rule of thumb for the funding level could be based on the practice at the best universities of providing faculty with sabbatical leave at half pay every six years, which would suggest funds and other resources adequate to provide training to at least 20 percent of the labor force every year. Such a training fund level compares favorably to the sink fund set up for replacing a machine when it is purchased. Individual employers, however, would be unwilling to allocate these resources because of (1) the nature of competition in the United States and (2) the general assumption that a worker in whom a firm has invested training is likely to leave the firm, costing the firm its investment, or worse, that the worker will join a competing firm, so that the firm ends up subsidizing its own competition. These difficulties could be avoided if the training facilities were set up jointly by firms through their industry associations. These associations would, of course, need to expand their activities in order to set up training institutes. Once the principle was accepted, it would not be difficult to fill in the practical details for these training institutes.

MOTIVATION

Skill formation is only part of the story. The potential of the level of work effort is also important. To realize this potential in work effort, a worker has to be motivated to give his or her best. Proponents of every civilization have boasted about the capacity of their system to provide a large quantity and variety of material goods, some even justifying their system on the basis of such production. Labor, generally, involves giving up one's own goals to pursue those of an employer or organization.[24] The question is how to persuade a person to give up his or her own goals and instead pursue those of an employer. Part of the answer to this question lies in theories of motivation. Four ways by which individuals may be persuaded to give up their own goals and pursue those of an employer have been identified.[25] One is sheer use, or the threat of use, of force. An individual may be compelled to work at the cost of punishment. This is motivation by force or compulsion.[26] The second motivating force is the pecuniary reward, or wage payment, which depends on the pecuniary motive and the available alternatives. The effectiveness of this motivation is based on the level of need and greed of the worker being persuaded; if a person is starving, the pecuniary motive works wonders.[27] In this sense, this motivation is the same as the compulsion motive. As wages go up and a society become affluent, however, the pecuniary motive loses its appeal and effectiveness. Both of these motives treat labor as purely physical ability and do not consider that labor has intelligence potential. The level of intelligence potential that they realize is minuscule. As is being discovered, again and again, the compulsion motive uses labor inefficiently and is the least productive so that it loses quickly in a competitive situation.[28] Some suggest that the techno-economic paradigm represented by the mass production culture based its motivation for production on the compulsive motive via wage labor.

The third motivation category is identification, wherein labor identifies itself with the goals of the employer or organization. By identification, they change their own goals and bring them in conformity with those of their employers. They are thus willing to work hard for these goals.[29] A variation of the identification motivation is that of adaptation. In this fourth category of motivation for work, an individual not only identifies with the goals of the employer but also believes that these goals can be changed to conform to his/her goals. In identification the goals of the person are reviewed in accordance with the given goals of the employer. In adaptation, on the other hand, the goals of the employer or organization are revised in conformity with the given or perceived goals of the labor involved. Obviously, the difference between identification and adaptation is more analytical than real. In high-tech industries, where technology is rapidly changing, it is the identification motive that is most relevant. Capital-labor complementarity relates to, and requires, this type of motivation.

There are two different technology regimes defined by (1) mass production techniques, and (2) high technologies. The mass production–based technology regime uses wage labor motivation, which contains elements of compulsion, for production. This, perhaps, explains existing neoclassical economic theory, which treats labor as a commodity based on providing physical abilities. Theories of learning by doing and human capital attempt to take some of the skills embodied in labor into consideration, but they are "add-ons" to theory without in any way changing its basic assumptions. New technology regimes, on the other hand, require less of the physical abilities embodied in labor and depend more on its intelligence potential. Because it depends on labor's state of mind and its emotional capacities to achieve production the new technology regime uses the identification motivation. Economic theory has not yet incorporated this motivation effectively, although a number of sporadic efforts have been made.[30] Our findings suggest that the issues of values, perceptions, and related institutions need to be discussed and eventually integrated into a revised economic theory. These issues are vital to the development of helpful policies for strengthening the competitiveness of the U.S. high-tech sector.

VALUES, PERCEPTIONS OF SELF-WORTH, AND RULES OF THE GAME

The identification motive requires that labor change its goals and accept those of the employer. Once this change has taken place, labor considers the employer's goals as its own and therefore works hard to achieve these goals. Since these are, now, the goals of the worker, a worker puts in his/her very best, which fosters the realization of a worker's highest intelligence potential. This makes the system most productive. The question then is how to promote the identification motive. Since this motivation depends on a worker changing goals *voluntarily*, the worker has to *feel* a sense of belonging to the production system.[31] Values, perceptions, and the rules of game become important here. The three factors that determine how a worker feels about work, that affect one's willingness to change one's goals in favor of those of the employer, are (1) general perceptions in the society as a whole about the nature of work and the value that is attached to work. These values provide the very basis for the possibility of changing worker's values to those of the employers. We identify these as "values" of a society,[32] which are basic to any social system. (2) Worker "perceptions of self-worth." Worker's perceived self-worth depends on how workers perceive a production process and their role in it and how workers perceive their own opportunities and capabilities. These issues can place a worker's goal in a context so that changes to employer's goals are possible. (3) Worker perceptions about the attitudes of management toward labor. How does management treat labor? How is labor rewarded? These are the "rules of the game" that are defined for labor and by which labor has to change its goals in favor of those of the employer.

Values

U.S. society generally perceives that work is not pleasant. The idea of a labor market in economic theory is that one has to be paid for work, in the form of a wage rate, which implies that work has disutility. Justification of this disutility is that by getting a wage, a worker obtains equal or greater utility in terms of the consumption goods such wage makes possible. The difficulty with this formulation is that work is something that a person does not look forward to and would like to give up at the earliest possibility. Accordingly, labor is perceived as a lamentable activity. Only a few centuries ago, society considered working for wages the greatest misfortune to befall a person so that in terms of status a laborer was considered far below a poor and destitute person. A laborer was a social outcast, one who was not accepted in society and so could not obtain a livelihood from within social relations.[33] Some of this abhorrence for labor still survives. Workers often consider their work derogatory and demeaning.[34] The way management treats labor confirms this perception. Even government action has sometimes furthered such values; particularly in its dealings with labor unions and its enforcement of occupation safety rules.[35] Such attitudes are consistent with the paradigm that labor is a cost that has to be minimized. This paradigm implies that labor is replaceable, is useful only at low cost, its work is not that important, and worker demands are, by definition, unacceptable. This value paradigm has been consistent with the mass production technology regime. It is not consistent with the new emerging technology regimes of high technology where labor is a complement of capital and an asset that has to be cared for. The idea that labor is an asset is not consistent with these social attitudes. Instead the underlying premise of the social attitude has been, and still is, that labor is a cost that has to be reduced. For the promotion of the U.S. high-tech sector, these social attitudes have to change. This is a paradigm shift and a revolutionary change. It must come about, either slowly or by some serious accident, because this change is a prerequisite of the new techno-economic paradigm.

Perceptions of Self-Worth

The perception of labor about its work and worth, in the United States, is deplorable. In the mass production technology regime, labor is involved in such repetitive work that it deprives the person, who embodies this labor, of humanity.[36] The psychological impact of such work on personality is by now well known and well documented. Furthermore the work is not obviously satisfying in the sense that the worker does not feel he/she has made a meaningful contribution. It does not lead to a sense of self-worth.[37] Without self-worth, labor cannot be an asset. The transference of the paradigm from labor as a cost to labor as an asset takes place when work involves most faculties of the worker—physical abilities and intelligence potential. Once intelligence potential comes into play, a worker is transformed from pure labor to a human being with skills. Crafts, in the old days, promoted an image of self-worth precisely because a craftsman was a person with a craft. The new techno-economic paradigm requires the use of skills and has therefore to treat a worker as a human being with skills. The need of high technology then is to develop a work culture in which a worker perceives self-worth. Achieving this involves some amount of decision making in work; work that takes place in organizations where value is placed on loyalty, loyalty in both directions, from a worker to an employer and from an employer towards a worker; and a workplace where work is done in teams. Given the history in which people have become accustomed to feeling ignored and mistreated in work places, the change in the new paradigm will take considered and consistent efforts. What is certain is that without the worker gaining self-worth, production culture will find it difficult to adapt to the new emerging high-technology regimes and to compete internationally.

Rules of the Game

One of the serious deficiencies of what the MIT Commission on Industrial Productivity has called "outdated strategies," follows from the management's idea about labor. Management ideas relate to the mass production technology regime. Accordingly it treats labor as a cost item; something that has to be minimized. The economists have rationalized the idea of labor being a cost by a number of theoretical subterfuges: (1) wage costs are considered a variable. In the concept of value added, this is the only variable cost. Also, labor is the only variable factor. Capital by comparison is a fixed factor and a stock variable. (2) The wage rate is determined by marginal product.[38] Replacing labor to reduce cost, therefore, is good policy. Labor can be easily acquired in labor markets. The issue of motivation by identification is unimportant; it is introduced via the increment in the wage if there are increases in productivity. The presumption is that pecuniary gain is sufficient to provide the desired level of motivation. The conventional wisdom is that without supervision, the worker will not bring forth the desired labor. The idea that labor has knowledge and can make suggestions does not arise. Labor is tolerated as long as it satisfies the desired need to do the physical work. Since the matter is purely economic, feelings do not enter into the management process. Labor is a cost. It can be reduced if possible. Hence the need and desirability to hire and fire at will. In such a scheme of things, long-term, much less life-term, employment becomes a costly affair to be avoided at any cost.[39] Union busting becomes a profitable strategy.

The existing reward structure of giving small increments to individuals, supposedly on the basis of productivity, is also outdated. There is no empirical basis for such increments. There is no way individual productivity can be identified, much less quantified. The existing reward structure is an institutionalization of the irrational reward structure where the owner-boss distributed pecuniary rewards basically as personal favors. In the institutionalization of the personal favor system, the rewards now are based on political considerations and favoritism. Once it is realized that the rewards are given on the basis of the prejudices of the boss, these incentives shift away from production and toward appealing to the boss's prejudices. What suffers most is morale and productivity. This reward structure further alienates a worker from contributing his/her best. It defines a game in which neither the worker nor the quality of work can easily succeed, except in the very long run and in very exceptional cases.

The rules of the game as defined by management's attitude toward labor and the reward system are not in conformity with our findings that labor is a complement of capital and an asset. In the new techno-economic paradigm and the international competitive world of high technology, the paradigm about labor as a cost is outdated. There is a need for the management to change its attitudes and ideas about labor. As new technologies grow and the industrial structure changes, these attitudes will change. Similarly, a change in the reward structure is over due. There are various ways that a reward system can be structured. To improve reward structure and motivate work effort, we suggest the institutionalization of a bonus system for production teams. These teams in turn would distribute the bonus among their members based on well-defined criteria. The bonus could be directly related to the level of production by the production team. However, such a bonus scheme has to be well defined so that a production team can itself estimate the amount of bonus to which it is entitled. This, however, requires changes in the institutional framework.

INSTITUTIONAL FRAMEWORK

Societal values, perceptions of self-worth, and the rules by which work is rewarded and motivation promoted are enforced by an institutional framework. Technological regimes not only require selection and application of technology but also an institutional framework within which workers can be motivated, work evaluated, and decisions that favor adoption of such technology made and implemented. In the mass production technology regime, these institutions are the corporate structure for decision making, the market for labor, and a reward structure that treats workers as individuals. Since this paradigm has been based on the idea that labor is a cost, the relationship between management and labor have been, and are, mostly confrontational.

Given the emergence of new and high technologies, the new technology regime requires a different institutional framework because its paradigm is different. As we have found in our empirical results, labor is a complement of capital and is an asset in a production process. Accordingly, such a technology regime needs different societal values about work, different perceptions about the self-worth of a worker, different mechanisms to make decisions, and different ways to evaluate and reward work. A worker needs to have better self-worth, which requires more education and training. Once training has been imparted to a worker, it becomes more economic to keep the worker than to let him/her go. Lifetime tenure becomes an efficient objective. One feels valued if one participates in decision making. Once these changes are introduced in the production system, identification motivation becomes operative. The institutional framework for these paradigms has different elements. Since we are interested here only in terms of capital-labor complementarity, we discuss below two such institutions; namely (1) team work and (2) hierarchy.

Team Work

Neoclassical economics is formulated in terms of individual productivity. In the real world, production work is rarely done individually. The training that a worker receives depends fundamentally on the support and help of co-workers. The workers work as a team; even when the management discourages it. Team work provides a sense of belonging and security to a worker. The learning process is mostly a result of well-developed team work. A worker is hired, joins a production group, makes friends with co-workers over time, learns from them various intricacies of diverse tasks and the short cuts of different processes, provides in return support to them by looking after their interests and suggesting new ways of doing the assigned tasks, and develops a relationship of mutual respect and trust. This all takes time. If there is a good relationship between co-workers such that they work together as a team, then productivity goes up.[40]

Economists have looked at the relationship of productivity and the time period workers have been on the job.[41] When there is an increased productivity in this relationship, that is, the relationship is positive, they have called it the learning curve or the learning process. It is also called experience in common parlance. Experience is always valued; at least in hiring if not in wage payments. In fact it is mostly team work and harmony among workers in a production process that ensures productivity. In the last analysis, productivity follows from team work.[42] For team work to develop, and the learning curve to operate, harmony in working relations is necessary. Successful managements support team work and promote learning. It has been suggested by many observers that the Japanese management methods encourage team work. In fact, they consider team work an essential part of their management function. For team work to function, the members of the team need to work together for quite some time so that they can know each other and develop mutual trust. Since job mobility is disruptive of team work, a certain level of security of tenure becomes an important element in a policy to develop team work. Lifetime tenure and team work go well together and seem to have been a source of high productivity in Japanese manufacturing where they are most practised.[43] By contrast, the U.S. production culture has been based on individualism; its desirability, growth, and emphasis on job mobility. It is now being recognized that the cost of individualism, particularly to the growth in the

U.S. high-tech sector, may be high since it is not in conformity with the emerging new technology regime. All commissions, and various reports, dealing with issues of competitiveness have stressed the need for encouraging team work. They have, one and all, recommended that changes be made both in educational programs and in production methods that help students and workers to work together as a team instead of competing with one another.

Hierarchy in Decision Making

What will be produced? How it will be produced? Who will perform what function? These are important decisions. In the U.S. corporate structure, these decisions are made by management at the top and are handed down to middle management to implement through supervision of workers who are told what they have to do and how they must perform. Workers are responsible to their foreman who reports to a higher boss and the ladder continues until it reaches the chief executive officer who is supposed to be all knowing and able to sift the quality of performance. In fact this system is not far different from a military command. This concentration of decision making by top management is also reflected in highly inflated executive salaries, and other benefits, which many times are one hundred to a thousand times those of the lowest paid.[44] This structure is consistent with the paradigm that labor is a cost and is replaceable. It is not consistent with emerging new technology regimes of high technology where worker motivation is an essential input in production.

The success of the U.S. high-tech sector requires that labor be treated as an integral part of production, which also involves decision making. Workers on the shop floor know best and can make meaningful contributions to quality production and cost reduction, but to be able to do so, they have to participate in decision making. The decision making structure needs to be changed such that a worker, and groups of workers, can be assigned meaningful responsibilities. Their responsibilities should not simply be being on the shop floor and attending to an assembly line. The needed changes involve processes in which a worker or a group of workers are expected to make decisions and implement them. The results could be improvements in the product, improvements in the production process, slowing or accelerating the speed of the assembly line, introduction of new methods and materials, and so on. The decision making structure has to be such that the workers can initiate a change and have enough financial authority to experiment and thereby persuade the management to effect the desired change. A few companies have recently followed this idea and made some changes. As the newspaper reports suggest, these have been successful in raising productivity. This leads to less hierarchical organizations.[45] There are some logical implications of such changes. The reward structure that is currently prevalent needs to be changed to reduce the inordinate inequality between the wages of the workers and the salaries of the executives. So far as productivity and international competitiveness is concerned, this level of income inequality is counterproductive. In the new techno-economic paradigm, equity is necessary for efficiency and productivity.[46] In the final analysis, promotion of high technologies needs and encourages cooperation between management and labor.

MANAGEMENT-LABOR COOPERATION

Capital-labor complementarity presumes management-labor cooperation, whereas capital-labor substitution is based on a conflict between labor and management.[47] The history of labor-management relations in the United Kingdom and United States has generally been confrontational.[48] In the past, labor was treated quite harshly. The standard rule was "if you cannot come on Sunday, do not come on Monday." In other words, a worker could be fired without notice or cause. Labor unions arose out of a need by the workers to protect their jobs, safety, and incomes.[49] The entrepreneurs, owners of capital and factories, and management did not accept the legitimacy of unions in the beginning. The result was that the movement for labor unionization became a major source of conflict between the workers and management. This necessitated labor union militancy. Because of this history, the relations between management and labor have remained confrontational. The structure of unions, management, and regulation reinforces the confrontational attitudes. The history and culture of labor-management relations is full of conflicts. The folklore among labor is that the management will not even provide humane and safe facilities for work without a concerted and confrontational effort by labor. Management, on its side, follows policies of union busting through legal and illegal means. Practitioners of the law also join in this process of union busting so that confrontational relations harden. This is one of the major weaknesses in the U.S. production system since it increases costs of operation, reduces flexibility, and discourages innovative practices and processes, thereby making the producing unit less competitive.[50]

The worst part of labor-management relations is that neither trusts the other.[51] Management distrusts labor. It worries that labor will sabotage machinery, have zero or negative productivity, and not provide the necessary work and help when it is most needed. Because of this distrust and such worries, it pushes policies of severe supervision, threatens bureaucratic action leading to firing, and demonstrates an unwillingness to understand the human needs of those who embody labor.[52] These policies, in turn, further accentuate the distrust labor has of management. As it is, labor distrust management. They worry that their work will not be recognised, their wages will not be paid, they will be fired unfairly, and their work conditions will not be safe; in other words, they will be exploited. To avoid the possibility of exploitation, they do the minimum necessary work. This further adds to the distrust management has of labor. This is the standard negative game of the prisoner's dilemma in which both parties try to protect their own interests, but in the end both lose. Unfortunately, this dynamic process is a vicious cycle, and the basic element of this negative game is the lack of trust.

The confrontational relations between labor and management are most inimical to the new technology regime and the growth of the U.S. high-tech sector. They are based on the paradigm that labor is a cost while new technology regime implies the other paradigm, namely, labor is an asset. What is needed, therefore, is cooperation between management and labor. This follows from capital-labor complementarity and there is a growing consensus on the issue. Recent commission reports argue in favor of this cooperation.[53] The need for cooperation is becoming obvious, and excellent companies in the United States follow policies that foster it. Japanese and German production systems are considered more productive and innovative partly because they have managed to develop cooperative relations between management and labor.

The most relevant question, in this respect, is what management-labor cooperation means. Is it possible in a structure where labor unions and management coexist? Are labor unions obsolete and unnecessary? Is this cooperation possible within the existing decision making hierarchies? Are such hierarchies obsolete and unnecessary? Is management-labor cooperation efficient and productive? In its most basic form, management-labor cooperation means that management and labor recognize that they work together toward a common objective and are trusting of each other. They have different roles to play and both acknowledge that these roles are necessary. This implies that workers participate in decision making. Worker participation is fundamentally different from their performing given tasks. Participation means that they share both the risks and benefits in decision making process. The sharing of decisions makes them responsible and cooperation means that both respect each other's decisions. The important thing here is that workers participate, explicitly, in the decision-making roles of management; the emphasis is on the term *explicitly*. In the confrontational relationship there is no sharing by labor in the decision making process.

Some argue that worker participation enhances both worker welfare and firm productivity.[54] This argument is logically correct and empirically compelling. The reasons for greater productivity and welfare are not hard to see. Participation leads to responsibility, which gives labor a sense of belonging and a feeling that they can make a real contribution. The fact that labor knows the production processes in detail, since they are fully involved with it on a daily basis, means they are the most competent people to introduce meaningful changes that make their work easier, product quality higher, and the production process more efficient.[55] Participation leads to efficiency because it relates to motivation by identification. This motivation relates to high-technology regimes and leads to higher work effort because it makes a worker feel like a partner in the production process. Perceived self-interest belongs to the category of a positive motive that remains strong all the time. Participation, therefore, releases positive energy that promotes both productivity and worker well-being.

Although management-labor cooperation is efficient, the question remains whether it is possible. The existing structure of management is that management makes all the decisions and negotiates for the wages, employee benefits, and occasionally work conditions, with the unions. Since management considers labor a commodity to be hired and fired at convenience, it finds the union a serious handicap to the flexibility of its decision making. Now that production conditions are changing, international competition becoming intense, and technical change taking place continuously, the perception of management that unions are a serious obstacle is further intensified. They are getting rid of the unions by locating production units in Third-World countries where wages are low, unions non-existent, and governments supportive of free labor markets. Some perceive labor unions as part of the problem of the non-competitiveness of U.S. industry. Such a view is fallacious. The existence of unions satisfies a perceived or genuine need. Unions came into being because of the nature of decision making by management. If this decision making process changes so that labor does not feel threatened, unions will simply wither away.[56] The real issue is not the existence of unions, but the nature of management; its hierarchy, its decision making process, its attitudes toward labor, and its priorities. So long as management excludes labor from participation, pushes policies that alienate labor, and keeps a military type hierarchy, the unions will remain necessary. If they do not exist, they will be created, as in the past.[57] The policy issue therefore relates to how management structures and systems can be changed to encourage worker participation. It is interesting to note that virtually all commission reports and studies suggest the need for such a reform.

If a change in management structures is to be supportive of worker participation, the question is what the nature of this change should be. The basic principle in worker participation is the sharing of decision making by the workers. There are a number of management forms that ensure such participation. These forms, defining a continuum from zero to full participation by labor, may be outlined as follows: (1) At the extreme end is the worker ownership. The best known case of worker ownership is Mondragon.[58] Mondragon, started as a small experiment by a priest attempting to provide a base of skills and incomes to the local community, now spans over half a million members. In this program, there are no separate workers and managers. All members are workers and owners. Over the more than 40 years of its existence it has expanded into numerous cooperatives. The structural form has been maintained at a small scale so that owner/workers have complete information and control. It started as a successful producer cooperative that produced consumer durables for export. It has maintained this activity and is still able to compete internationally in the market for these products. (2) Corporation managers do make mistakes and mismanage so that they are not able to compete in the global market. They get out of such mistakes by declaring bankruptcy, thereby shifting the costs of these mistakes to the community and the country.[59] In some cases, when management decided to declare bankruptcy of a particular production unit and lay off the work force, labor supported by the community, has purchased the production facility and has run it as a worker-owned company. Some of these companies have been successful and continue to compete in global markets. Some of the small, successful and specialized steel plants are being run by such cooperative efforts. Much depends on the initial conditions and the amount of commitment that labor brings to the plant as well as the level of financial support provided by the community and the government. However, this has not been the norm in America. (3) The next case is that of cooperatives where a production unit is run by the workers jointly with management on a profit sharing scheme. The cooperatives do not, necessarily, have to have a profit sharing or co-ownership with workers. Generally, motivation for such cooperatives has come from the idea of sharing and providing labor participation. There is a good-sized cooperative sector in the United States. There is also a good deal of literature on such cooperatives; particularly worker managed companies.[60] Their record is mixed; one can find both successful and unsuccessful stories. In U.S. manufactures, however, these cooperatives form a small proportion. Also cooperatives have operated on a small scale and small scale is not consistent with the mass production technology regimes. The impact of these cooperatives in the past, therefore, has not been significant. (4) The largest industrial organizational form remains a corporation where the managers deal with unions who speak for the workers. To introduce worker participation would require a change in this form and the introduction of new management structures. Some argue that Japanese management structure provides meaningful participation with labor. They are consistent with the paradigm of the high-technology regime and labor-management cooperation. In fact, one implies the other. The Japanese management system has been extensively studied in the United States.[61] There is a growing consensus to orient the American management system toward the Japanese system. Some of the practices of the "excellent companies" are similar to those of Japanese management. The issue is what policies would promote such organizational reform.

Policies are implemented by the actors whose interests these policies serve. It is hardly in the interest of the labor unions to promote worker participation since once worker participation becomes common and accepted, the unions will wither away. Labor unions, as currently organized, are not the right actors to implement the needed policies. The current make-up of the management is also not interested in cooperation. To make this actor interested, pressures would have to come from outside. The pressure of global competition is building as more and more firms are losing their market share and profitability. Pressure is also coming from public opinion. Public opinion works over a long time, however, public opinion in favor of worker participation is growing even though existing management and its supportive structure is fighting back. What is visible is that there are pressures on the part of the management itself to reform. There are, however, no incentives. On the contrary, all the incentives are negative. The existing organizational forms assure management's privileges of non-accountability and high pecuniary gains. Organizational changes consistent with worker participation will reduce management's power, make it more accountable, and result in lower pecuniary gains for the senior management. These penalties partly explain the slow diffusion of Japanese management systems among American companies.

The encouragement for organizational changes that promote worker participation has to come from outside, especially from government. The U.S. government has influenced changes in the organizational structure indirectly through some of its regulatory legislation, particularly the anti-trust laws. On the whole, it has followed a policy of non-interference in the inner working of privately owned organizations. Government has become involved in the inner workings of organizations only when forced to do so either because of the conflict between various parties[62] or due to bankruptcies.[63] The reason for non-interference by the government lies in the acceptance of the idea that private enterprise is efficient and government bureaucratic activity inefficient. The conclusion follows: government interference can only lead to inefficiencies. So long as this ideology prevails, the government cannot play a meaningful role in promoting worker participation. As U.S. industry keeps on losing in the international markets, as layoffs become more widespread, as the diffusion of Japanese management system gathers momentum, the grip of this idea is bound to weaken. Then government action will be perceived as beneficial for organizational reform.[64] It would be useful for the government to have some well thought out policies to encourage this change. Tax policies can help; if tax incentives are given, for example, for team work, an organization feeling the pressures from international competition will look at such changes favorably. Again, if taxes on excessive salaries and remunerations of executives and managements are high and their expenses not tax deductible, the advantages of large pecuniary gains will be reduced so that organizational changes will not have such heavy penalties. Tax incentives provide indirect influences. If an activist government accepts the proposition that worker participation is in the national interest, it can then take an active part in promoting it through providing incentives for the diffusion of Japanese type management, cooperative systems of production, and worker profit sharing and ownership. It is not difficult to work out outlines of an incentive program with the objective of promoting work participation.[65] Such experiments have been carried on in many countries. We can learn a great deal from other countries and adopt what seems to be the best approach in our environment.[66] However we do it, it is essential that cooperation between labor and management be encouraged if the U.S. high-tech sector has to grow and compete internationally.

CONCLUSIONS

In chapter 7 we discovered empirically that capital and labor in the U.S. high-tech sector have become complements over time. When labor input was disaggregated between skilled and unskilled labor, we found that capital is a substitute for unskilled labor but a complement to skilled labor. Capital-skilled labor complementarity is an important finding because of its large policy implications. At a theoretical level, it raises serious questions about many theorems in neoclassical economics, which are based on the assumption of capital-labor substitution. There are few economic theorems that assume, or can deal with, capital-labor complementarity. At a paradigm level, this finding questions the proposition that labor is a cost consistent with the mass production techno-economic paradigm of the past.

Capital-labor complementarity implies a new paradigm that labor is an asset. This is consistent with the new emerging high technology–based regime. Our other finding is that growth of the U.S. high-tech sector is associated with the growth of the proportion of skilled labor in total labor force, it being both a cause and effect. Policies to promote the U.S. high-tech sector then need to encourage skill formation. Skill formation follows from quality and availability of education. The U.S. education system at high school level is now in crisis. At the college and university level curricula need to be directed toward hands on experience in engineering and greater emphasis on international studies. Skill formation also entails training. In the current U.S. economic system, training is a free good so that no individual employer is willing to provide it. We offer the specific suggestion that management needs to set up a special fund for training and retraining its workers. For it to be meaningful and to be taken seriously, this fund has to be at a level that is sufficient to provide meaningful training to a majority of willing workers. The object of this training fund is not to provide rewards for good behavior, as is done in some firms, but to provide genuine training to a good-sized part of the labor force. Unless management and labor perceive that any one can obtain the necessary training, and that there are sufficient funds as well as resources to do so, such a training fund will not achieve its goal. A good rule of the thumb for the funding level could be based on the practice at the best universities of providing faculty a sabbatical leave at half pay every six years, which would suggest funds and other resources adequate to provide training to at least 20 percent of the labor force every year. Such a training fund level compares favorably to the sink fund set up for replacing a machine when it is purchased. Individual employers, however, would be unwilling to allocate these resources because of (1) the nature of competition in the United States and (2) the general assumption that a worker in whom a firm has invested training is likely to leave the firm, costing the firm its investment, or worse, that the worker will join a competing firm, so that the firm ends up subsidizing its own competition. These difficulties could be avoided if the training facilities were set up jointly by firms through their industry associations. These associations would, of course, need to expand their activities in order to set up training institutes. Once the principles were accepted, it would not be difficult to fill in the practical details for these training institutes.

Skill formation, however, is not enough. A change in societal values about the nature of work is needed. Work in our society is considered derogatory. In high-technology regimes, work is not derogatory, it can be satisfying in view of the realization of a person's intelligence potential. Societal values are also related to a worker's perception of self-worth. The low esteem that many workers in America have of themselves follows mostly from the rules of the game in production where they have no part in decision making and where the reward structure does not adequately reflect inputs of effort. To improve the reward structure and motivate work effort, we suggest the institutionalization of a bonus system for production teams. These teams in turn distribute the bonus among their members based on well-defined criteria. The bonus can be directly related to the level of production by the production team. However, such a bonus scheme has to be well defined so that a production team can itself estimate the amount of bonus to which it is entitled.

This, however, requires changes in the institutional framework, because the institutional framework has placed all decision making authority in the hands of top management. This system is not consistent with our findings of capital-labor complementarity and is inimical to the growth potential of high technology. A different institutional framework is required that places team work in the center of the production process and changes hierarchical decision making processes by worker participation. Labor participation, in its turn, needs supporting organizational forms based on the principle of management-labor cooperation—forms that are consistent with the paradigm that labor is an asset, with the new emerging high-technology regime, and with the necessity for the growth of the U.S. high-tech sector.

NOTES

1. The McNeil-Lehrer Report devoted the whole week of June 26–30, 1989, to discussions of the importance of the high-tech sector. The *New York Times* has devoted a lot of space to this topic, on and off its editorial pages. Other influential dailies and weeklies provide continuous coverage of this issue.

2. This study summarizes the basic findings of other reports. It is listed as Dertouzos et al. (1989).

3. Nelson (1984) projects a strong distrust of government and an equally strong belief in the private enterprise system.

4. Nelson (1984) makes this argument.

5. The argument concerning whether manufacturing matters has been discussed by a number of researchers, including Cohen and Zysman (1987), Tyson et al. (1988), and Dertouzos et al. (1989).

6. One of the advantages and sources of success of capitalist modes of production is exactly this capacity to substitute capital for labor. The socialist and planned economies are criticized for their incapacity to perform such substitution so that there are always more workers than needed, and capital is not properly and efficiently used.

7. Without the assumption of capital-labor substitution, the Solow (1956) growth path loses its stability and certainty. Instead, "razor edge" solutions become more likely and theoretically credible.

8. One reason for the lack of popularity of the Leontief-type production function is this discontinuity so that marginal calculus becomes difficult.

9. "The economics of the text books and of graduate schools not only still teaches the price-auction model but is moving toward narrower and narrower interpretations. The mathematical sophistication intensifies as an understanding of the real world diminishes" Thurow (1984), p. 236.

10. "Wage rigidity, therefore, is not a 'market imperfection' producing inefficiency,

but is instead a functional market adjustment producing long-run efficiency; more output is produced with it than without it," Thurow (1984), p. 212.

11. Arrow (1962) defines learning by doing by the total output produced. Others define it in terms of the level of capital investment.

12. Becker's idea about human capital is now classic.

13. "Anyone who has tried to assess individual productivity in the real world can tell you that it is not fixed and known, but variable, unknown, and perhaps unknowable. Each worker undoubtedly has some maximum level of productivity that he can bring to the work place, but depending on motivation, he can also provide his employer any productivity between his maximum and nothing" Thurow (1984), p. 201. It is the zero productivity that the employer tries to avoid through supervision and the fear of firing.

14. "But the word 'motivation' is strangely absent from the vocabulary of the price auction theorist. Wages, it is assumed, do not motivate workers but rather compensate workers for their productivity" Thurow (1984), p. 201.

15. The importance of education is well recognized. The Cuomo Commission (1988) report states, "Quality education produces prosperity for society as a whole," p. 122.

16. This is how Richard D. Lamm, former Governor of Colorado, describes this deterioration, "In practically every town in America, the best building is the hospital (40 percent empty) and the worst a school (usually overcrowded). The highest paid professionals are doctors; the lowest paid professionals are teachers. We are overtreating our sick and undereducating our kids." Op. Ed., *New York Times,* August 2, 1989, under the title, "Saving a Few, Sacrificing Many—at Great Cost." The piece is on health care and not on education.

17. This is the title of a major report on the status of high school education in the United States. National Commission on Excellence in Education, 1983.

18. School buildings are crowded and have become areas where drugs are sold. The teachers are full of fear. Cases where teachers take revolvers to school for safety are not unknown.

19. During the presidential campaign in 1988, George Bush projected himself as an education president.

20. "There is no need to prove the importance of education, but it should be remarked that for modern nations, which have founded themselves on reason in its various uses more than any nation in the past, a crisis in the university, the home of reason, is perhaps the profoundest crisis they face" Bloom (1987), p. 22.

21. "The society's problems have moved into the university, defiling its intellectual freedom. The university has become society's conceptual warehouse of often harmful influences," Saul Bellow in his foreword to Bloom (1987), p. 18. He adds, "Any proposed reforms of liberal education which might bring the university into conflict with the whole of the U.S.A. are unthinkable. Increasingly, the people 'inside' are identical in their appetites and motives with the people 'outside' the university."

22. Reich (1983) and Peters and Waterman (1982) give examples of the unrealism of the rationalist approach.

23. Details are given in chapter 12 of the report. Hopefully, the MIT faculty will pay heed to these recommendations and set a trend in the country for other colleges and universities to follow.

24. Diwan (1985a) distinguishes "stranger-defined work" from "self-defined work." Most work in industrial societies is "stranger-defined work."

25. Galbraith (1967) follows these four categories from his ideas about technostruc-

ture. Diwan (1985a) has argued that these ways may define Western theories of motivation. Eastern theories involve additional categories. The difference is that Western theories of motivation relate to stranger-defined work, while he articulates motivation of caring and loving that explains self-defined work.

26. This was a common motivation in slave societies. It is practiced today in a number of illegal activities, such as, prostitution, drug sales, and smuggling.

27. This is why Marxian economics has argued that a "reserve army of unemployed" is fundamental to capitalism, which believes in wage markets. This also explains why conservatives are so much against social programs that provide subsistence living to the poor and unemployed.

28. Genevose (1965) has argued, persuasively, that slavery, which is fundamentally based on this motivation, was a cause of both the U.S. civil war and the defeat of the South because this system of production was inefficient and could not withstand competition.

29. Vogel (1979) and Pascal and Athos (1981) argue that this is perhaps the secret of the success of Japanese management.

30. Leibenstein's concept of X-efficiency, the idea of voice, and exit disequilibrium analyses are some of the attempts to introduce these factors. Diwan (1989) argues that many concepts in economic theory are not consistent with the implications of new techno-economic paradigm, particularly flexible manufacturing.

31. Economic theory tries to stay away from facts of how a person feels, not because it is not real but because the theory has not been able to grapple with this reality. As a result it has simply assumed it away.

32. Societal values are particularly important for development. Diwan (1968b,c) deals with specific development issues that in the final analysis are based on societal values.

33. Illich (1981). How far have we come through changes in the industrial modes of production?

34. Terkel interviewed a number of persons and asked them what they thought of their work. He collected their perceptions in *Working*. According to him, "This book being about work, is, by its very nature, about violence—to the spirit as well as to the body. It is about ulcers as well as accidents, about shouting matches as well as fistfights, about nervous breakdown as well as kicking the dog around. It is above all (or beneath all) about daily humiliations. To survive the day is triumph enough for the walking wounded among the great many of us. The scars, psychic as well as physical, brought home to the supper table and the TV set, may have touched, malignantly, the soul of our society," Terkel (1972), p. xii.

35. The reaction of the Reagan administration to the PATCO strike promoted an attitude of union busting thereby implying that labor is irrelevant except when working on the terms prescribed by employers.

36. "Norma Watson may have said it most succinctly, 'I think most of us are looking for a calling, not a job. Most of us, like the assembly line worker, have jobs that are too small for our spirit. Jobs are not big enough for people,' " Terkel (1972), p. xxix.

37. "No matter how bewildering the times, no matter how dissembling the official language, those we call ordinary are aware of a sense of personal worth—or more often a lack of it—in the work they do. Tom Patrick, the Brooklyn fireman whose reflections end the book, similarly brings this essay to a close. 'The fuckin' world's so fucked up, the country is fucked up. But the firemen, you actually see them produce. You see them put out a fire. You see them come out with babies in their hands. You see them give mouth-to-

mouth when a guy's dying. You can't get around that shit. That's real. To me, that's what I want to be. I worked in a bank—you know, it's just paper. It's not real. Nine to five and it's shit. You are lookin' at numbers. But I can look back and say, "I helped put out a fire. I helped saved somebody. It shows something I did on earth,'" Terkel (1972), pp. xxix–xxx.

38. Economics text books carry forward the fiction that the marginal product of labor can be determined. Like Clapham's many other empty boxes, the concept of marginal product has no counterpart in reality. These conclusions are derived by making stringent and obviously unrealistic assumptions about the nature of the labor market. It is assumed that the total product is a linear sum of individual products that are known and fixed, the market for labor is competitive where skills and physical labor are acquired exogeneously, and the utility of the worker is determined by wage alone.

39. Diwan (1990) comments on a study dealing with issues of long-tenure and productivity comparing U.S. and Japanese firms.

40. "In practice, most production processes also require a degree of teamwork that can only be acquired through common on-the-job experiences, a high degree of internal harmony, and a substantial period of working together. Team and not individual productivity dominates industrial processes," Thurow (1984), p. 204.

41. Tan (1985) provides an example of such studies.

42. Individuals working separately in a jungle environment do not produce; like animals they become beasts of prey.

43. Vogel (1979) and many other writers on Japan have commented on this fact.

44. Interestingly, there is no economic theory worth its salt that can explain the basis for the salaries of the executives. Theories based on productivity, limited supply, human capital, and risk taking founder when confronted with empirical facts. The only meaningful explanation lies in the idea that these groups decide their own salaries and are not accountable to anyone.

45. Tomer (1987) discusses implications of different organizational structures.

46. The fact is that the changing economic conditions will not be able to support such an unequal wage structure. Either management follows a policy to reduce inequalities or else the global competition will force it on the firms that stay in business; others will simply go bankrupt and out of the market.

47. The underlying assumption is that management represents capital. This assumption is one of the unwritten axioms of capitalist modes of production.

48. There is ample evidence on the nature of this relationship in theory, history, and literature. Marxian analysis is based on the nature and necessity of this conflict. Braverman (1974) details some of this history and its theoretical implications.

49. The film, *Salt of The Earth*, provides vivid details about the needs for safety and jobs and the necessity of a labor union as well as the dynamics of management-labor relations.

50. The MIT Commission on Industrial Productivity (1989) report considers this as one of the major weaknesses and a part of outdated strategies.

51. The nature of the procedures required to set up a labor union speak a lot about this distrust. The workers interviewed by Terkel (1972) not only question the meaninglessness of work but also talk of their distrust.

52. The current debate on family leave bill, vetoed by President Bush, reflects a lack of appreciation of the fact that labor is embodied in a human being whose human needs are important.

53. "Of the many seedlings of change in the broad field of American industry, perhaps no other deserves our care and attention more than this movement towards participation and cooperation" Cuomo Commission Report (1988), p. 166. It goes on to say that the American formula depends heavily on workers feeling that they are part of the process of change and beneficiaries of improved cooperation. The MIT Commission on Industrial Productivity (1989) report also emphasizes the need for labor-management cooperation.

54. Tomer (1987) provides theoretical analyses to explain the empirical evidence on increase in productivity and worker welfare as a result of participation. To quote from his conclusion: "Increasingly, both theory and empirical findings lead to the conclusion that higher productivity and worker well being are possible through organizational change which introduces greater worker participation," p. 112.

55. It has been suggested, and empirically verified, that labor in Japanese manufactures makes regular and innumerable suggestions right from the shop floor. Many of these suggestions are normally put into practice. These changes improve the quality of products and the efficiency of production.

56. The united automobile workers (UAW) union has been trying to organize workers in the Nissan auto factory in Arkansas. The issue came to a vote in July 1989. It is interesting to note that the workers rejected the union by a margin of two to one. The workers have been saying, so it seems, that they are satisfied with working conditions and do not need a union to mediate for them. It is generally known that Japanese management is different from U.S. management.

57. As industry relocates in Third-World countries, a movement toward unionization in these countries is starting to emerge.

58. Mondragon has been heavily researched because it is a successful form of holistic society. The economic analysis is done by a number of economists. Diwan (1985b) discusses the relevance of its structure to productivity.

59. Galbraith (1967) has called this phenomenon "socialism through bankruptcies."

60. Vanek (1978) has discussed at length the economic argument in favor of cooperatives.

61. Vogel (1979), Reich (1987), and Tomer (1987), to name a few, provide information on Japanese management and their labor-management relations.

62. OSHA follows from the conflict between management and labor about working conditions. Currently the secretary of the Department of Energy is forcing government owned facilities to open up information regarding toxic impact on communities. Such measures will eventually influence changes in the organization of the privately owned companies.

63. The current bail-out scheme for the savings and loan institutions (S&Ls) is the largest of its kind. It is expected to cost the federal government some $500+ billion in subsidies. These bail outs will fundamentally change the structure of the S&Ls and therefore also of other companies.

64. Both the MIT Commission on Industrial Productivity (1989) report and the Cuomo Commission (1988) report recommend action by and cooperation with government.

65. West German law has institutionalized co-determination. Considering the growth rate of the economy, its exports, and the rate of its innovation, this seems to have worked well.

66. As the MIT Commission on Industrial Productivity (1989) argues, one of the weaknesses of the U.S. industrial sector lies in its "parochialism," which is basically its incapacity to learn from, and about, other cultures and experiences.

9

Promoting Technological Change

INTRODUCTION

The findings of this empirical research on the U.S. high-technology sector are that capital and skilled labor are complements, technological change is non-neutral, and the largest contribution to costs is in terms of the material input. We have already discussed the implications of capital-labor complementarity in chapter 8. The other two findings deal basically with technological change. In chapter 7 we tested the hypothesis whether technological change is neutral or non-neutral by comparing Model II with Model I. Our tests suggested that technological change is non-neutral. It is embodied in the three inputs in our analysis. We estimated both neutral and non-neutral technological change by a translog cost function in chapter 7. Our result about neutral technological change, defined in terms of Hicksian neutrality, was that $a_R = -0.03$. However, when we decomposed labor input into skilled and unskilled labor, the estimate of this coefficient fell by half, a_R in this case was -0.015. We also found that the coefficients of interaction terms of technological change with the inputs, namely, a_{Ri}, $i = K$, L, and M, are non-zero; which means that technological change is non-neutral. We estimated the magnitude of this non-neutral technological change, BTC, to compare it with the coefficient for neutral technological change. We found that BTC $= -0.06$, twice the value of a_R which is -0.03. Thus technological change is both important and embodied in the inputs capital, labor, and materials.

These findings agree with our general thesis that high technologies belong to a new emerging techno-economic paradigm. A new technology regime emerges when three conditions are satisfied: (1) the price of the basic elements of this technology falls continuously, (2) the supply of material embodying these tech-

nologies is sufficiently large to avoid bottlenecks, and (3) these technologies are
pervasive. This technology regime is based on new technologies that have come
into being in the past two decades or so. The technologies in this regime are
radically different from those in an earlier regime, which was specified in terms
of mass production technologies. The major characteristics of these new high
technologies are: (1) they are international in character so that production processes, markets and competition are global, (2) they involve continuous changes
in technology. These technological changes are based on scientific principles and
advance, and (3) these technologies are the source of economic growth of both
the national and international economy—in terms of output, employment, and
productivity. The process of technological change involves the introduction of
new products, which introduction changes entirely the shapes of the isoquants.
There is no reason for the new isoquants to reflect purely parallel shifts. Much of
the literature on innovation, productivity, and high-tech industries corroborates
our empirical results. Our objective is to examine relevant policies that aid the
embodiment of technological change.[1]

In chapter 2, we argued that the U.S. economy generally, and manufacturing
especially, is losing its competitive edge in the global market. Our empirical
research is based on the proposition that the United States can regain its international competitive edge if it can maintain a lead in the high-technology industries. This involves strengthening and promoting the U.S. high-tech sector. In
chapter 8 we analyzed some of the implications for the advancement of this
sector in terms of work force skills and motivation. Developing of skills and
improving motivation is important; however, encouraging technological change
in the economy, particularly in high-tech industries where technological change
is the distinctive feature is equally important. In this chapter we discuss policies
to promote technological change. First, however, we will briefly go over the
process of technological change to point out the various constituents.

PROCESS OF TECHNOLOGICAL CHANGE

Technological change takes place when new knowledge in science and technology is introduced to a production process through its various inputs. Following Schumpeter,[2] economic literature distinguishes three well-defined stages in
this process; namely (1) invention, (2) innovation, and (3) diffusion of innovations. These three stages differ in essential ways.[3] The mix of actors, factors, and
rules of the game involved during each stage are sufficiently dissimilar to make
each stage distinct. Although distinct, these stages are sequential; innovations
follow inventions, and diffusion takes place after innovations have been made.
The process of technological change is an aggregate of these three stages so that
analyzing the three stages individually furthers an understanding of the process
of technological change.

Invention

Invention is a commonly understood phenomenon yet it is hard to describe. It follows from a creative activity that involves ingenuity, and in the process of technological change, this creative activity involves science and technology. For an invention to take place, two conditions must be satisfied. First, there must be an extension of the frontiers of scientific and technological knowledge. The scientists, particularly those dealing with basic science, are continuously involved in such extensions; a Nobel prize in one of the sciences is generally a recognition of such an extension. Although conceptually the idea of an extension of a frontier is clear, it is not an easy concept to define in practice.[4] An extension of the frontier, however, is a necessary, but not a sufficient, condition for an invention to take place. Second, the extension of the frontier must be amenable to an application, which sometimes involves acquiring additional knowledge and takes time. It is not uncommon for some path breaking ideas to become applicable only after decades. Nobel prizes have been awarded to scientists for work done decades ago. This in fact may be the norm. For an extension of frontier to become applicable, equally important ideas have to be developed in related fields and then matched together. For the purpose of analysis, we have suggested that there is an important advance in the frontiers of knowledge first and development of related ideas later. Although scientific enquiry is a continuous process, ideas in the real world do not move in this sequential fashion. Instead, there is a simultaneity in advances to knowledge. Invention may, perhaps, be defined as a joint set of new ideas in many different, related fields with clear interrelationships and applicability. Once new interrelated ideas in different realms of knowledge reach a critical mass and have applications in many areas, an invention comes into being. This is a sufficient condition. The key elements here are applicability and interrelationships. The ideas that led to the development of steam engines and microchips, to name only two, exemplify how such ideas are the basic raw materials of major inventions.

The United States holds a lead in such research activity, which has been carried on by academic institutions where faculties have been the leaders in such research. In many universities, such research has become a part of the normal activity so that faculty are continuously evaluated on the basis of such research.[5] This is particularly true at universities that offer Ph.D. degrees. Today the United States has the largest number of such universities. However, there has been a visible decline in research activity in recent years. The universities find that their science and engineering departments are not able to attract a sufficiently large number of U.S. graduate students. Most graduate departments are dependent on foreign students.[6] This decline is due to a number of reasons. (1) The cost of graduate education has gone far higher than its rewards within universities so that U.S. graduates are choosing alternative opportunities to obtain higher incomes elsewhere. (2) There has also been a decline in the work ethic, and graduate studies are highly demanding. (3) The professoriate and research oriented faculty find that increasingly more effort and time has to be spent searching for research funding, which makes research work both uncertain and frustrating. Graduate students work closely with the faculty and such uncertainty and frustrations are contagious. With continuous declines in research funding, the future of research in the United States is growing more uncertain. Just as industry has laid off a large number of highly skilled workers, research funding cuts have reduced the stock of researchers as one research faculty member after another seeks different activities. Once the stock of research faculty is reduced, it will be very difficult, if not impossible, to replenish because it takes about 20 years to build an effective research faculty. The impact on the U.S. capacity to create new ideas and inventions will be devastating indeed.

Innovation

Once ideas with clear applications become available, the entrepreneur enters and initiates the process whereby these ideas can be translated into commodities. This is the development part of R&D. It leads to the creation of innovations. The Penguin dictionary defines innovation as "an act or process of introducing something new, making changes." The emphasis here is on something new. Innovation is analytically different from invention. Invention suggests the possibility of something new; innovation encompasses the materialization of this possibility. In a market system, it involves not only the technical tasks but also the associated market activities such as raising funds, developing markets, and setting up a relevant organization.[7] Randomness in the process that leads to important inventions is considerable. Interestingly, many inventions that precipitated major innovations have been quite inexpensive. Although it is necessary to maintain inventions of all sorts for the innovative process to become significant, some inventions may not lead to any innovations. Similarly, innovations may emerge without any clear reference to any particular invention. Innovation can be conceived as a setting up of a new production function. Innovations are relevant and important to an economy. Schumpeter formulated his theory of development around the idea of major innovations. The most important actor for these innovations, in his view, was the entrepreneur with the capacity to take risks, introduce new products, and move into uncharted markets.[8] He argued that innovations entail new plants and equipment, which implies that new innovations are embodied in new business leaders.[9] Another hypothesis states that innovations are made by the technostructure.[10] There is no unique answer as to which relevant economic agent introduces innovations in an economy; innovations derive from a large set that is difficult to define precisely. On the other hand, innovation is a real phenomenon that needs to be taken seriously.

Once an innovation has been introduced, it has a significant effect on the market for a particular good and a related industry. When innovations are major, their influence is so large that they disrupt the existing economic equilibrium, by making old products and/or old methods of production obsolete. The larger the rate of innovations, the higher the rate of obsolence. Innovations start new dynamic processes. Employment of all sorts of inputs, including factors of production, increases in the innovative activities while there is a simultaneous decline and unemployment in competing industries. The growing demand for new innovative activity initiates the next process of technical change—diffusion.

Diffusion

Diffusion results as more firms adopt the new technology.[11] Once the new technology has become profitable, existing firms find it profitable to introduce new technologies, making it feasible to introduce these technologies into new capital goods. Firms with these new capital goods are able to compete successfully in the product market; they earn profits and increase their market share. Supplier firms find that there is a market for new capital goods.[12] New firms, as well as renovated old firms, purchase these new capital goods, finding it cheaper to purchase new capital goods in the market than to adapt existing capital. Over a period of time, the proportion of new capital goods embodying new technologies increases until it becomes the dominant technology. At this point, the new technology has become the standard, and the diffusion process is complete. Spurred by competition, the adoption of new technologies by a majority of firms reduces the competitive advantage, until enterprising firms look to still newer technologies. Theoretical and empirical analysis of the diffusion process involves a study of such subjects as the rate of diffusion, rationales for diffusion and their timing, and so on.[13]

In the mass production techno-economic paradigm, technologies were discovered and introduced sequentially and technological change was represented by a step function.[14] A technology was introduced; this technology diffused and, for some period, became only standard technology in operation; then, a new technology was introduced and the process of technological change started anew. The rate of technological change is low and the process of diffusion rather long. High, and new, technologies follow a different paradigm. Here, technological change is denoted by a continuous function, which makes the process of technological change far more complex. Diffusion is not separate from the innovate process. When a firm adopts a new innovation it also introduces some additional innovative parts to it. In other words, there is an integration of the two processes of innovation and diffusion, which follows partly from the fact that these technologies result from a continuous advance in and application of science and technology to production. This integration alters the process of technological change in an essential way[15] that relates to the theory of evolution.[16] In view of the essentiality of science and technology in this process of technological change, R&D becomes highly significant.

ENCOURAGING RESEARCH AND DEVELOPMENT

Our empirical result that technological change is important for productivity in the U.S. high-tech industries results from two propositions: (1) technological change is embodied, and (2) R&D is an integral part of this embodiment hypothesis. We now turn to the importance of R&D in the process of technological change and relevant policies to promote R&D. There is a large literature on R&D, which we do not propose to review here. However, this literature contains a consensus that R&D is important for the growth of the U.S. economy. The contribution of R&D has been obtained by constructing an R&D stock, similar to capital stock. Various studies suggest that the R&D stock contributes about 0.2 and 0.3 per cent annually to productivity growth;[17] however, these studies estimate only the direct effects of R&D. R&D, however, has indirect effects as well, which may be equally large. If indirect effects are taken into consideration, the contribution of R&D is higher still. A recent study estimates that even the direct contribution of R&D to productivity growth for the period 1948–1987 may have been as high as 0.4 per cent.[18] To place these numbers in context, the same study found that the contribution of the capital stock to productivity growth was around 0.8 percent. Considering that R&D is relevant to the U.S. high-tech sector, which has a higher growth rate and growth potential, the contribution of R&D becomes all the more significant.

An important question is how R&D is linked to various processes of technological change. This is particularly crucial for the formulation of meaningful policy. For purposes of policy formulation, we need to specify the form of the linkage between R&D and technological change. The appropriate form of this linkage defines a causal relationship. Is R&D a cause or an effect of technological change? The relationship, especially over time, is highly intertwined. Depending on its objective, one can argue in favor of either position. In this analysis, we take the point of view that R&D is a cause of technological change. This argument is implied in much of the literature on technological change where R&D is introduced as an independent variable.[19] Our interest here is to determine relevant policy options that encourage R&D, therefore R&D becomes a policy variable. In this sense it is an exogenous variable and a source of technological change. The policy objective is defined by questioning how an increase in R&D promotes improvements in technology. An answer requires unmasking of the link between R&D and technological change. R&D and technological change are sets with different elements, and by looking into the various elements of these sets we can discern if there is a mapping between the elements of the two sets. We have pointed out above that there are three parts of the process of technological change; namely invention, innovation, and diffusion. Therefore we need to ask how R&D relates to these three processes. In turn, R&D itself is a large aggregate that can be divided into (1) research and development and (2) basic and applied research. Generally it is divided into (1) basic research and (2) development including applied research. Encouragement of R&D involves encouraging basic research and development.

DECLINE IN FUNDING FOR BASIC RESEARCH

A relationship exists between basic research and inventions and some part of innovations. Although inventions come from what seem like random events, basic research is aimed at extending the frontiers of knowledge that raise the probability of such random events. Basic research has been the hallmark of the U.S. science and government science and research policy. It has attracted scholars and scientists from all over the world to U.S. universities and research institutions. The United States has always taken pride in the fact that it has the largest number of Nobel laureates. American universities boast of the number of such eminent scientists on their faculties. In recent years, however, a strong attack has been leveled at basic research. In science policy literature a controversy has grown about the usefulness of basic research. Some argue that basic research does not lead to any direct effects in terms of production of goods and services or reduction in costs. Furthermore, because all basic research is published in scientific journals so that it is available to scientists in every part of the world, it does not help the competitive position of an economy. This argument became potent in the 1980s with growing government budget deficits and declining U.S. competitive strength. As a result, the efficiency of expenditures on research, defined in terms of returns to economic growth and competitiveness, has been used as a policy instrument. The administration in the Office of Management and Budget (OMB) has regularly cut the budget of research institutions but Congress has consistently restored these budgets, rescinding the OMB cuts. Apologists for science policy then point to the total of available research funds and conclude that they have not diminished. Although actual dollars have not diminished, the fact remains that, from the point of view of scholars, less money is available for basic research, particularly from the two major research funding institutions, the National Institutes of Health (NIH) and the National Science Foundation (NSF). Within these institutions, large chunks of funding have been earmarked for what can, at best, be considered applied research if not purely development, however these funds are not available for basic research. A look at the situation of researchers in science clarifies this fact. A decade and a half ago, it was common for the NIH and NSF to fund 40 to 50 percent of the research proposals approved by peers, but the percentage has steadily declined to the point that in 1989, it is estimated that only 10 to 12 percent of such proposals will be funded.[20] The shortage of funds for basic research is real and is affecting the scientific output in basic research.

The arguments on which these reductions of funding are based are, at best, erroneous and flawed, if not false. They are also seriously misguided. Let us look the arguments one by one. (1) Evidence from quantitative studies refute the argument of low returns from basic research. Instead they show high returns to basic research, particularly when one takes into consideration both social and private rates of return.[21] Inventions, and a large proportion of innovations, are social, not private, phenomena, which are supported by a society and not by an individual. In a sense, these refer to the technological environment in a society. (2) The argument that basic research is not helpful to the competitive strength of an economy is also mistaken. The fallacy of this argument follows from an overemphasis on a particular element of basic research; namely, published research. True, results of basic research are published in international journals. Research generally, and scientific advance particularly, depends fundamentally on independent reconfirmation of hypotheses and experiments as well as replication of results.[22] Openness of basic research is necessary. (3) Publication is only one element of basic research, larger and more important elements are advanced learning and laboratories, without which such published research is incomprehensible. Highly trained and research-oriented personnel are crucial to basic research. And this faculty and research group has large externalities. They provide most of the scientific personnel for applied and developmental research. Every scientist, researcher or faculty member engaged in basic research influences (a) colleagues to whom she/he communicates scientific knowledge and discovery, (b) doctoral graduates who cooperate in research, and (c) graduate students, some of whom, in the end, provide the necessary expertise for developmental work. Publication is a particular stage of this process in which a whole team is engaged. Basic research is defined by both the process and the team.

COUNTER PRODUCTIVITY OF RESEARCH FUNDING

The current policy and institutional arrangements for research funding is inefficient, ineffective, and counter productive. The objective of research funds provided by the U.S. government and channeled through such funding agencies as the NIH and NSF should be to encourage basic research. The process for research funding is as follows. A researcher, in a university or research institution, makes a research proposal and submits it through the institution to a research funding agency, say the NIH or NSF. The proposal has a cost, which is made up of (1) funds needed to perform the scientific tasks required in the proposal, and (2) indirect or overhead costs charged by the institution for allowing, or enabling, the researcher to carry on the research. These overhead charges are quite high; sometimes more than the costs of the scientific research. The overhead costs are primarily administrative; although, in a number of institutions, real administrative costs are also pushed onto the researcher. The research proposal, in multiple copies, goes to the funding institution, which then sets up a process of peer review the form of which varies with the institution. After 9 months or so a researcher learns whether or not the proposal will be funded. If only 10 percent of proposals, judged to be scientifically desirable, are funded, a researcher has to apply, on the average, ten times to get one proposal funded. Given the time, effort, and intellectual and emotional energy involved in writing a proposal and going through the administrative and bureaucratic steps, such as xeroxing copies and getting the signatures of a list of administrators, a researcher often finds that more of his/her time is spent on writing proposals than in doing basic science. As the percentage of approved proposals funded decreases, institutions collectively spend more and more of their time and resources in the process of forwarding proposals, and funding agencies spends more and more of their resources and time reviewing these proposals. This is a vicious cycle. The dynamics of this process ensure that more time, financial and other resources, and intellectual and emotional energy are wasted in producing and reviewing proposals than in helping scientists and researchers to do basic research. This mechanism has become counter productive in many scientific fields; more money is spent, fewer researchers are supported, and less science is being done. The source of this counter productivity is the congestion[23] that is caused by a shortage of funds and an increase in researchers seeking them. A spiraling increase in administrative costs ensues, both in institutions through which proposals are initiated and in funding agencies that review proposals and allocate research funds. A major portion of scarce resources is being wasted; more resources are expended and much less per unit is achieved.

The present system has some additional problems, including the new vested interests it has created. Universities and research institutions consider grants from research funding agencies a useful input to their current budgets. Therefore, they increase their lobbying efforts to seek higher overhead costs and pressure scientists to send more proposals for funding. In the name of science, funding agencies have become a conduit for transferring resources to maintain the budgets of some research institutions and universities. This confluence of interests is now spilling into research for specific objectives such as cancer and AIDS. Large chunks of NIH funds are earmarked for particular research programs and concentrated on specific issues. Meanwhile, the NSF is spending large amounts to establish research centers. This process further reduces the availability of funds for doing basic scientific research, and the counter productivity rate goes up. Research intensity of these new centers is generally shallow and limited. Because of the comparatively large amounts involved the process has become political; Congress is getting into the action. Funds available for basic research are being further reduced. In addition, the situation is promoting costs and a growth in administrative and public relations activities. The social costs of the present system are colossal.

If this process continues, it is bound to weaken, if not destroy, a major scientific infrastructure built over many decades.[24] This infrastructure is made up of science faculties and research scientists who have been involved in scientific research over the past few decades. They are our most sophisticated and highly qualified national resource. The infrastructure's value translates into trillions of dollars. Once it is lost, it is permanently gone; because its gestation period spans over decades it could not be replaced even if there were trillions of dollars available. Like other infrastructures, in addition to being extremely valuable, this resource has a very high multiplier.[25] For example, a professor of science engaged in research advances frontiers of knowledge by his/her own research. In addition, this professor trains post-doctorals who will be able to take his/her place in a decade or two. Further, this professor prepares a number of graduates and doctors in scientific research who will become productive in science in the future. At the next level she/he influences a large number of graduate and undergraduate students who will provide the base for a future science and technology infrastructure. Once this professor has to give up his/her research, post-doctors will not be trained and students will not enter into graduate and doctoral work. We are now witnessing these effects.[26] The number of Ph.D.s in science and engineering has been decreasing. Fewer and fewer students want to go for doctoral degrees in science and engineering. In addition, an increasing number of graduate students are now from other parts of the world.[27] If the process continues to affect a number of such professors, in half a decade the level of scientific expertise will decline so much that this nation will not be able to maintain its universities, much less its preeminence in science and technology. This is a sure way to lose the competitive edge in the next decade.

POLICIES TO PROMOTE BASIC RESEARCH

If basic research has to be encouraged, it is necessary to change the existing system. The policy objective of such a change is simple; namely, to provide maximum funds to a maximum number of researchers, if not to all researchers. This is also the original policy objective. Ideally, it should be possible to provide research funds to all those whose research proposals are judged to be scientifically meritorious. This is not an unattainable ideal. In fact, in the 1960s and early 1970s this ideal was actually attained. Given a paucity of funds, an acceptable system should be able to provide funds to 50 percent of all proposals judged scientifically meritorious; the existing system was able to do so until the late 1970s. In the past decade, however, the system has not been able to perform at this level in spite of a small increase in funds. If we define efficiency of this system by its capacity to provide funds to 50 percent of the proposals judged scientifically meritorious, the existing system is highly inefficient. However, it could perform efficiently if funds available to the granting agencies were increased by a multiple of at least 5,[28] assuming that costs of administration do not accelerate. Currently, the NSF budget is around $4 billion and that of the NIH of the same order. Therefore, the existing system could perform well if the funding level were increased from $8 billion to $40 billion. Considering the importance of the issue, this is not an excessive amount, particularly for a trillion dollar budget. Such funds are available. The military or defence budget is around $300 billion. With the cold war coming to an end and the Union of Soviet Socialist Republics agreeable to disarmament, such funds could easily be transferred from defence spending.[29] The problem here is not lack of funds but lack of priorities.

Assuming that additional funds are not available, another solution lies in reducing unnecessary costs. There are two sources of costs that need to be looked into. First, administrative costs at the university or research institution level. Overhead costs at present are too high for funding agencies to afford, and these high overhead costs impose equally large administrative costs on the funding agencies. If these were eliminated completely the funds available for real research should virtually double.[30] Second, another source of reducible costs are the time costs that funding agencies pay to universities and research institutions so that faculty and researchers can work on their research. These are known as charge outs.[31] Charge outs could easily be eliminated; the NSF has, in fact, already eliminated some of them. A rough guess is that funds saved by eliminating charge outs could fund 10 percent of the accepted proposals.[32] Third, administrative costs at the level of proposal review and funding agencies need to be reduced. At present, the review process involves 10 to 12 expert readers with all sorts of implied costs. If these were reduced by half, and similar costs at the funding agencies were reduced by cutting administrative staff, approximately 10 percent more proposals could be funded. Additionally, if proposals now funded for short periods of one to three years were funded for a longer period, say four to six years, the costs of administration would fall by at least an additional 10 percent. Finally, if government stopped directing research into specific areas, large chunks of funds that have been siphoned off could be returned to basic research. With all these changes, the existing agencies with existing budgets should be able to perform their real function of promoting and enabling research activity. If the scientific and political leadership understands the importance of basic research, the nature of that research, and the necessity to maintain the scientific infrastructure that already exists, particularly for the promotion of the U.S. high-tech sector and our international competitiveness, it should not be difficult to introduce the above mentioned policies and promote basic research with existing funding levels and institutions.

POLICIES FOR APPLIED RESEARCH

Applied research and development expenditures link with the innovation and diffusion processes of technological change. A major function of applied research is to prepare a prototype, which not only displays relevant principles at work but is also useful to the development of a process or a product. Development expenditures push this prototype further to enable production of a particular product and/or a process. Analytically, applied research is distinct from what is known as development. Applied research has elements of enquiry, so it is proper research. Development is smoothing and getting the bugs out. By the time the development process begins, the scientific principles have been settled; there is not enquiry, no questioning. Experienced scientists and engineers are essential for applied research. In development stage, they can, at best, supervise. Development tasks can be performed by highly skilled technicians.[33] A large part of applied research is done in universities and established laboratories. Development work is mostly done in company labs. Just as basic research leads to publication, development work leads to patents; applied research lies somewhere between the two. Some applied research is published while other is patented. Basic research and development are distinct categories. Applied research is a continuum that connects these two categories. There is some commonality between basic and applied research, primarily for policy purposes.

Since basic research and development are distinct categories, policies relevant to these are also different. Basic research is a public good. It relates to, and depends on, public policy. Its support comes from government funds. Development, on the other hand, is a private good; private firms are engaged in it; and relevant policies have to operate through private agents. Since applied research lies between the two, policies that promote applied research follow from both directions. We have already discussed policies for basic research. We now take up policies that deal with development. The major policy objective here is to encourage processes of innovation and diffusion because applied research and development are means to that end. An underlying assumption for policy formulation is that an increased level of applied research and development is conducive to innovations and diffusion of technological change,[34] an important implication of which is that there is a positive monotonic relationship between development and applied research and technological change. It makes the objective of policy simple and clear: to promote applied research and development activity.

There are two approaches to this public policy objective: (1) to provide facilities and infrastructure for such R&D and (2) to develop incentives for private agents to engage in R&D. Although these two courses are somewhat interrelated in practice, conceptually and analytically they are different and need to be studied separately. Infrastructure relates primarily to applied research, the R in R&D, and incentives to development activity, the D in R&D. We will take R&D infrastructure first. It depends essentially on science and engineering faculties and their laboratories in universities, and on scientists and engineers in major national laboratories. The major, perhaps the only, instrument of public policy here is the provision of public funds to these scientists and engineers. This infrastructure relates to both basic and applied research. We have already commented above on the issue of basic research and a decline in this infrastructure. With growing budget deficits, increases in military spending, and declining funds for research and education, succeeding administrations, in this decade, have followed two policies: (1) to shift research funds toward weapons research, and (2) to shift funds from basic to applied research. Both these policies are short sighted. They have an adverse impact on this infrastructure. Weapons research in recent years does not seem to have beneficial effects on civilian and commercial research. As a result, the shifting of resources from civilian to weapons research involves reducing the availability of scientists and engineers for high-tech industries. This amounts to a reduction in infrastructure size. Also, weapons research funding has been volatile as it is highly political, which has brought an unusual level of uncertainty to scientific research. Shifting of resources from basic to applied research has also increased uncertainty in research funding. Funding of applied research has been justified by the country's need to concentrate on specific scientific tasks. These scientific tasks have been chosen not by the scientific community but by the users, commercial and political. Commercial and political priorities and targets are ever changing, which adds still another strong element of uncertainty to research funding, raising further the level of scientific obsolescence.[35] A meaningful policy would restore the level of funding for research commensurate with the objective of enabling a large percentage of scientists and engineers to do scientifically approved research.

POLICIES FOR DEVELOPMENT IN R&D

This brings us to development activity. Development relates to the diffusion stage in the process of technological change. However, in high technologies and the new technology regime, diffusion and innovation are somewhat integrated. Just as research is done by publicly funded scientists, development is primarily done by firms and companies. Development activity is private; it is taken up by private agents interested in economic returns. Companies treat this activity like any other—their choices are defined by what rate of return this activity will generate. Philosophically, and intellectually, this criterion seems rational and businesslike. In fact, and in the real world, however there is no rationality to this choice for the simple reason that there is no possible unique answer; it depends, crucially, on information about future returns, which can not be forecast accurately, particularly because development relates not to pure diffusion of a given technology but to some sort of innovative activity as well. In the case of the diffusion of a given technology, the market is well defined; if one can assume that one can sell the products, or processes, in this defined market, some estimates of future returns can be made with a certain associated level of probability. But in the case of innovative activity, where the market itself is not well defined and has to be created, estimates of future returns are a matter of opinion. Everything depends on the investors; on their capacity for risk taking, their expectations of future markets, and a host of similar factors. Although future returns are unknown and uncertain, current costs of such development activity are well defined. A firm contemplating such development activity has two issues to consider: how to reduce costs, and how to obtain larger returns in the future. Private agents involved in development activity have two concerns: to reduce (1) costs and (2) risks. The objective of public policy is to relate to these two concerns, which involves provision of incentives.

Cost reductions can be effected by tax policies. Taxes raise the cost function and the remission of taxes reduces it. Taxes favoring R&D were in place in the early 1980s, in the form of tax credits for investment in R&D. The lapse of these tax credits was not a helpful policy.[36] Tax credits are a form of a subsidy.[37] The

1986 Tax Reform Act reduced tax rates and attempted to place income from all sources on an equal par. With these lowered tax rates and the budget deficit, Congress may not be willing to institute a special favor for particular industries that could become a precedent and a loophole. The current budget deficit makes subsidies a politically unpopular issue. On the other hand, U.S. industry is vital. It is losing its competitive edge. R&D and technological improvements are essential if U.S. industry is to regain its competitive strength. R&D costs are high, particularly for high-tech industries where they are a continuous expense. Given the fact that U.S. firms are not spending sufficiently on R&D, a persuasive case can be made for the reintroduction of R&D tax credits for high-technology industries. For these tax credits to be effective, tax policy has to satisfy two criteria: (1) tax credits have to be sizable enough to be credible and an incentive. When marginal tax rates were high, any tax credit that reduced taxable income provided an incentive. With reduced tax rates, however, tax credits have to be larger in magnitude for the income effect to be operative.[38] (2) Tax credits have to be differential, favoring only high-tech industries, so that their substitutional effects are favorable. This could channel R&D toward the U.S. high-tech sector.

DEVELOPMENT RISKS AND PUBLIC POLICY

There are various types of risks that private R&D assumes: (1) There is no guarantee that bugs will be smoothed out in time. The nuclear industry in the United States has suffered particularly from this risk because it has not been able to satisfy concerns about safety. The general perception that nuclear plants are not safe has persisted. (2) Competitors may come out with a better product. The company finds that it has spent its resources on R&D; R&D has been successful in providing production of a new product; this product, however, is not competitive. The R&D effort and expense therefore is wasted. (3) A firm may spend lots of time and resources to develop a production technology. Once it is done, other producers may jump in with little of their own R&D because dissemination of knowledge regarding this production technology cannot be contained, or controlled. The original firm has to carry the R&D costs in addition to production costs, which makes its costs higher and hence it is less competitive and the firm is not able to achieve appropriate benefits from its expenditure. This is a standard case of public goods where benefits are external to a firm. Although their effects in terms of competitiveness and profitability are similar, these three types of risks belong to different categories and require different policies.

The risk regarding the difficulties of determining a product or a production technology can be reduced in only general terms. Development depends fundamentally on a team of scientists, engineers, and technicians. The quality of their work is directly proportional to their experience, expertise, cooperativeness, and a sense of identification with both the task at hand and the agency for which they are working.[39] The higher the quality of team work, the lower the risk that bugs will not be smoothed out. Once a team is in place, attitudes to work defined, management style given, not much can be done to reduce these risks. Private agents are on their own. This is where entrepreneurs become major players in promoting technological change.[40] It is not clear how public policy can encourage such risk taking. There is no direct role for public policy in this case. In the last analysis, such risk taking is a part of the cultural milieu of a society. Economics and public policy are but a small part of this cultural milieu.[41]

The risk associated with competitors winning a race can be contained to some extent by public policy. The risk here is that a company A develops a product but finds other competitors have a better product; or they managed to develop this product earlier than A. In a global market, company A has no recourse but to suffer the consequences of this risk. Public policy, however, can reduce this risk by helping company A in the domestic market. There are two policy instruments at government's disposal. The government can reward company A through its purchase policy; that is, government requires its purchases be made only from domestic producers. This policy is followed in all purchases for military and military related hardware; although, here too, economic and technological considerations have often resulted in purchase of goods from foreign companies.[42] Considering that government purchases reflect a sizable fraction of the domestic market, such a policy ensures a minimum market size to domestic producers. Economists, rightly, point out that this is nothing short of subsidy, particularly where prices charged by domestic producers are higher than those of foreign producers. They question if subsidies can, however, be justified on economic grounds. Once framed in a subsidy versus market dichotomy, the argument becomes academic and political. But the fact still remains that U.S. firms are losing competitiveness. Risk taking is necessary. Provision of incentives that encourage risk taking is a legitimate part of public policy. In the last analysis, public policy is a matter of costs and subsidies. Purchase policy is an acceptable form of public policy; consistent with its objective of reducing some of the risks in product and process development.

Another relevant policy in this context is trade policy, particularly import policy. In a sense, import policy is similar to government purchase policy in so far as both provide a part of the domestic market for domestic producers. The objective of an import policy is to improve the competitive edge of domestic producers by making the playing field favorable to them. The extreme case is forbidding imports so that the domestic market is available to domestic producers in its entirety. This is not only an extreme but also a rare case. Generally import policy has two instruments: (1) reducing the quantity supplied by foreign producers and (2) increasing the price of imported goods. Quantity restrictions are obtained through quotas, which are either negotiated, as in the case of Japan agreeing not to sell more than a certain quantity of cars in U.S. markets, or regulated, as in textiles where import quotas for different countries are determined and enforced. However, a quota is not a precise instrument and it is like a dangerous drug with large side effects. In high-tech industries where product design and quality are continuously changing, it is not possible to enforce quotas.

Also, textile quotas did not save the U.S. textile industry. In the case of automobiles, Japan has been able to get around the quota by selling upscale expensive cars, on the one hand, and starting production facilities in United States on the other. In the case of high-tech industries, where product designs are in flux, markets highly segmented and undergoing change, the quota is not a reliable policy instrument.

The second instrument of trade policy is a levy of import excise duties with the objective of making imported goods costlier.[43] This is also known as raising of tariff walls, where the height of the wall is defined by the steepness of excise duties. To be effective, tariff walls have to be raised sufficiently high so that foreign competitors cannot easily jump them. That is where the rub lies. High walls evoke a response from other governments which hurts international trade in general. Low walls are generally easy to hop. Unless there are other equally important objectives, trade policy as a whole is not an efficient way to reduce this type of risk in undertaking development expenditures. One has to seek other policy instruments. We will offer a specific suggestion after discussing other types of risks.

The risk of lack of appropriatability is a serious one. In the high-tech world it is also commonplace. The new techno-economic paradigm is still emerging. New technologies are coming on line; new products and processes appear continuously. A number of firms are regularly engaged in developing new products and processes. Once a product or process is created, however, competing firms can easily imitate and improve on it. It is impossible to keep secrets of technology, especially in the U.S. production structure where companies frequently hire and fire their scientists and engineers so that they seek economic advancement by moving from one company to another. As these scientists and engineers move from company to company, they also diffuse production technologies and development know how among competing companies. In such a climate, American companies feel that benefits from development expenses may not be appropriated. Over time, company after company has decided in favor of not taking this risk by not investing necessary amounts of resources in development. Although, in the short run, this has been a rational decision for individual companies, the social costs have been high since the society has lost its competitiveness. In the long run, it has been detrimental to these companies also.

Public policy in the past has tried to reduce this risk through patent law. The principle behind the patent law is that a firm that develops an innovative product or process deserves to appropriate benefits from the risk it has taken. Accordingly, this firm is encouraged to take out a patent for its new products or processes. Once a firm has taken a patent, the product or process is considered as private property. No other firm can produce a product or use a process that impinges on such a patent. A firm with a patent then acts as a monopoly that can charge a monopoly price and recover benefits from its research and development expenditures. In theory, patent law makes good sense. However, for it to work efficiently, rather stringent conditions are necessary. Products have to be very well defined and there can not be easy substitutes. Even in the old techno-economic paradigm of standardized goods and mass production it was difficult to satisfy this condition. In the real world, there are many substitutes close to any product, however well defined, as is evident from the hundreds and thousands of products patented regularly. Instead of defining a product, the patent has become a matter of legal interpretations, raising costs rather than providing monopolistic markets.[44] In the new techno-economic paradigm, where the definition of a product is likely to change in a short time, conditions necessary for the protection through patent law are virtually impossible to satisfy. Patent law has not been of much help in high-tech industries. One may argue that a part of the problem of inapplicability of patent law is that it provides a market-oriented solution. With a change in the techno-economic paradigm, market solutions have, perhaps, become inefficient. One has to seek solutions elsewhere.

PROPOSAL FOR A COOPERATIVE SOLUTION

One source of reducing this risk is provision of an environment where benefits from such risk taking can be appropriated, but with market globalization and internationalization of production and technology, such an environment no longer exists. Another source of reducing these risks is to collaborate with those who are liable to appropriate the benefits without taking risks. In other words, risks can be spread over a number of producers who share these risks jointly. The American production system, with its oligopolistic market structure and history, has not been helpful in a search for solutions in this direction. Part of the responsibility lies with the U.S. anti-trust laws. Anti-trust laws were introduced to break up monopolies and ensure market competition so that consumers could be protected.[45] Although the Federal Trade Commission, responsible for enforcing anti-trust laws, has not enforced them in this decade, private corporations still shy away from joint collaborations within the United States even for development purposes. There is a slow change in this practice—U.S. corporations do collaborate with foreign corporations. For example, every U.S. auto manufacturer has a collaboration with a Japanese manufacturer. Recently, these corporations are recognizing a need for joint collaboration. SEMATECH and U.S. MEMORIES are recent examples of such joint collaboration.[46] Congress is looking into changes in anti-trust laws that will make such cooperation easier. However, there are no institutions in the United States that can facilitate such cooperation. There are associations of manufacturers and trade associations, but these bodies consider that their functions are to lobby for subsidies and do public relations. They have neither the status nor the foresight to seek cooperative solutions for the lack of competitiveness of their industry or trade.

The U.S. government has not been involved in developing cooperative efforts among different, and sometimes competing, firms; yet, government is an appropriate body to do so. Captains of industry recognize this need and are now asking for it. The National Advisory Committee on Semiconductors is made up pri-

marily of the executives of major U.S. semiconductor and computer corporations. In their report, they are recommending that the U.S. government should
set up a multi-billion dollar venture capital fund to promote the U.S. semiconductor industry so as to enable it to obtain a competitive, if not a leading, place in
the global market. Spreading risk among companies, so as to reduce the risks of
research and development to each, and promoting cooperation among competing
firms to enhance technological change are significant objectives of public policy.
The essence of the new techno-economic paradigm implies that governments
recognize such policy objectives. Governments in Europe and Japan are involved
in pursuing these policy objectives. Not only are governments promoting cooperation among private firms, European governments themselves are joining together and providing incentives for firms from different European countries to
cooperate for R&D in high-tech industries. Competitive strategies, the prece-
dents set by other governments, and the compulsions of new techno-economic
paradigm require that the U.S. government accept this policy objective and
devise the necessary mechanisms to achieve it.

To achieve the objectives of reducing these risks by spreading them among
different firms and encouraging cooperation among competing U.S. firms, we
need an institutional framework. The U.S. government can provide such an
institutional framework through one of its departments. The underlying principles for such an institutional framework to be effective are that it have (1) high
enough status to evoke cooperation and eventual compliance at the highest levels
of private industry and (2) enough resources to initiate an activity with even a
small number of participating firms. We suggest that the secretary of the U.S.
Department of Commerce would be able to provide such an institutional framework; certainly in the initial stages. The secretary has cabinet status and being in
charge of a department, she/he has command of enough resources to follow these
policy objectives. However, the secretary has to be involved at his/her level. To
do so, the secretary would need to develop a cell under its chairpersonship in the
department that oversees relevant activities to achieve these objectives. Once the
process has been started, other institutional frameworks could be worked out. A
policy with the clear objective of encouraging development expenditures and
reducing different risks through cooperative risk taking pursued at the cabinet
level is bound to be effective.[47]

PROMOTING TECHNICAL CHANGE

Our objective is to formulate policies to encourage the process of technological
change that will keep the U.S. high-tech industries internationally competitive.
The underlying assumption, based on the conclusions in chapter 2, is that the
United States has not been able to keep pace with the processes of technological
change taking place internationally. There are three actors in these policies;
namely government, firms or corporations, and the science and technology establishment (STE). Generally, the STE is denoted by R&D. We have discussed

the role of R&D above. However, we suggest that the STE is much larger than R&D. It includes not only R&D but also agencies that promote the cultural context within which R&D is carried on, such as departments of education in both federal and state governments, non-government funding agencies for science and technology, and universities. We question how these actors help in the acceleration of the various processes of technological change.

INDUSTRIAL ORGANIZATION AND HIGH TECHNOLOGY

Firms and corporations are directly responsible for the adoption of the most recent technologies in their production processes. The conventional wisdom is that firms operate on signals from the market. If it is profitable to invest in new technologies, it is in their interest to make such investments. Economic and business theories make the assumption that these firms and corporations are rational. If firms in the United States have not been investing in new technologies, the reason may be that the market has not provided such signals. This point of view is advocated by a group of economists and businessmen. They argue that the real interest rates in the United States have been particularly high compared with those of other countries. Accordingly, rational corporations have invested their resources to obtain higher returns instead of investing in new technologies. The difficulty with this argument is that it assumes (1) the rationality of firms and (2) the capacity of markets to provide meaningful signals for long-term investments. Profitability of long-term investment is virtually impossible to define or estimate;[48] there are all sorts of uncertainties in the long run so that it is not even possible to ascribe probabilities. Long-term investment, in the final analysis, depends fundamentally on the risk taking propensities of large investors. The Schumpeterian theory of development depends essentially not on rational investors but on risk-taking entrepreneurs. It is instructive to note that corporations in other countries do make long-term investments in technological change. Their long-term investment in new capital goods explains their competitive advantage in a global market. After all, markets have become global, particularly the financial markets. Finance now moves rather fast from one country to another. If corporation managers in other countries behave equally rationally, all they have to do is to follow signals in U.S. markets.[49] This would imply that they would not be making long-term investments. The facts, however, do not support this rationality thesis. The reasons for long-term investments in technological change by firms in other countries have to be sought in different quarters.

Although the argument that U.S. corporations are not making long-term investments because of their economic rationality is not persuasive, the fact remains that such investments are not being made. We have suggested that such investment involves risk-taking. The question is why U.S. corporations do not take risks. There are two ways to look at this question based on managerial makeup and the nature of institutional arrangements. Some argue that a new crop of managers has come to occupy decision making authority in most U.S. corporations.[50] These are people brought up by business schools through their M.B.A. programs. These managers are adept in financial management and consider it most important. All investment projects are filtered through financial returns. Proposals that offer greater probability of yielding a quick and/or a high level of financial returns are accepted. Long-term investments in new technologies have high uncertainties. They do not normally meet these criteria and are thus left out. A number of studies have faulted U.S. schools of business for pushing this idea.[51] Since uncertainties cannot be quantified, decision processes based on probabilities of financial returns make the decision maker avoid risk taking.

Another school of thought maintains that the source of this deficiency lies in the nature of the institutional arrangements.[52] The argument is based on the following propositions: (1) the market for most industrial goods and processes is defined by large oligopolies. In virtually every commodity, between three to ten firms control most of the output and supply. The competition that we witness is not of text book type. It is instead monopolistic competition about which there are no well-defined economic theories. (2) These large oligopolies are able to reverse the logic of production. The standard market logic is that a producer produces goods demanded by a consumer whose preferences are formed independently. According to this argument, consumer preferences are not independent of the production by these oligopolies. These oligopolies decide what is feasible to produce, then change consumer preferences through advertisement and government policy so that they will demand these goods. The production-consumption sequence is reversed. The sequence now is that producers have the sovereignty to decide about production. Once supply has been created, market and non-market mechanism are used to create the necessary demand to match this supply. (3) Production decisions are made by a techno-structure that is not accountable to either market or shareholders. If one accepts this thesis it follows that decisions to make long-term investments are made by the techno-structure.[53] The techno-structure has well-defined interests. Risky and uncertain long-term investment in new technologies do not advance its interests. By its nature, the techno-structure is conservative and not conducive to risk taking.

There is validity to both these arguments. Decision makers are too preoccupied with short-term financial gains.[54] The decision making structure seems to be immune to market conditions except when it is too late. There are two types of policies that support decisions to invest in new technologies: (1) Our business community has to define success in terms of technological achievements, instead of financial gains. The decision makers then have to have technological knowledge rather than financial expertise. There is a need to change the criteria for selecting and promoting people to higher levels of executive positions. A technological background has to become one of the more important qualifications. This will emphasize the scientific and technological considerations in the operation of a corporation and promote the introduction of new technologies in its production processes. Some incentives can be devised to encourage such a change. For example, banks may be encouraged to give preferential loans for investments in new technologies. Policy panels for the government may seek technologically trained executives instead of people who just happen to be at a higher level of a corporation hierarchy. The financial reward structure also needs to be revised so that inequalities and discrepancies in salaries and emoluments between technologically qualified people and purely financial M.B.A. types are eliminated. These policies will change the makeup of the decision makers and thereby bring technologically relevant issues to the fore.

(2) The oligopolistic structure needs to be replaced. A major weakness of this oligopolistic structure lies in its very strength—its capacity to influence consumers. Since these producers do not produce to satisfy consumer demand, they are vulnerable to competition from other producers who are able to do so. This is most apparent in the automobile market. The Japanese are able to compete successfully simply because consumers now believe that Japanese producers satisfy their demand for efficient, maintenance free, and reliable cars. Japanese producers are producing for consumers with given preferences and not trying to change their preferences. They thus invest in new technologies that can perform engineering functions efficiently. Since the U.S. manufacturers could sell inefficient and unreliable cars to their customers, they have not been in a hurry to keep pace with new technologies. Instead they devoted more resources on advertisements, financial discounts, and government lobbying to stay legislation proposing fuel efficiency and passenger safety. Changes in oligopolistic structure would require an adversarial, or at least a less cozy, relationship with the government.[55] If it is not changed by policy, it will be fundamentally altered by global competition—this process of change, through the pressure of global competition, is already in operation.[56]

A significant change in the nature and objectives of advertisement is also needed. Advertisement has two effects; first, to shift the aggregate demand, and second, to increase the advertiser's share in the market.[57] The fact that the tobacco industry spent a billion dollars in 1980 to promote smoking would suggest that industry believes in the effectiveness of advertisement in shifting demand as a whole. Similarly, beef producers and cheese producers are now spending 20 to 22 million dollars a year; their only objective is to raise consumption of these commodities. Although empirical economic analysis is not able to satisfactorily quantify advertisement effects on demand, a general perception for policy is that advertisement does increase total consumption. Once a large corporation feels it can sell its product by advertisement, not only is its need to make meaningful investments in engineering the product reduced, it also forces other companies to shift resources toward advertisement campaigns. Product quality and long-term investment suffer.[58] There is now a great deal of empirical evidence that small firms have been more venturesome in investments, particularly in new technologies.[59] The collusion between advertising agencies, manufacturers, and the media is partly responsible for maintaining an oligopolistic market structure. This collusive market structure has not been helpful to investments for technological change.

ROLE OF GOVERNMENT IN PROMOTING
TECHNOLOGICAL CHANGE

The preceding makes it clear that the U.S. corporate sector is not in a position to bring about the changes necessary for long-term investment in technological change. Except for enlightened leaders, nothing in the leadership makeup or the rules of short-term profitability encourages one to believe that such changes can be made without outside prodding or pressures. This brings one to government, which acts on behalf of a society. In other competing countries, such as France, Japan, South Korea, and West Germany, governments have played an important role. In the past, the U.S. government also played an important role in moving this country forward and establishing the highest living standards. In recent years however, particularly during the Reagan administration, a proposition has been advanced that government can do no good. This is obviously a mistaken idea. Problems keep on escalating. The U.S. government seems to be less effective.[60] Still the U.S. government is particularly important in promoting investments in particular directions. The U.S. lead in major technologies had been the direct result of government policy and expenditures. The aerospace industry has depended essentially on defense contracts for all its major technological and innovative investments. Because of this, it still maintains a lead in the world. The United States once had a commanding lead in semiconductors, which were a spin off of the space program. The argument then is not that government direction and expenditures are not an important source of technological advance, neither is it that the U.S. government has not been involved in directing technological changes in different industries. The real issue is that in recent years U.S. government policy has not been directed specifically to the issue of international competitiveness.[61] What is needed is a recognition of the usefulness of government expenditures and policy direction in encouraging investments in technological change.

EUROPEAN GOVERNMENTS' INVOLVEMENT
IN NEW TECHNOLOGIES

Other countries and their governments have already started the process to make major investments in new technologies. The Japanese government and its agent MITI is now well known. With 1992 on the horizon, governments in European Economic Community (EEC) countries are not only helping their industries, they are joining with other governments to create large organizations in virtually all high-tech fields. A number of projects are already in existence.[62]

1. *Airbus* is a consortium of aerospace companies from Britain, France, Spain and West German. Airbus, with help from these governments, has already become the world's second largest manufacturer of passenger

aircraft and is providing tough competition to U.S. companies such as Boeing.

2. *Arianespace* is an 11-nation European space launch consortium. It has already put 58 satellites in orbit. With the *Challenger* disaster, the United States lost its capacity to launch satellites and all commercial business shifted to Arianespace.

3. *Cern* is a 14-nation research laboratory. It is a European laboratory for particle physics and has the world's largest atom smasher, the 17-mile long electron-positron collider.[63]

4. *Esprit* is a multi-billion dollar European community program. It has many cooperative projects to seek improvements in microelectronic technology in such areas as integrated circuit design and computer-aided manufacturing.

5. *Eureka-A* is a 19-nation program where governments provide as much as 40 percent of the funds for some projects. It is already involved in 297 research projects in which corporations cooperate to develop the most scientifically advanced systems, such as high-definition television standards and external automobile guidance systems.

6. *Eurofighter* is a four-nation (Britain, Italy, Spain and West Germany), $30 billion project. A number of companies in this program are building 800 new fighter aircraft.

7. *Euromissile* is a French-German consortium. It builds anti-tank and anti-aircraft missiles.

8. *European Space Agency* is a 13-nation program. It is now building the $4.8 billion *Hermes* space shuttle and also part of the planned international space station. It has also built 28 satellites for weather, telecommunications, and research.

9. *Jessi* is a European program for submicron silicon. It is a $5 billion program to develop a new generation of semiconductors and the machines to build them.

10. *Jet* is a 14-nation project. Its objective is to develop a prototype nuclear fusion reactor.

11. *Race* is a $1.5 billion European program that deals with new technologies in telecommunication areas such as data transmission and video telephones.

Europeans are taking international competitiveness seriously. They are gearing up to compete with both Japan and the United States. These efforts are based on two basic assumptions: (1) the investments needed to introduce new technologies are large and beyond the capacity of individual corporations, even governments.

Governments in the European Community have to be directly involved. (2) Technical progress requires cooperation among competing corporations. There are many arguments in favor of cooperation, including, economies of scale, usefulness of other points of view, larger learning experience, and the strength in mixing cultural experiences.[64] This is consistent with Japanese experience and strategy. MITI has been successful in bringing a number of competing corporations together and helping them cooperate in making joint investments. Since these are successful strategies in global competition, it follows that these will have to be adopted by the United States.

A PROPOSAL FOR THE U.S. GOVERNMENT TO PROMOTE TECHNOLOGICAL CHANGE

U.S. companies are recognizing the need for such cooperative efforts and are becoming willing to imitate Europe.[65] They are also moving in this direction, even if slowly. SEMATECH is a research consortium of 14 semiconductor companies with a $1 billion budget over five years; the U.S. government is expected to pay half of this budget. There was an unsuccessful attempt to set up U.S. MEMORIES as a consortium of 7 companies. Despite these examples, the U.S. market structure is not helpful to such cooperative efforts. What is needed is government help and direction. Whenever such activities, such as SEMATECH, the 59-mile particle collider, are brought into being, government expenditures are considered necessary. None of these activities can get off the ground without government financial help. The issue is that government is not pursuing a well-designed policy to focus investments in new technologies where international competitiveness is intense. Without a focused policy, such government expenditures remain unproductive. Given the dynamics of international competitiveness, the U.S. government will need to be increasingly involved. Once we accept that government will be involved, the relevant question is, how U.S. government policy can be made more effective. As in competing countries, the U.S. government policy needs to have two objectives: (1) to encourage investment in new technologies and (2) to promote cooperative efforts among competing corporations. Both these objectives are necessary and government initiative and financial support can promote both. Given the oligopolistic market structure, an individual corporation is not in a position to either make investment at the desired level or persuade other producers to join together. By and large, oligopolistic markets enforce a zero-sum game, wherein its members try to increase their market share. The government can help change this into a positive game. At present, the U.S. government has neither such policy goals nor any instruments whereby such objectives can be achieved. Both anti-trust laws and regulations are reactive instead of being proactive.

Since the United States is losing its competitive edge in the global market, its competitive strength requires a continuous investment in new and high technologies. Our policies, in the past, have been directed toward promotion of technological advance through the defense industries. These policies have provided subsidies to different groups of people. Given these facts, all the elements of the government involvement in investment for technological change are there. The only remaining question is whether the U.S. government should take initiatives to encourage high technologies as other governments have done. Our sense is that the U.S. government is the only body that can influence private corporations and markets in this direction. There is no endogenous solution to the problem of lack of investment in technological advances and new technologies. What is needed is an exogenous push. The only source of this push is the U.S. government.

Accordingly, we propose that the U.S. government define its policy objectives to maintain and improve our international competitive position similar to its national security interests. In fact, without a capacity for new and high technologies, our defense capabilities also suffer.[66] There is a consensus on this among different sectors of the economy. This idea has two implications: (1) government policy has to direct investment in high technologies, which means that the U.S. government needs a body of experts from different fields of science and business who study, investigate, and forecast, on a regular basis, about new technologies on the horizon. At present this work is done, in a sporadic fashion, by the National Academy of Science and Engineering. There is a need to upgrade this function either through the national academy itself or by assigning this responsibility to a senior government office. We suggest that the Office of the Science Advisor to the President be upgraded to the level of the cabinet and assigned this task. Such an institutional arrangement would provide continuity, prestige, and resources for this task. The structure could be similar to The Council of Economic Advisors. This would not only provide the necessary information on a regular basis but also set the tone by providing important and relevant information. It would also promote policies for research in basic science.

(2) The U.S. government needs to develop a capacity to organize various corporations to cooperate in the promotion of technological advances, and even their eventual production if necessary in particular fields. This would involve some investment by the government itself as well as power to persuade corporations at the most senior level, the chief executive officers (CEOs). In fact, corporations should welcome such an initiative since it would avoid duplication of efforts and reduce risks. Given the need for large investment and shortage of supply of capital, a number of groups are suggesting that the government should provide funds and leadership. Groups of corporations, such as SEMATECH, suffer from the proverbial deficiency—too little and too late. Since the initiative of SEMATECH came from different private sources, most of their time and energy are spent in raising funds through the Congress and other corporations. By the time these arrangements are set up for actual business, competitors in other countries have already moved ahead. A department of government with a well-defined objective and responsibility would be more effective and efficient.

For example, an advisory committee on semiconductors is recommending that the government set up a mechanism to provide large help to this industry.[67] This is a function for the U.S. Department of Commerce, which already has an office, supervised by an assistant secretary, that deals with issues of technology and productivity. This office, however, is inadequate for this purpose. What is needed instead is the direct involvement of the secretary of commerce. There has to be a cell or a division in the U.S. Department of Commerce supervised directly by the secretary, whose function is to bring together various corporations and businesses with the clear object of promoting investment in particular technologies. If such a function is defined for the commerce secretary, it will be easy to move forward fast. Government's persuasive powers are at their best at the level of a secretary. This proposal also takes into consideration the issue of risk sharing suggested above. If these policy objectives are identified and institutional arrangements made, the United States should be able to channel investments in high technologies and regain its lead in the global market.

CONCLUSION

One of our empirical findings is that technological change in the U.S. high-technology sector is embodied in different inputs. We have used stock of R&D expenditures as a proxy variable for technological change. This finding is consistent with the idea of emerging technology regimes based on high technologies. We also found that the United States is losing its international competitiveness in the global market. According to our results, one way to strengthen U.S. competitiveness is to make investments in high technologies. We have analyzed some of the policy implications of these results.

The new techno-economic paradigm essentially depends on all the various stages in a process of technological change; namely invention, innovation, and diffusion. However, innovation and diffusion are now integrated. R&D deals with both these processes. A tax credit policy for investment in R&D is helpful in this process and we suggest the reintroduction of a tax credit in favor of genuine R&D that is sufficiently large to have an incentive value and sufficiently differential so that it can discriminate between useful and paper R&D. Over the past decades, the United States has developed an excellent infrastructure in basic and applied science in the form of university faculties. This infrastructure is in a process of decay, with a large detrimental impact on economic growth. Rebuilding this structure will take decades. Research funding for basic science has declined. The process for science funding has become counter productive, in the sense that more effort, money, resources, and time are being devoted while research output is declining. The system needs a change. We have outlined an approach to stop this counter productivity and decay with the objective of providing research funding to at least 50 percent of the proposals judged meritorious on scientific grounds. This suggestion is that, assuming additional funds are not available, the solution lies in reducing unnecessary costs. First, if overhead administrative costs at the university or research institution level are eliminated completely, it should double the funds available for real research. Second, charge outs can be easily eliminated. A rough guess is that these funds may be able to fund 10 percent of the accepted proposals. Third, at present, review process involves 10 to 12 expert readers with all sorts of implied costs. If these were reduced by half, approximately 10 percent of these proposals could be funded. Additionally, if proposals were funded for longer periods, the costs of administration would fall by at least another 10 percent. Finally, large chunks of funds that have been siphoned off should be returned to the basic research. With all these changes, the existing agencies with existing budgets should be able to perform their real function of promoting and enabling research activity.

Development activity relates to innovation and diffusion. There are three risks associated with such activity: (1) engineering a product, (2) winning a race, and (3) lack of appropriability. Engineering a product depends on the development of a team and needs a culture that values teams. Winning the race can be helped by the government purchase and import policies. There are limits to both these policies. Patent law attempts to protect appropriability, but it is neither sufficient nor relevant in high-technology regimes where maintaining secrecy about production techniques is impossible. This is perhaps the most serious risk in view of the essentiality and continuity of technical change.

Improvements in lack of appropriability require risk sharing by cooperative efforts. The market structure in the United States and its history of anti-trust laws are not helpful for promoting such cooperative investments and risk sharing. Japanese and European governments have initiated cooperative efforts with and for private corporations. The U.S. government should formulate a policy objective to promote technological change by bringing together U.S. firms for investment in high technologies. It would require an institutional framework whose underlying principles have to be: (1) high enough status to evoke cooperation and eventual compliance at the highest level of private industry, and (2) availability of sufficient resources to enable the taking of an initiative for starting an activity. The objectives of such an institution, which have to be well defined, are: (1) to encourage investment in high technologies and (2) to promote cooperative efforts among competing corporations so that risks can be shared. Both these objectives are necessary. We have offered specific suggestions. First, the Office of the Science Advisor to the President should be upgraded to the level of the cabinet, similar to the Council of Economic Advisors, and charged with the specific tasks of studying, investigating, and forecasting, on a regular basis, about new technologies on the horizon. Second, the secretary of the Department of Commerce should be charged with the task of promoting investment in high-technology industries by bringing together competing corporations in cooperative projects. These principles and institutional changes would promote technological change and investment in high technologies and enable the U.S. high-technology sector to grow and compete internationally.

NOTES

1. Thirtle and Ruttan (1987) refer to some of these.

2. Schumpeter was not interested in an analysis of the process of technological change. His objective was economic development itself. He distinguished these stages because he thought that the development process goes through various stages wherein a particular process of technological change becomes important.

3. Qureshi and Diwan (1990) suggest another intermediate stage between invention and innovation, which can be called pre-innovation and distinguished from innovation proper.

4. This is a question that faculty committees find extremely difficult to deal with in their deliberations on faculty appointments, promotions, and tenure. Similarly, the so-called peer groups evaluating research proposals at funding agencies face this issue. Convention has placed this decision in the hands of journal editors. Papers published in some particular journals are defined as extensions of the frontiers; not because these are genuine extensions to the frontier but because this has become the convention. Success here depends on the ethical standards of decision makers.

5. Research is an extremely complex phenomenon and its evaluation is fraught with all sorts of pitfalls. Considering good and path breaking ideas takes a good deal of time—decades; evaluation at the time of germination is often misleading. Some faculty feel that any evaluation criteria will have to depend either on simple indices such as number of publications, which is highly misleading, or on judgment of some people, which is basically political. Some suggest that the system of relating evaluation of research to faculty productivity has promoted simplistic and mechanistic research.

6. The National Science Foundation has reported that there is going to be a serious deficiency of U.S. Ph.D.s in science and engineering.

7. Schumpeter was perhaps the first economist to articulate a clear distinction among three parts of the technological change process; namely invention, innovation, and diffusion. "Invention to him was the act of conceiving a new product or process and solving the purely technical problems associated with its application. Innovation comprised the entrepreneurial function required to carry a new technical possibility into economic practice for the first time" Scherer (1980), p. 411.

8. "In the evolutionary process, as it is normally conceived in Schumpeterian economics, innovations are at the root of cyclical movements. The principal economic agent is the entrepreneur, who establishes new combinations by introducing new products as well as new production methods" Hanusch (1988), p. 2.

9. He later recognized the importance of big business and its capacity to introduce new innovations. However, he did seem to suggest that innovations in big business would occur with the emergence of new business leaders in the organization. Considering this idea, he introduced the concepts of "trustified capitalism" as against "competitive capitalism."

10. Galbraith (1967) introduced the idea of technostructure. There is a controversy about the relationship of innovative activity and firm size. This is an empirical question. The evidence seems to go in both directions. Diwan (1989) refers to this evidence. However, it is difficult to settle this controversy by empirical research because innovative activity is not easy to define empirically.

11. Schumpeter was not particularly interested in the issue of diffusion. He more or less assumed that once major innovations had taken place the force of market competition would ensure their diffusion.

12. Supplier firms are distinguished from user firms. In recent literature this distinction has been emphasized particularly with reference to the question of who promotes what innovative activity. Pavitt (1984) considers the role of supplier firms significant in advancing technological change.

13. Thirtle and Ruttan (1987) devote a good part of their essay to these issues.

14. A large part of the literature on technological change is based on this proposition although it is not explicitly stated. The argument is often phrased in terms of either neutral technological change or parallel shifts in the production function, particularly in empirical studies, partly because it is easier to develop an empirical methodology on this basis.

15. It has implications for theory, empirical analysis, and policy. This is a new proposition and little has been written on it.

16. Schumpeter can be understood in promoting the idea of a theory of evolution. This, certainly, is the contention of the neo-Schumpeterians. Nelson and Winter (1982) articulate this view point. It is still quite recent and needs to be subjected to detailed analysis and discussion.

17. Griliches (1980) and Terleckyj (1982b).

18. U.S. Department of Labor, Bureau of Labor Statistics (1989).

19. Some studies present a model in which R&D and other variables are jointly determined so that it is neither a cause nor an effect. Such studies are somewhat limited. Another set of studies and models present R&D as a dependent variable. The object of these studies, generally, is to explain R&D itself and not to discover a linkage between it and technological change. In many of these studies, R&D is considered synonymous with technological change.

20. "At last month's meeting of the National Institute of Child Health and Development advisory council, money available could fund only 13 percent of grants approved by the panels of experts judging research requests to the National Institute of Health. The National Institute for Neurologic Disease and Blindness will fund only 11 percent of approved grants, and reports from other N.I.H. institutes are equally bleak. This will seriously impair our biomedical research. These constraints come at a time of spectacular success for biomedical research" Letter to the Editor, "Give Us Biomedical Research, Not Bombs" *New York Times,* October 31, 1989 by Joseph B. Warshaw, M.D. pp. A26. Professor Warshaw is the Chairman of Pediatrics, Yale University School of Medicine.

21. Mansfield (1980) and Link (1978).

22. Interestingly, one major weakness of economic research is the virtual impossibility of replication of empirical results for lack of data availability. Economic journals do not value this scientific attitude.

23. Illich (1974) makes a persuasive case for congestion as a source of counterproductivity in many fields; automobiles on a road, education in schools.

24. Adams and Sveiskaskaus (1990) suggest that this infrastructure is one of the most important sources of economic growth even though its gestation period is around 20 years.

25. Diwan (1971b) argues that education is a source of increases in labor efficiency.

26. Bowen and Sosa (1989) have estimated the demand and supply of faculty in the next 5 years. They suggest a large shortfall.

27. Finding that professors are struggling to keep their research activity going, these students consider the hassles of professional life too risky and unrewarding. They therefore shy away from the advanced degree programs.

28. This is an extremely rough estimate, but the logic is simple. If current expenditures can fund 10 percent of the scientifically acceptable proposals, five times the current expenditures should be able to fund 50 percent of these proposals. The objective here is to

illustrate the principle rather than provide a fine tuned estimate. Such an estimate could easily be made by an interested office of a funding agency.

29. The government is already spending more on a bail out of the Savings and Loan institutions. This bail out is expected to cost more than half a trillion dollars. The government has come up with these funds even with the budget deficit. The interesting thing is that these bail-out funds have little growth potential for the economy. Some suggest that the peace dividend has already been mortgaged to the S&L bailout.

30. This course would involve a major policy change since it would have a profound impact on the administrative structure of universities and research institutions.

31. In fact, institutions charge overhead on charge outs. The costs are thus twice inflated. Incidentally, the bureaucracies of research institutions negotiate with those of funding agencies about the size of these charge outs and overheads.

32. On the assumption that a researcher charges out 25 percent of his/her time, 10 percent is an under estimate.

33. Highly skilled technicians are highly educated and generally have a M.S. degree or its equivalent in experience. The difference between such highly skilled technicians and research scientists is a matter of education and interest. The object here is to make a finer distinction between a research scientist and a highly skilled technician.

34. It will be appreciated that this is a somewhat heroic assumption similar to bigger is better. In some situations, quality of development and applied research may be more important than quantity.

35. It is commonplace to observe teams of scientists collected for particular tasks lying waste after there has been a change in priorities. Interdisciplinary teams were created under the Research Applied to National Needs (RANN) program in the NSF. But when the program was discontinued a major part of the research work done for a specific objective became obsolete. The one saving grace was that RANN funds did not cut deeply into funds generally available for what we have called the research infrastructure. The recent wave of actually shifting funds has had much more harmful effects.

36. Some parts of the R&D tax credits continued a little longer, for multi-nationals particularly. Allocation and apportionment of research expenses allowed multi-national corporations to make fuller use of their R&D tax credits based on foreign tax payments. This provision also expired in 1987.

37. Economists who consider the market as a regulator of investment decisions are not particularly fond of subsidies, even through taxes.

38. Congress considered the reintroduction of R&D tax credits in the fall of 1989 that would allow companies to take a 20 percent credit for annual increases in spending on research. Formulae for calculating eligible increases in spending have still to be worked out. "Lawmakers Are Scrambling to Save Tax Breaks," *New York Times,* November 15, 1989, p. D6. This is a step in the right direction but it is not clear whether it satisfies the principles laid down above.

39. In U.S. management circles, motivational force and intensity of identification has not been fully recognized.

40. Remember that Schumpeterian entrepreneurs are risk takers. Kaldor (1967) also argued in a similar vein when he suggested that economic growth depends on "animal spirits."

41. Reich (1987) finds it necessary to deal with culture as a whole.

42. This is particularly true of parts of some technological products. There is some concern in military circles that the United States may be losing its military independence as a result of its industry's incapability to produce goods needed for military purposes.

43. This is not the only objective of import duties. Another objective is to obtain a certain level of revenues for the government. In the context of our discussion, this is not a relevant objective. This has not been a major objective of the U.S. import policy.

44. What might seem like a success of patent policy was in fact the result of mass production techniques that required immense capital investments, which in turn provided somewhat monolopist or oligopolistic control to these producers.

45. Collusion among producers to raise prices and gouge consumers is as old as Adam Smith who stated that whenever producers meet together at a social gathering they end up making a pact for curtailing competition, raising prices, and lowering wages.

46. U.S. MEMORIES did not last long and died because of lack of finance and cooperation. SEMATECH still continues, however. It has not been able to get the level of support needed from the government.

47. This has similarities to the functioning of MITI in Japan.

48. It is not even clear if one can ever define long term. In Keynes language, "in the long run we are all dead."

49. On Friday, October 13, 1989, the New York Stock Market registered a 190.58 drop in the Dow Jones Industrial Averages in one and a half hours of trading before the close of the market. Financiers, central banks, and treasury departments in all the industrialized countries were jittery and were looking toward the Japanese Stock Market on Monday, the next trading day. The markets in Japan, Europe, and the United States seemed to be looking toward each other for signals.

50. This argument has been advanced by a number of scholars, such as Peters (1988) and Reich and Magaziner (1981).

51. Peters and Waterman (1982), Abernathy et al. (1983) have made a strong case against the business schools.

52. Galbraith (1967) is the most articulate exponent of this school.

53. Needless to say, this thesis is controversial. A number of economists do not accept it and question its various propositions.

54. One has only to read the daily newspapers to appreciate the merger mania that has been going on many years, locking up large sums of financial capital, raising costs and stock prices, adding to financial risk for productive enterprises, and making the climate for future investment unfavorable.

55. One may argue that the U.S. system is already adversarial. Although in form the relationship is quite adversarial, in practice industry, especially large corporations, wields enormous influence in government policy. This has been particularly true during Republican administrations. Because of this influence, U.S. industry has been able to consistently thwart legislation aimed at helping consumer interests.

56. Such a shift will be rather painful, causing unemployment and a decline in the standard of living.

57. There is however a controversy among economists about advertisement's capacity to increase aggregate demand for a product in general. This controversy has been particularly related to the effect of advertisement on cigarette smoking. Hamilton (1972) and Schmalensee (1972) argue that advertising affects shares between companies. Bishop and Yoo (1985) find that it also shifts the demand curve as a whole.

58. We are now witnessing similar negative effects of mass advertisements of political campaigns. It makes it difficult for decent, sincere candidates to get elected.

59. Studies by Carlsson (1989) and Zoltan and Audretsch (1988) confirm this evidence and refer to other such studies.

60. Even the conservative *Time* has now come to recognize how mistaken this idea is.

Its cover page headline reads, "Is Government Dead: Unwilling to lead, politicians are letting America slip into paralysis," *Time,* October 23, 1989. A short quote gives the flavor of this argument, "Surely he (Ronald Reagan) did not seriously propose to dismantle an institution that had brought the U.S. through two world wars, restored stability during the Depression and played a major part in developing one of the highest standards of living on earth. Or did he? If Washington was 'the problem' when Reagan took office in 1981, it looks like a costly irrelevancy today," p. 28.

61. Magaziner and Reich (1983) make a persuasive case in this direction.

62. These were reported in the *New York Times,* "Europeans Are Working Together to Compete with Japan and the U.S." August 21, 1989, p. D8.

63. The U.S. government is thinking in terms of setting up a 59-mile collider in Texas, but financing this joint project is problematic. The actual laboratory, if it comes into existence, is still years away.

64. "Cooperation sometimes forces you to accept that the other guy might have a better idea than you do. . . . Cooperative research mixes cultures and is effective in fighting inbreeding" *New York Times,* August 21, 1989, "Europeans Are Working Together to Compete with Japan and the U.S.," p. D8.

65. "Despite the problems, Europe's push for cooperation has caught the eye of many American officials and companies, and there is increasing talk about seeking to imitate the Europeans," *ibid.*

66. U.S. firms are reportedly using foreign subcontractors to provide necessary parts and materials for U.S. weapons, making the defense system vulnerable. Some Japanese authors even suggest that Japan determines the balance of power between the United States and the Union of Soviet Socialist Republics by virtue of its strength and advances in electronic technology.

67. "In a report that will be delivered to the President this week, a national advisory committee on semiconductors will recommend that the Government establish a multibillion-dollar venture capital operation intended to resurrect the American consumer electronics industry," "U.S. Aid Sought for Electronics," *New York Times,* October 30, 1989, p. D1.

10

Conclusions

Half a century ago, after the Second World War, the United States emerged as the largest and fastest growing economy in the world. It was an undisputed world leader with little competition from any quarter. However, in these fifty years, technology and the world economy has undergone major changes. Two major countries that lost the war have experienced high growth rates in their GNP and exports so that they are now serious competitors in the world markets. Also new technologies are emerging and developing a new technology regime. This technology regime is radically different from the earlier technology regime identified by mass production technologies. The new technology regime is international in character and is conducive to the emergence of a global market, particularly in new technologies.

The question is whether the United States can maintain its competitive strength in the global market. There are various responses to this question. This book starts with the assumption, on which there is now a wide consensus, that manufacturing generally, and high technologies particularly, are important, even essential, for the maintenance of U.S. economic health and international competitiveness. Accordingly, this book analyzes high-technology industries in the United States in great detail. It places the high-technology issue in its larger context. It makes the first attempt to define a U.S. high-tech sector in terms of output and important inputs over the historical period of 1967 to 1982. The year 1967 is perhaps the beginning when high-tech industries could be considered separately from manufacturing in general. The series ends in 1982 because detailed data needed for such definitions are not available beyond that and some of these data have not been collected—a casualty of budget cuts in the last decade. It analyzes these historical times series data for changes in productivity through a translog cost function.

The quantitative information presented here confirms the view that the United States has historically had a competitive advantage in high-technology production. Several indicators reveal that high-technology industries have been a source of strength in the overall U.S. manufacturing trade balance. The products of these industries comprise an increasing proportion of U.S. exports. There has been a trade surplus in high-technology products over virtually the whole period. The United States still maintains a strong competitive advantage in high-technology trade and exports. It is still the largest exporter both in terms of the world trade and in the third country market.

In recent years, however, there has been a noticeable shift in the pattern of trade in high-technology products. There are several indications that the U.S. dominance in world trade of high-technology products is beginning to erode. Since the U.S. domestic markets form a large part of the global market, these trends affect the production and sale of high-technology goods in domestic market as well. Import penetration ratios suggest that virtually every industry is feeling the heat of international competition. The U.S. market share both in world exports and third country exports has been declining. The primary source of competition in the world market is Japan, and in the third country market, West Germany and France. For the United States to gain back its world shares, it is necessary to promote high-technology industries. To develop meaningful policies, it is useful to analyze its structure of production and nature of technological change.

There are various productivity concepts; the most common are partial and total factor productivity. There are various approaches to the measurement of these concepts; namely econometric, index number, and non-parametric. Total factor productivity is a form of technological change. Technological change is either neutral, representing shifts in production or cost functions, or embodied in different factors of production that change the slope of the isoquants. All measures of productivity and technological change are based on assumptions, implicit or explicit, about the form of a production function or its dual, a cost function. Neoclassical production functions are based on stringent assumptions about separability of inputs, input aggregation, and the relevant form of a measure of output, gross or value added. Various forms of production functions, such as the CES and the VES, have been estimated. To relax some stringent conditions, duality-based production functions have been developed. The translog cost function follows from the duality theory. Its estimation still involves stringent conditions regarding homogeneity, separability, and homotheticity. To estimate the parameters of these functions, we have first to develop data series on output and input prices in the U.S. high-tech sector.

Because this study is the first to provide time series data set for the U.S. high-technology sector it defines, for the first time, the U.S. high-tech sector historically. The high-tech sector forms more than one-fifth to one-fourth of the U.S. manufacturing sector, and this proportion is increasing. We have developed these data set for the U.S. high-technology sector for the period 1967–1982, because

1967 marks the beginning of a trade surplus in high-technology goods while 1982 is the last year for which data, at the level of detail with which we have worked, are available. In our data set we quantify all the important concepts in production theory: output, capital, labor, materials, and research and development, and divide labor further into skilled and unskilled. Our data set provides data for both quantities and prices of these variables and a time series of unit costs and cost shares of labor, capital, and materials. For R&D we quantify a stock concept. These data have been divided into four periods on the basis of GNP peaks in 1969, 1973, and 1979 in order to facilitate a comparative analysis of business cycles as well as the upswing and downswing phases of a cycle. These periods are (1) 1967–1969, representing an upswing, (2) 1969–1973, a business cycle, (3) 1973–1979, a business cycle, and (4) 1979–1982, reflecting a downswing phase.

Our findings are that high-technology sector output conforms to the business cycle of the U.S. GNP. The mean value of this output, in terms of 1972 constant dollars, is $163 billion with a maximum of $228 billion. There is large variability in output over the years. By comparison, variability in inputs is low. The growth path of materials and total labor is cyclical, consistent with output cycles. Average employment during this period is 4 million workers with a maximum of 4.6. Employment has not been growing; however, our findings reveal little cycles in skilled labor employment, and an increase of the share of skilled labor in total labor. In recent years it forms an even larger part. Capital and materials each form 40 percent of costs, the remaining 20 percent being due to labor.

Output in the U.S. high-tech sector has been growing at an average 3 percent per year rate. Materials are growing at double this rate and capital at 4 percent per year, so that output is becoming capital and material intensive. Employment, on the other hand, has been stagnant. The largest contribution to growth in output comes from materials and a lesser one from total factor productivity. Labor productivity has been growing at a rate of 3.5 percent per year. Here too, the major source contributing to this growth is materials. Material productivity, on the other hand, has been declining. These are consistent with casual observations. The behavior over the two business cycles and their different phases is different. Total factor productivity played a major role in the 1967–1969 upswing. Part of the reason that total factor productivity does not contribute to growth may be that technological change is embodied in capital and labor.

We designed tests in two different sequences to choose the maintained hypothesis, and among the four models tested, our test statistics accepts the least restrictive model of a translog function with non-neutral technological change. Accordingly, we estimated a translog cost function with three inputs, capital, labor, and material. We also had a semi-shift variable in stock of R&D as a proxy for technological change. In view of the clear data shifts after 1972, we designed a dummy variable that takes the value zero for 1969 to 1972 and one for 1973 onward. These two variables defined our augmented translog cost function. We estimated this function for the U.S. high-tech sector for the period 1967–1982, spanning two business cycles, one upswing and another downswing, and obtained acceptable results both from statistical and *a priori* expectations.

We found that own elasticities of input substitution are elastic. Own elasticity of materials, numerically, is the highest and that of capital the lowest. Own elasticities of materials and capital move opposite to each other over time. Substitution elasticity for materials falls over the period, while that of capital rises. Cross elasticity for capital-labor switches sign over the period, implying a change in the relationship from substitution to complementarity. We decomposed the input labor into skilled and unskilled workers and reestimated the translog cost function, to further verify these results and found that our estimates for disaggregated labor confirmed earlier results. The own elasticities become more elastic. Cross elasticity between capital and skilled labor implies a relationship of complementarity. The relationship between capital and unskilled labor is substitution.

Our empirical results confirmed our hypothesis about non-neutral technological change, which implies embodied technological change. For the case of aggregate labor, neutral technological change had a coefficient of -0.03, implying a cost reduction of 3 percent per year. When we decomposed labor into skilled and unskilled labor, this number fell to -0.015; shifts in cost function reduced cost by much less. When we estimated the coefficient for biased technological change, we obtained the value as -0.06, implying that embodied technological change reduces costs by 6 per cent per year; twice the rate of neutral shifts in the cost function.

The costs of production have gone up by 7.5 percent per year. Although wage costs have gone up, the cost due to labor input has gone down, implying reduction in employment. Growth in materials costs explain 57 percent of the growth in total cost. This is due to an increase in both the price and quantity of materials input. Materials costs have grown over time; capital costs have declined.

The empirical finding that capital and labor in the U.S. high-tech sector have become complements over time is interesting. When labor input was disaggregated between skilled and unskilled labor, we found that capital is a substitute for unskilled labor but a complement to skilled labor. Capital-skilled labor complementarity is an important finding since it has large policy implications. At a theoretical level, it raises serious questions about many theorems in neoclassical economics, which are based on the assumption of capital-labor substitution. There are few economic theorems that assume, or can deal with, capital-labor complementarity. At a paradigm level, this finding questions the proposition that labor is a cost; a paradigm consistent with the mass production techno-economic paradigm of the past.

Capital-labor complementarity implies a new paradigm that labor is an asset. This is consistent with the new emerging high technology–based regime. Our other finding is that growth of the U.S. high-tech sector is associated with the growth of the proportion of skilled labor in total labor force, it being both a cause and effect. Policies to promote the U.S. high-tech sector then need to encourage skill formation. Skill formation follows from quality and availability of education. The U.S. education system at the high school level is now in crisis. At college and university levels, curricula need to be directed toward hands on experience in engineering and greater emphasis on international studies. Skill formation also entails training. In the current U.S. economic system, training is a free good so that no individual employer is willing to provide it. We offered the suggestion that management needs to set up a special fund for the training and retraining of its workers, a fund sufficient to provide meaningful training to the majority of willing workers, which could amount to at least 20 percent. Because individual employers would most likely be unwilling to allocate these resources, we suggest that training facilities be set up jointly by firms through their industry associations, which would need to expand their activities to set up training institutes. Once this principle is accepted, it should not be difficult to fill in the practical details for these training institutes.

Beyond skill formation, what is needed is a change in societal values concerning the nature of work. Work in our society is considered derogatory. In high-technology regimes, work can be perceived as satisfying in view of the realization of a person's intelligence potential. Societal values are related to a worker's perception of self-worth. The low esteem that many workers in America have of themselves follows mostly from the rules of the game in production where they have no part in decision making and where reward structures do not reflect inputs of effort. To improve reward structure and motivate work effort, we suggest the institutionalization of a bonus system for production teams, where teams in turn distribute the bonus among their members on well-defined criteria related directly to productivity levels.

The institutional framework that places all decision making authority in the hands of top management is inconsistent with our findings of capital-labor complementarity and inimical to the growth potential of high technology. We suggest a different institutional framework, one that places team work in the center of the production process and changes hierarchical decision making processes by worker participation, as necessary for the growth of the U.S. high-tech sector.

One of our empirical findings is that technological change in the U.S. high-technology sector is embodied in different inputs. We have used a stock of R&D expenditures as a proxy variable for technological change. This finding is consistent with the idea of emerging technology regimes based on high technologies. We also found that the U.S. is losing its international competitiveness in the global market. According to our results, one way to strengthen the U.S. competitiveness is to make investments in high technologies.

The new techno-economic paradigm essentially depends on all the various stages in a process of technological change; namely, invention, innovation, and diffusion. However, innovation and diffusion are now integrated. Because R&D deals with both these processes, we suggest a tax credit policy that encourages investment in R&D organized in a way that favors the development of the high-tech sector.

Another problem that seriously threatens the U.S. economy is the recent decay of the infrastructure that accomplishes research in basic and applied science, the university faculties. A cause of the decay of this infrastructure is the decline of research funding for basic science. In addition, the procedure for acquiring science funding has become counter productive in the sense that more effort, money, resources, and time are being devoted to the search for funding while research output is declining. To halt the decay, we recommend providing research funding to at least 50 percent of the proposals judged scientifically meritorious. Assuming additional funds are not available, this could be achieved by eliminating unnecessary costs, including overhead administrative costs at universities and research institutions, which could double available funds, and charge outs, the elimination of which could fund 10 percent of acceptable proposals. In addition, halving the number of expert readers in the review process could fund another 10 percent of proposals and funding proposals for longer periods could cut administrative costs at least another 10 percent. Finally funds siphoned off for "specific studies" should be returned to basic research. With these changes, existing agencies with existing budgets should be able to promote and enable essential research.

Development activity, which relates to innovation and diffusion, involves three risks: engineering a product, winning a race, and lack of appropriability. Engineering a product depends upon the development of a team and needs a culture that values teams, whereas winning the race can best be ensured by government purchase and import policies. Both of these policies, however, have limits. Patent law's attempts to protect appropriability are neither sufficient nor relevant in high-technology regimes where maintaining secrecy about production techniques is impossible. In view of the essentiality and continuity of technological change, this is perhaps the most serious risk.

A resolution to the lack of appropriability problem requires risk sharing and cooperative investments, elements that neither the market structure in the United States nor its history of anti-trust laws have helped to promote. On the other hand, Japanese and European governments have initiated cooperative efforts with, and for, private corporations. The U.S. government needs to formulate policy objectives to promote technological change by bringing together U.S. firms for investment in high technologies. Achieving this end would require an institutional framework with (1) high enough status to evoke cooperation and eventual compliance at the highest level of private industry, and (2) availability of sufficient resources to enable the taking of an initiative for starting an activity. The objective of such an institution should be to encourage investment in high technologies, and to promote cooperative efforts among competing corporations so that risks an be shared. Both these objectives are necessary and we have suggested that the Office of the Science Advisor to the President be upgraded to the level of the cabinet, similar to the Council of Economic Advisors, and charged with the specific tasks of studying, investigating, and forecasting new technologies on a regular basis. In addition, the secretary of the Department of

Commerce should undertake the task of promoting investment in high-technology industries by bringing competing corporations together in cooperative projects. These principles and institutional changes would promote technological change and investment in high technologies that would enable the U.S. high-technology sector to grow and compete internationally.

Appendix Tables

Table A1
Output and Inputs in U.S. High-Technology Sector: 1967–1982
(Billion Dollars)

Year	Output	Capital*	Total Wage	Production Worker Wage	Non-Production Worker Wage	Material
1967	109.88	48.33	25.91	15.99	9.92	35.64
1968	118.22	51.44	26.53	16.19	10.34	40.25
1969	125.18	60.47	24.70	17.54	7.16	40.01
1970	123.17	60.79	22.94	16.96	5.98	39.44
1971	122.99	58.44	25.14	16.17	8.97	39.41
1972	135.58	47.14	34.39	17.22	17.17	54.05
1973	156.80	54.76	38.25	19.45	18.80	63.79
1974	188.69	67.45	42.00	21.09	20.91	79.24
1975	191.06	67.42	42.51	20.37	22.14	81.13
1976	218.69	80.81	46.03	22.11	23.92	91.85
1977	252.38	94.38	52.00	25.30	26.70	106.00
1978	287.70	105.09	59.71	29.27	30.44	122.90
1979	339.65	127.29	67.66	33.47	34.19	144.70
1980	386.01	147.71	75.00	36.63	38.37	163.30
1981	425.10	166.55	85.75	39.83	45.90	172.80
1982	402.55	134.78	90.87	36.63	54.24	175.90

*Current dollar value of output is equivalent to capital cost and is taken to be defined as a residual. Written in equation form, cost of capital = total cost − total wage − total material cost.

Table A2
Output, Capital, Material, and R&D in U.S. High-Technology Sector:
1967–1982 (Billions of Constant Dollars)

Year	Total Output	Capital*	Material	Research and Development*
1967	119.93	52.75	42.01	46.56
1968	127.94	52.87	46.24	49.14
1969	133.88	56.21	44.45	50.95
1970	126.77	59.04	41.96	52.56
1971	123.85	61.16	40.53	53.50
1972	135.58	63.09	54.05	54.61
1973	152.89	65.60	54.05	55.85
1974	158.07	69.49	52.79	56.92
1975	139.89	72.61	46.49	57.93
1976	154.32	73.90	49.17	60.01
1977	172.90	79.40	53.00	62.14
1978	191.12	83.38	57.73	63.34
1979	211.62	88.48	57.90	65.65
1980	225.76	95.97	59.47	67.16
1981	227.69	102.20	56.67	70.30
1982	211.91	107.80	58.27	74.03

*Both capital and research and development are stock values.

231

Table A3
Workers and Work Hours in U.S. High-Technology Sector: 1967–1982
(In Millions)

Year	Total Labor	Total Work Hour	No. of Production Worker	Production Worker Hour	No. of Non-Production Worker*	Non-Production Worker Hour*
1967	4.06	8.57	2.41	4.99	1.66	3.58
1968	4.20	8.71	2.18	4.78	2.02	3.93
1969	4.18	8.84	2.39	4.93	1.78	3.91
1970	3.96	8.30	2.20	4.47	1.76	3.83
1971	3.63	7.59	1.86	3.98	1.77	3.61
1972	3.66	7.68	2.04	3.99	1.61	3.69
1973	3.92	8.24	2.20	4.06	1.71	4.18
1974	4.02	8.40	2.22	4.31	1.79	4.09
1975	3.70	7.68	1.95	3.57	1.75	4.11
1976	3.76	7.86	1.97	3.79	1.78	4.07
1977	3.93	8.24	2.03	4.15	1.89	4.09
1978	4.18	8.81	2.26	4.33	1.92	4.48
1979	4.23	9.43	2.28	4.63	1.94	4.80
1980	4.57	9.57	2.38	4.57	2.18	5.00
1981	4.60	9.63	2.33	4.50	2.26	5.13
1982	4.46	9.24	2.38	4.57	2.07	4.67

*Number and hours of non-production workers are residual measures. Number of non-production workers is measured by the difference between total labor and number of production workers. Non-production worker hours , is measured by the difference between total work-hour and production worker hour.

232

Table A4

Price Indices of Output and Inputs in U.S. High-Technology Sector: 1967–1982 (1967 = 100)

Year	Price of Output*	Price of Capital*	Price of Total Labor**	Price of Production Worker**	Price of Non-Production Worker**	Price of Material*
1967	100.00	100.00	100.00	100.00	100.00	100.00
1968	100.85	106.19	98.98	111.89	85.19	102.32
1969	102.05	117.42	92.59	110.43	66.68	107.28
1970	106.04	112.38	90.77	116.14	56.55	109.64
1971	108.39	104.29	108.52	130.83	84.44	111.42
1972	109.15	81.55	147.23	126.61	177.38	113.23
1973	111.94	91.11	152.90	133.01	182.32	117.27
1974	130.29	105.94	163.72	142.67	194.09	125.73
1975	149.07	101.34	180.03	157.54	210.32	132.01
1976	154.67	119.35	191.83	168.66	223.03	131.40
1977	154.67	129.74	207.34	187.03	234.87	135.45
1978	159.32	137.57	223.84	195.12	263.86	144.68
1979	164.29	157.02	250.63	220.68	292.55	157.38
1980	175.18	167.99	257.15	231.77	291.74	169.96
1981	186.63	177.86	292.10	256.78	337.72	183.67
1982	207.34	136.46	319.25	231.77	434.20	195.54

* Price is measured by the ratio between current dollar value and constant dollar value.
**Price is obtained by dividing the total wage for the category of labor by the number of workers in the particular, category.

233

Table A5
Cost Shares of Inputs in the U.S. High-Technology Sector: 1967–1982

Year	Share of Capital	Share of Material	Share of Production Worker	Share of Non-Production Worker
1967	0.4398	0.3244	0.1455	0.0903
1968	0.4351	0.3405	0.1370	0.0875
1969	0.4831	0.3196	0.1401	0.0572
1970	0.4936	0.3202	0.1377	0.0486
1971	0.4752	0.3204	0.1315	0.0729
1972	0.3477	0.3987	0.1270	0.1266
1973	0.3492	0.4068	0.1240	0.1199
1974	0.3757	0.4199	0.1118	0.1108
1975	0.3529	0.4246	0.1066	0.1159
1976	0.3695	0.4200	0.1011	0.1084
1977	0.3740	0.4200	0.1003	0.1058
1978	0.3653	0.4272	0.1017	0.1058
1979	0.3748	0.4260	0.0985	0.1007
1980	0.3827	0.4281	0.0949	0.0994
1981	0.3918	0.4065	0.0937	0.1079
1982	0.3348	0.4395	0.0909	0.1347

Note: Share of an input is defined as the ratio between current dollar value of the input concerned and the total cost.

Table B1
Coefficients of Translog Cost Function for U.S. High Technology

Coefficients	Model I	Model II	Model III	Model IV
a_0	-0.06883	-0.06623	-0.06925	-0.08158
	(0.0083)	(0.0089)	(0.0124)	(0.0098)
a_K	0.37449	0.37333	0.38407	0.38700
	(0.0035)	(0.0043)	(0.0107)	(0.0109)
a_L	0.21752	0.21178	0.22119	0.21678
	(0.0024)	(0.0035)	(0.0046)	(0.0045)
a_M	0.40799	0.41489	0.39474	0.39622
	(0.0038)	(0.0035)	(0.0110)	(0.0111)
a_R	-0.01421	-0.01229	-0.01124	-0.01322
	(0.0517)	(0.0529)	(0.0735)	(0.0741)
a_{RR}	-1.5206	-2.2349	-1.7023	---
	(0.6507)	(0.7331)	(1.0292)	
a_{KK}	0.20618	0.20756	0.03799	---
	(0.0447)	(0.0316)	(0.0134)	
a_{KL}	-0.14477	-0.14402	-0.03799	---
	(0.0223)	(0.0141)	(0.0134)	
a_{KM}	-0.05141	-0.06354	---	---
	(0.0447)	(0.0316)		
a_{KR}	0.05795	---		---
	(0.0447)			
a_{LL}	0.04855	-0.03018	0.03799	---
	(0.0158)	(0.0115)	(0.013361)	
a_{LM}	0.10622	0.17420	---	---
	(0.0227)	(0.0140)		

(continued)

Table B1
(Continued)

Coefficients	Model I	Model II	Model III	Model IV
a_{LR}	-0.16235	---	---	---
	(0.0274)			
a_{MM}	-0.05481	-0.11066	---	---
	(0.0406)	(0.0330)		
a_{MR}	0.10440	---	---	---
	(0.0396)			
Log of Likelihood	126.20	121.42	98.42	95.86

Table B2
Coefficients for Translog Production Function for U.S. High Technology

Coefficient	Model I	Model II	Model III	Model IV
a_0	0.23053	0.24204	0.19337	0.22678
	(0.0035)	(0.0038)	(0.0073)	(0.0091)
a_K	0.22758	0.25025	0.39575	0.33858
	(0.0141)	(0.0113)	(0.0118)	(0.0118)
a_L	0.18425	0.11608	0.16790	0.17923
	(0.0123)	(0.0087)	(0.0052)	(0.0055)
a_M	0.58817	0.63367	0.43635	0.49219
	(0.0110)	(0.0083)	(0.0159)	(0.0177)
a_R	0.27009	0.44302	0.38997	1.0686
	(0.0279)	(0.0215)	(0.0318)	(0.0498)
a_{RR}	-0.78133	-1.8462	-1.19650	---
	(0.2643)	(0.2849)	(0.3744)	
a_{KK}	0.01894	-0.13343	0.07637	---
	(0.0644)	(0.0241)	(0.0259)	
a_{KL}	0.14685	0.22716	-0.07637	---
	(0.0632)	(0.0224)	(0.0259)	
a_{KM}	-0.16579	-0.09373	---	---
	(0.0282)	(0.0141)		
a_{KR}	-0.08771	---	---	---
	(0.0894)			
a_{LL}	-0.14373	-0.07159	0.07637	---
	(0.0655)	(0.0291)	(0.0259)	
a_{LM}	-0.00312	-0.15557	---	---
	(0.0257)	(0.0198)		

(continued)

237

Table B2
(*Continued*)

Coefficient	Model I	Model II	Model III	Model IV
a_{LR}	-0.29717	---	---	---
	(0.0896)			
a_{MM}	0.16891	0.24930	---	---
	(0.0249)	(0.0198)		
a_{MR}	0.38488	---	---	---
	(0.0494)			
Log of Likelihood	115.73	109.97	89.60	83.68

Table C1
Elasticities of Substitution for Model with Aggregated Labor

Year	Own Elasticities*			Cross Elasticities**		
	σ_{KK}	σ_{MM}	σ_{LL}	σ_{LK}	σ_{LM}	σ_{KM}
1967	-1.0719	-2.2569	-1.3519	0.2174	0.6879	1.2955
1968	-1.0922	-2.0949	-1.3705	0.1688	0.6875	1.2846
1969	-0.9029	-2.3077	-1.3703	0.1485	0.6215	1.2730
1970	-0.8660	-2.3013	-1.3941	0.1170	0.5997	1.2667
1971	-0.9318	-2.2989	-1.3785	0.1644	0.6355	1.2769
1972	-1.5535	-1.6235	-1.3100	0.0797	0.7639	1.3041
1973	-1.5436	-1.5686	-1.3344	0.0473	0.7594	1.2967
1974	-1.4423	-1.4849	-1.3727	-0.0200	0.7446	1.2808
1975	-1.5207	-1.4564	-1.3728	-0.0337	0.7473	1.2813
1976	-1.4206	-1.4846	-1.3803	-0.0435	0.7299	1.2716
1977	-1.3952	-1.4846	-1.3794	-0.0533	0.7241	1.2684
1978	-1.4453	-1.4411	-1.3799	-0.0702	0.7307	1.2702
1979	-1.1323	-1.7985	-1.3732	-0.0437	0.6802	1.2640
1980	-1.3469	-1.4660	-1.3646	-0.0915	0.7096	1.2624
1981	-1.2983	-1.5707	-1.3762	-0.0269	0.7088	1.2647
1982	-1.6387	-1.3703	-1.3688	-0.0737	0.7593	1.2865

* σ_{ii} = Own elasticity of substitution for ith input.

** σ_{ij} = Cross elasticity of substitution between ith and jth input. $(i \neq j)$.

Table C2
Elasticities of Substitution for Model with Disaggregated Labor

| | Own Elasticities | | | |
Year	σ_{KK}	σ_{MM}	σ_{UU}	σ_{NN}
1967	-1.5357	-2.4738	-7.3264	-3.5911
1968	-1.5661	-2.2917	-7.9441	-3.5233
1969	-1.2875	-2.5310	-7.7055	-0.3238
1970	-1.2344	-2.5238	-7.8865	2.8285
1971	-1.3292	-2.5211	-8.3883	-2.7734
1972	-2.2957	-1.7670	-8.7827	-3.6004
1973	-2.2793	-1.7064	-9.0637	-3.6633
1974	-2.1945	-1.6143	-10.4120	-3.7195
1975	-2.0412	-1.5829	-11.0890	-3.6931
1976	-2.0777	-1.6139	-11.9050	-3.7274
1977	-2.0368	-1.6139	-12.0400	-3.7295
1978	-2.1178	-1.5662	-11.8050	-3.7295
1979	-1.6267	-1.9609	-12.3200	-3.7175
1980	-1.9597	-1.5934	-12.9590	-3.7247
1981	-1.8828	-1.7088	-13.7100	-3.5101
1982	-2.4391	-1.4884	-6.4808	-2.5553

Cross Elasticities*

Year	σ_{UK}	σ_{NK}	σ_{UM}	σ_{NM}	σ_{UN}	σ_{KM}
1967	0.9418	−0.6082	1.7843	1.4610	0.8097	0.9339
1968	0.9375	−0.6780	1.7940	1.4534	0.7912	0.9364
1969	0.9450	−1.3116	1.8266	1.7385	0.6880	0.9389
1970	0.9452	−1.6651	1.8396	1.8684	0.6260	0.9403
1971	0.9404	−0.8428	1.8788	1.5777	0.7392	0.9381
1972	0.9157	−0.4503	1.7311	1.2674	0.8445	0.9320
1973	0.9141	−0.5251	1.7336	1.2768	0.8319	0.9337
1974	0.9068	−0.6120	1.7887	1.2901	0.7981	0.9372
1975	0.9011	−0.5617	1.8177	1.2744	0.7976	0.9371
1976	0.9004	−0.5799	1.8718	1.2939	0.7739	0.9393
1977	0.9007	−0.6142	1.8792	1.3038	0.7642	0.9400
1978	0.8999	−0.6524	1.8518	1.2987	0.7677	0.9396
1979	0.9113	−0.4891	2.0024	1.3579	0.7479	0.9410
1980	0.8975	−0.5456	1.9222	1.2956	0.7559	0.9418
1981	0.8956	−0.2097	2.0009	1.2465	0.7960	0.9408
1982	0.9303	−0.0948	1.5282	1.1458	0.9256	0.9359

*σ_{ij} = Cross elasticity of substitution between ith and jth inputs.

Table C3
Elasticities of Factor Demand for Model with Aggregated Labor

Year	Own Elasticities*		
	ξ_{LL}	ξ_{KK}	ξ_{MM}
1967	−0.3187	−0.4714	−0.7320
1968	−0.3076	−0.4752	−0.7132
1969	−0.2704	−0.4361	−0.7375
1970	−0.2498	−0.4274	−0.7368
1971	−0.2817	−0.4427	−0.7366
1972	−0.3322	−0.5401	−0.6471
1973	−0.3255	−0.5390	−0.6381
1974	−0.3055	−0.5334	−0.6235
1975	−0.3054	−0.5365	−0.6184
1976	−0.2905	−0.5249	−0.6235
1977	−0.2842	−0.5217	−0.6235
1978	−0.2863	−0.5279	−0.6156
1979	−0.2735	−0.4824	−0.6740
1980	−0.2651	−0.5154	−0.6201
1981	−0.2776	−0.5086	−0.6384
1982	−0.3089	−0.5486	−0.6021

* ξ_{ii} = Elasticity of demand for the ith input.

Cross Elasticities*

Year	ξ_{LK}	ξ_{KL}	ξ_{LM}	ξ_{ML}	ξ_{KM}	ξ_{MK}
1967	0.0954	0.0511	0.2231	0.1622	0.4201	0.5698
1968	0.0732	0.0377	0.2341	0.1543	0.4375	0.5589
1969	0.0715	0.0292	0.1986	0.1226	0.4068	0.6149
1970	0.0575	0.0217	0.1920	0.1117	0.4056	0.6252
1971	0.0779	0.0335	0.2036	0.1299	0.4091	0.6067
1972	0.0275	0.0201	0.3045	0.1937	0.5199	0.4534
1973	0.0163	0.0114	0.3089	0.1852	0.5275	0.4528
1974	−0.0073	−0.0045	0.3127	0.1657	0.5378	0.4578
1975	−0.0120	−0.0076	0.3173	0.1662	0.5440	0.4521
1976	−0.0162	−0.0092	0.3065	0.1536	0.5340	0.4698
1977	−0.0201	−0.0110	0.3041	0.1492	0.5327	0.4743
1978	−0.0259	−0.0147	0.3121	0.1516	0.5425	0.4639
1979	0.0184	0.0086	0.2549	0.1355	0.4737	0.5385
1980	−0.0352	−0.0178	0.3002	0.1378	0.5332	0.4823
1981	−0.0107	−0.0053	0.2881	0.1430	0.5140	0.4954
1982	−0.0248	−0.0167	0.3337	0.1714	0.5653	0.4307

* ξ_{ij} $(i \neq j)$ = Cross elasticity of demand for ith and jth input.

243

Table C4
Elasticities of Factor Demand for Model with Disaggregated Labor

	Own Elasticities			
Year	ξ_{KK}	ξ_{MM}	ξ_{UU}	ξ_{NN}
1967	-0.3851	-0.8023	-1.0661	-0.3242
1968	-0.3879	-0.7802	-1.0797	-0.3081
1969	-0.3577	-0.8092	-1.0801	-0.0287
1970	-0.3575	-0.8089	-1.0797	-0.0185
1971	-0.3504	-0.8081	-1.0860	0.1373
1972	-0.3627	-0.8087	-1.1028	-0.2022
1973	-0.4308	-0.7044	-1.1155	-0.4559
1974	-0.4302	-0.6942	-1.1243	-0.4392
1975	-0.4271	-0.6779	-1.1638	-0.4121
1976	-0.4289	-0.6721	-1.1823	-0.4279
1977	-0.4221	-0.6778	-1.2035	-0.4073
1978	-0.4239	-0.6690	-1.2010	-0.3945
1979	-0.3932	-0.7349	-1.2140	-0.3742
1980	-0.4161	-0.6741	-1.2297	-0.3688
1981	-0.4116	-0.6946	-1.2398	-0.4024
1982	-0.4352	-0.6540	-1.2475	-0.4729

Cross Elasticities

Year	ξ_{KM}	ξ_{MK}	ξ_{KU}	ξ_{UK}	ξ_{KN}	ξ_{NK}
1967	0.3029	0.4108	0.1371	0.4144	-0.0547	-0.2668
1968	0.3188	0.4074	0.1284	0.4081	-0.0591	-0.2943
1969	0.3001	0.4535	0.1324	0.4566	-0.0748	-0.6325
1970	0.3011	0.4641	0.1302	0.4666	-0.0807	-0.8205
1971	0.3006	0.4457	0.1236	0.4470	-0.0613	-0.3996
1972	0.3715	0.3240	0.1163	0.3185	-0.0568	-0.1561
1973	0.3798	0.3260	0.1134	0.3194	-0.0627	-0.1828
1974	0.3936	0.3350	0.1014	0.3243	-0.0676	-0.2182
1975	0.3979	0.3306	0.0961	0.3181	-0.0649	-0.1977
1976	0.3945	0.3470	0.0910	0.3329	-0.0632	-0.2137
1977	0.3948	0.3515	0.0903	0.3370	-0.0648	-0.2291
1978	0.4013	0.3432	0.0916	0.3289	-0.0688	-0.2377
1979	0.3526	0.4008	0.0898	0.3884	-0.0490	-0.2077
1980	0.3984	0.3603	0.0852	0.3436	-0.0673	-0.2591
1981	0.3824	0.3686	0.0842	0.3523	-0.0548	-0.1991
1982	0.4113	0.3133	0.0799	0.2941	-0.0558	-0.1386

Table C4
(Continued)

Cross Elasticities

Year	ξ_{MU}	ξ_{UM}	ξ_{MN}	ξ_{NM}	ξ_{UN}	ξ_{NU}
1967	0.2595	0.5786	0.1319	0.4738	0.0731	0.1178
1968	0.2456	0.6106	0.1271	0.4948	0.0692	0.1083
1969	0.2558	0.5836	0.0994	0.5556	0.0393	0.0964
1970	0.2532	0.5889	0.0907	0.5982	0.0303	0.0862
1971	0.2469	0.6018	0.1150	0.5055	0.0539	0.0971
1972	0.2198	0.6899	0.1605	0.5052	0.1069	0.1072
1973	0.2149	0.7051	0.1530	0.5194	0.0997	0.1031
1974	0.1998	0.7509	0.1429	0.5417	0.0884	0.0892
1975	0.1937	0.7716	0.1476	0.5411	0.0924	0.0850
1976	0.1892	0.7859	0.1415	0.5434	0.0846	0.0782
1977	0.1883	0.7890	0.1379	0.5476	0.0808	0.0766
1978	0.1883	0.7908	0.1374	0.5547	0.0812	0.0781
1979	0.1972	0.7502	0.1366	0.5088	0.0752	0.0737
1980	0.1823	0.8129	0.1313	0.5588	0.0730	0.0697
1981	0.1847	0.8012	0.1411	0.5315	0.0813	0.0705
1982	0.1751	0.8460	0.1654	0.5396	0.1072	0.0724

References

Abbott, Thomas; Robert McGuckin; Paul Herrick; and Leroy Norfolk. 1989. "Measuring the Trade Balance in Advanced Technology Products," *Discussion Paper*. Center for Economics Studies, Bureau of the Census, U.S. Department of Economics.

Abernathy, William J.; Kim B. Clark; Alan M. Kantrow. 1983. *Industrial Renaissance: Producing a Competitive Future for America*. New York: Basic Books.

Acs, Zoltan, and David Audretsch. 1988. "Innovation in Large and Small Firms: An Empirical Analysis," *American Economic Review* pp. 678–690.

Adams, James D., and L. Sveiskaskaus. 1990. "Fundamental Stock of Knowledge and Productivity Growth." Mimeo.

Aganbegyan, Abel G. 1988. *The Economic Challenge of Perestroika*. Bloomington, Indiana: Indiana University Press.

Aho, C.M., and H.F. Rosen. 1981. "Trends in Technology-Intensive Trade: With Special Reference to U.S. Competitiveness," *Economic Discussion Paper 9*. Washington, D.C.: Department of Labor, Bureau of International Labor Affairs.

Andrikopoulos, A.; J.A. Brox; and E. Carvalho. 1986. "Inter-fuel Substitution in the Canadian Manufacturing Sector: An Alternative Modeling Approach," *Applied Simulation and Modelling*, D.O. Koval ed. Calgary: Acta Press, pp. 484–88.

Arrow, Kenneth J. 1962. "The Economic Implications of Learning by Doing," *Review of Economic Studies* 29, no. 2.

Bailey, Martin Neil. 1986. "What Has Happened to the Productivity Growth?" *Science* 234, no. 4775 (24 October), pp. 443–51.

———, and Alok K. Chakrabarti. 1988. *Innovation and The Productivity Crisis*. Washington, D.C.: Brookings Institution.

Barten, A.P. 1969. "Maximum Likelihood Estimation of a Complete System of Demand Equations," *European Economic Review* 1, pp. 7–73.

Batra, R. 1989. *Surviving The Great Depression of 1990*. New York: Dell Books.

Baumol, William; Sue Anne Batey Blackman; and Edward Wolff. 1989. *Productivity and American Leadership*. Cambridge, Mass.: M.I.T. Press.

Baumol, William J., and Kenneth McHennan. 1985. *Productivity Growth and U.S. Competitiveness.* New York: Oxford University Press.

Berndt, E.R., and M.A. Fuss. 1986. "Productivity Measurement with Adjustment for Variations in Capacity Utilization and other Forms of Temporary Equilibrium," *Journal of Econometrics* 33, pp. 7–29.

———; C.J. Morrison; and G.C. Watkins. 1981. "Dynamic Models of Energy Demand: An Assessment and Comparison," *Measuring and Modeling Natural Resource Substitution,* Berndt, E.R. and B.C. Field eds., Cambridge, Mass.: M.I.T. Press. pp. 259–89.

———. 1980. "Energy Price Increases and the Productivity Slowdown in United States Manufacturing," *Decline in Productivity Growth,* Proceedings of Conference, Edgartown, Massachusetts.

———; and M.S. Khaled. 1979. "Parametric Productivity Measurement and Choice among Flexible Functional Forms," *Journal of Political Economy* 87, pp. 1220–1245.

———, and David O. Wood. 1975. "Technology, Prices and Derived Demand for Energy," *Review of Economics and Statistics* LVII, no. 3, pp. 259–68.

———. 1974. "Testing for the Existence of a Consistent Aggregate Index of Labor Input," *American Economic Review* 44, pp. 391–404.

———, and L.R. Christensen. 1973a. "The Internal Structure of Functional Relationships: Separability, Substitution and Aggregation," *Review of Economic Studies* 40, pp. 403–11.

———, and L.R. Christensen. 1973b. "The Translog Function and the Substitution of Equipment, Structures, and Labor in U.S. Manufacturing 1929–1968," *Journal of Econometrics* 1, pp. 81–114.

Bernstein, Jeffrey I., and M. Ishaq Nadiri. 1988. "Industry R&D Spillovers, Rates of Return, and Production in High-Tech Industries," *American Economic Review* 78, no. 2 (May), pp. 429–434.

Best, Michael H. 1982. "The Political Economy of Socially Irrational Products," *Cambridge Journal of Economics* pp. 53–64.

Binswanger, H.P. 1974a. "The Measurement of Technical Change Biases with Many Factors of Production," *American Economic Review* 64, pp. 964–76.

———. 1974b. "The Measurement of Elasticities of Factor Demand and Elasticities of Substitution," *American Journal of Agricultural Economics* 72, pp. 377–386.

Bishop, John A., and Jang H. Yoo. 1985. "'Health Care,' Excise Taxes and Advertising Ban on Cigarette Demand and Supply," *Southern Economic Journal* 52, pp. 402–11.

Bloom, Alan. 1987. *The Closing of The American Mind.* New York: Simon and Schuster.

Boretsky, M. 1982. "The Threat to U.S. High-Technology Industries: Economics and National Security Implications," Draft. Washington, D.C.: U.S. Department of Commerce, International Trade Administration.

———. 1980. "The Role of Innovation," *Challenge* 23, pp. 9–15.

———. 1975. "Trends in U.S. Technology: A Political Economist's View," *American Scientists* 63, pp. 70–82.

Bowen, William G., and Julie Ann Sosa. 1989. *Prospects for Faculty in Arts and Science.* Princeton, N.J.: Princeton University Press.

Braverman, Harry. 1974. *Labor and Monopoly Capital.* New York: Monthly Review Press.

Brown, R.S.; D.W. Caves; and L.R. Christensen. 1979. "Modeling the Structure of Cost and Production for Multiproduct Firms," *Southern Economic Journal* 46, pp. 256–70.

Brown, R.S., and L.R. Christensen. 1982. "Estimating Elasticities of Substitution in a Model of Partial Static Equilibrium: An Application to U.S. Agriculture, 1947–74," *Measuring and Modeling Natural Resource Substitution*. Berndt, E.R. and B.C. Fields, (eds.) Cambridge, Mass.: M.I.T. Press.

Brox, J.; Emanuel Carvalho; and Dino Lusetti. 1988. "Input Substitution in Canadian Manufacturing: An Application of the CES-Translog Production Function," *Atlantic Economic Journal* 16, pp. 21–46.

Burgan, John. 1985. "Cyclical Behavior of High-Tech Industries," *Monthly Labor Review* 108 (May), pp. 9–15.

Carlsson, Bo. 1989. "The Evolution of Manufacturing Technology and Its Impact on Industrial Structure: An International Study," *Small Business Economics* 1, pp. 21–37.

Caves, Douglas W.; Laurits R. Christensen; and Joseph A. Swanson. 1981. "Productivity Growth, Scale Economies and Capacity Utilization in U.S. Railroads, 1955–74," *American Economic Review* 71, no. 5, pp. 994–1002.

———. 1980. "Productivity in U.S. Railroads, 1955–74," *Bell Journal of Economics* 11, no. 1, pp. 166–81.

Chakraborty, Chandana, and Romesh Diwan. 1989. "R&D Components and Technical Change," *Eastern Economic Journal*, XV, pp. 365–72.

Christensen, L.R., and D.W. Caves. 1980. "Global Properties of Flexible Functional Forms," *American Economic Review* 70, pp. 422–32.

———; D. Cummings; and D.W. Jorgenson. 1980. "Economic Growth, 1947–73: An International Comparison," *New Development in Productivity Measurement and Analysis*, J.W. Kendrick and B. Vaccara, eds. Chicago: The University of Chicago Press.

———; D.W. Jorgenson; and L.J. Lau. 1973. "Transcendental Logarithmic Production Frontier," *The Review of Economics and Statistics* 55, pp. 25–45.

———. 1971. "Conjugate Duality and the Transcendental Logarithmic Production Function," *Econometrica* 39, pp. 225–56.

———, and D.W. Jorgenson. 1970. "U.S. Real Product and Real Factor Input 1929–67," *Review of Income and Wealth* 16, pp. 19–50.

———. 1969. "The Measurement of U.S. Real Capital Input, 1929–67," *Review of Income and Wealth* 15, pp. 293–320.

Cobb, C., and P.H. Douglas. 1928. "A Theory of Production," *American Economic Review* 18, pp. 139–65.

Cockburn, Ian, and Zvi Griliches. 1988. "Industry Effects and Appropriability Measures in the Stock Market's Valuation of R&D and Patents," *American Economic Review* 78 (May), pp. 419–423.

Cohen, Stephen, and John Zysman. 1987. *Manufacturing Matters: The Myth of The Post Industrial Economy*. New York: Basic Books.

Cowing, T.G., and R.E. Stevenson, eds. 1981. *Productivity Measurement in Regulated Industries*. New York: Academic Press.

The Cuomo Commission on Trade and Development. 1988. *The Cuomo Commission Report: A New American Formula for a Strong Economy*, New York: Simon and Schuster.

Davis, L.A. 1982. "Technology Intensity of U.S. Output and Trade," Mimeo. Washington, D.C.: Department of Commerce, International Trade Administration.

Denison, E.F. 1989. *Estimates of Productivity Change by Industry*. Washington, D.C.: The Brookings Institute.

———. 1980. *Accounting for Slower Growth*. Washington, D.C.: Brookings Institution.

———. 1979. "Explanations of Declining Productivity Growth," *Survey of Current Business* 59, pp. 1–24.

———. 1978. "Some Major Issues in Productivity Analysis: An Examination of Estimates by Jorgenson and Griliches," *Survey of Current Business* 58, pp. 21–44.

———. 1962. *Sources of Economic Growth in the United States and the Alternatives Before Us*. New York: Committee for Economic Development.

Denny, M., and Fuss M. 1981. "Substitution Possibilities For Energy: Evidence from U.S. and Canadian Manufacturing Industries," *Measuring and Modeling Natural Resource Substitution*, Berndt, E.R. and B.C. Field eds. Cambridge, Mass.: MIT Press.

———, and L. Waverman. 1981. The Measurement and Interpretation of Total Factor Productivity in Regulated Industries with an Application to Canadian Telecommunications," *Productivity Growth in Regulated Industries*, Cowing, T.G. and Stevenson, R.E., eds. New York: Academic Press.

———, and L. Waverman. 1979. "Energy and the Cost Structure of Canadian Manufacturing Industries," Institute for Policy Analysis, Technical Paper 12, University of Toronto.

———. 1977. "The Use of Approximation Analysis to Test for Separability and the Existence of Consistent Aggregates," *Economic Journal* 67, pp. 492–97.

Dertouzos, Michael L.; Richard K. Lester; and Robert M. Solow. 1989. *Made in America: Regaining the Productive Edge*. The MIT Commission on Industrial Productivity, Cambridge, Mass.: MIT Press.

Diewert, W.E. and C.J. Morrison. 1985. "Assessing the Effect of Changes in Terms of Trade on Productivity Growth: A Comparison of Japan and the U.S." Paper presented at the NBER Conference on U.S. Japan Productivity Growth. Boston, Mass.

———. 1982. "Duality Approaches to Microeconomic Theory," *Handbook of Mathematical Economics*. Arrow, Kenneth J. and Michael D. Intriligator, eds. Amsterdam: North Holland.

———. 1981. "The Theory of Total Factor Productivity Measurement in Regulated Industries," *Productivity Measurement in Regulated Industries*, T.G. Cowing and R.E. Stevenson eds. New York: Academic Press.

———. 1980. "Capital and the Theory of Productivity Measurement," *American Economic Review*, 70, no. 2, pp. 260–67.

———, and C. Parkan. 1979. "Linear Programming, Test of Regularity Conditions for Productivity Functions," Discussion Paper, no. 79-01, University of British Columbia.

Diewert, W.E. 1978. "Superlative Index Number and Consistency in Aggregation," *Econometrica* 46, 883–900.

———. 1976. "Exact and Superlative Index Numbers," *Journal of Econometrics* 4, no. 4, pp. 115–45.

———. 1971. "An Application of the Shephard Duality Theorem: A Generalized Leontief Production Function," *Journal of Political Economy* 79, pp. 481–507.

Diwan, Romesh. 1990. "Comment on Human Capital and Technical Change: A Comparison of the U.S. and Japanese Labor Markets," *A Comparison of Productivity Growth in Japan and the United States,* Charles R. Hulten ed. Chicago: University of Chicago Press.

———, and Chandana Chakraborty. 1990. "Input Substitution and Technical Change in U.S. High Tech Industry," *Economic Letters* 32, no. 1, pp. 141–145.

———, and Suresh Desai. 1990a. "Perestroika and Gandhian Economics," *International Journal of Social Economics* 17, no. 5, pp. 4–17.

———, and Suresh Desai. 1990b. "Market Globalization and International Competitiveness: Implications for U.S. Business," *Issues in International Business* 6, no. 2 (Spring), pp. 1–7.

Diwan, Romesh. 1989. "Small Business and The Economics of Flexible Manufacturing," *Small Business Economics* 1, no. 2, pp. 101–109.

———. 1988. "High Tech Development: Gandhi Towards An Understanding of The Quality of Living," *Development: Journal of the Society for International Development* no. 4, pp. 64–70.

———. 1987. "Mahatma Gandhi and The Economics of Non-Exploitation," *International Journal of Social Economics* 14, no. 2, pp. 39–52. Also reprinted in *International Review of Economics and Ethics* 2, no. 1.

———, and Mark Lutz, eds. 1987. *Essays in Gandhian Economics.* New York: Intermediate Technology Development Group of North America, republication. First publisher: Gandhi Peace Foundation, New Delhi, 1985.

———, and Nirjhar Leonardson. 1986. "Productivity, Technical Change and Capital-Labor Substitution in Indian Industry," *Indian Journal of Quantitative Economics* 1, no. 2, pp. 1–16.

———, and Renu Kallianpur. 1986. *Productivity and Technical Change in Foodgrains.* New Delhi: Tata McGraw-Hill.

Diwan, Romesh. 1985a. "Economics Of Bread Labor," *Essays in Gandhian Economics,* Romesh Diwan and Mark Lutz eds. New Delhi: Gandhi Peace Foundation, pp. 109–127.

———. 1985b. "On The Relevance Of Gandhian Economics," *Indian Economics Association Conference Volume,* (keynote paper). December, pp. 13–33.

———, and Renu Kallianpur. 1985. "Biological Technology and Land Productivity: Fertilizers and Food Production in India," *World Development,* 13, no. 5 (May), pp. 627–638.

Diwan, Romesh. 1982. "Economics Of Love," *Journal of Economic Issues* 16, no. 2 (June), pp. 413–433.

———. 1981. "Transfers of Hard Technologies and Debasement of Human Rights," *Human Rights Quarterly,* November, pp. 19–44.

———, and Dennis Livington. 1979. *Alternative Development Strategies and Appropriate Technology: Science Policy For An Equitable World Order.* Elmsford, N.Y.: Pergamon Press.

———, and Kanta Marwah. 1976. "Transfers From Poor To Rich Countries: An Analysis of World Exports," *Economic and Political Weekly, Annual Number* 11, nos. 5, 6, and 7, pp. 191–205.

Diwan, Romesh. 1973. "Trade Between Unequal Partners," *Economic and Political Weekly, Annual Number* 8, nos. 4, 5, and 6, pp. 213–220.

———. 1971a. "Planning For The Poor," *Economic and Political Weekly* 6, no. 34 (August 21), pp. 1809–1814.

————. 1971b. "Impact of Education On Labor Efficiency," *Applied Economics* 3, no. 2, pp. 127–136.

————. 1970. "About The Growth Path Of The Firms," *American Economic Review* 60 (March), pp. 30–43.

————. 1968a. "On The Cobb Douglas Production Function," *Southern Economic Journal* 34, no. 3, pp. 410–414.

————. 1968b. "Effect of Price on Savings," *Economic Development and Cultural Change* 16, no. 3, pp. 430–435.

————. 1968c. "A Test Of The Two Gap Theory of Development," *Journal of Development Studies* 4, no. 4, pp. 529–537.

————. 1968d. "Bias In The Measurement of Technical Change," *Journal of Financial and Quantitative Analysis* 3, no. 4, pp. 417–427.

————, and D. Gujerati. 1968. "Employment and Productivity in Indian Industries: Some Questions of Theory and Policy," *Arthvinjana* 10, no. 1, pp. 29–67.

Diwan, Romesh. 1966. "Alternative Specification of Economies of Scale," *Economica* 33, no. 132, pp. 442–454.

————. 1965. "An Empirical Estimate of The Constant Elasticity of Substitution Production Function," *Indian Economic Journal* XII, no. 4, pp. 347–366.

Dosi, Giovanni; Christopher Freeman; Richard Nelson; Gerald Silverberg; and Luc Soete eds. 1988. *Technical Change and Economic Theory*. London: Printer Publishers.

Drucker, Peter F. 1988. "Management and the World's Work," *Harvard Business Review* September–October, pp. 65–74.

Eisinger, Peter K. 1988. *The Rise of the Entrepreneurial State*. Madison: The University of Wisconsin Press.

Eliasson, Gunnar. 1988. "Schumpeterian Innovation, Market Structure, and the Stability of Industrial Development," *Evolutionary Economics*, H. Hanusch ed., pp. 151–198.

Fabricant, S. 1983. "Productivity Measurement and Analysis: An Overview," *Measuring Productivity, Trends and Comparisons*, First International Productivity Symposium, UNIPUB, N.Y.

Feenstra, Robert C. 1988. "Quality Change Under Trade Restraints in Japanese Autos," *The Quarterly Journal of Economics* February, vol. 103, pp. 131–146.

Feldstein, Martin, ed., 1987. *Taxes and Capital Formation*. Chicago: The University of Chicago Press, National Bureau of Economic Research.

Felemban, Fareed, 1989. "Productivity Growth and Competitiveness of The United States Petroleum Industry," Ph.D. thesis, Managerial Economics, RPI, Troy, New York.

Fields, George. 1983. *From Bonsai To Levi's: When West Meets East*. New York: Macmillan Publishing Co.

Frank, Robert H. 1988. *Passions Within Reason*. New York: W.W. Norton.

Freeman, Christopher and Carlotta Perez. 1988. "Structural Crisis of Adjustment, Business Cycle and Investment Behaviour," *Technical Change and Economic Growth*, Dosi et al. eds. London: Printer Publishers, pp. 38–66.

Freeman, Christopher. 1974. *The Economics of Industrial Innovation*. Harmondsworth, England: Penguin.

Fuss, M.A., and L. Waverman. 1985. "Productivity Growth in the Automobile Industry, 1970–80: A Comparison of Canada, Japan and the U.S.," Conference on U.S.-Japan Productivity Growth, Cambridge, Mass.: August 25–28.

Fuss, M.A.; D. McFadden; and Y. Mundlak. 1978. "A Survey of Functional Forms in the Economic Analysis of Production," *Production Functions: A Dual Approach to Theory and Applications,* M.A. Fuss and D. McFadden eds. Amsterdam: North-Holland Publishing, pp. 219–364.

Fuss, M.A. 1977. "The Demand for Energy in Canadian Manufacturing: An Example of the Estimation of Production Structures With Many Inputs," *Journal of Econometrics* 5, pp. 89–116.

Galbraith, John Kenneth. 1988. "Time and the New Industrial State," *American Economic Review* 78, no. 2 (May), pp. 373–376.

———. 1967. *The New Industrial State.* Boston, Mass.: Houghton-Mifflin.

Gandhi, Mohandas Karmachnad. 1962. *Hind Swaraj.* Ahmedabad: Navjivan Press. [This is the first publication of Gandhi's classic 1908 work].

Genevose, Eugene D. 1961. *The Political Economy of Slavery.* New York: Random House.

Goldberg, L. 1979. "The Influence of Federal R&D Funding on the Demand for and Returns to Industrial R&D," Center for Naval Analysis, CRC, 388.

Gollop, F.M., and M.J. Roberts. 1981. "The Sources of Economic Growth in the U.S. Electric Power Industry," *Productivity Measurement in Regulated Industries,* Cowing T.G. and R.E. Stevenson eds. New York: Academic Press.

Gorbachev, Mikhail. 1987. *Perestroika: New Thinking for Our Country and The World.* New York: Harper and Row, Publishers.

Griliches, Zvi. 1988. "Productivity Puzzles and R&D: Another Nonexplanation," *The Journal of Economic Perspectives* 2, no. 4 (Fall), pp. 9–22.

———. 1986. "Productivity, R&D, and Basic Research at the Firm Level in the 1970s," *American Economic Review* 76, no. 1, pp. 141–54.

———, ed. 1984. *R&D, Patents, and Productivity.* Chicago: University of Chicago Press.

———, and R. Litchenberg. 1984. "Research and Development and Productivity at the Industry Level: Is There Still a Relationship," *R&D, Patents, and Productivity,* Griliches ed. Chicago: University of Chicago Press, pp. 465–96.

Griliches, Zvi. 1980. "R&D and the Productivity Slowdown," *American Economic Review* 70 (May), pp. 343–348.

———. 1971. *Price Indexes and Quality Change.* Cambridge, Mass.: Harvard University Press.

———, and V. Ringstad. 1971. *Economies of Scale and the Form of the Production Function: An Econometric Study of Norwegian Manufacturing Establishment Data.* Amsterdam: North-Holland Publishing Co.

Gunn, Thomas G. 1987. *Manufacturing for Competitive Advantage: Becoming a World Class Manufacturer.* Cambridge, Mass.: Ballinger.

Hamilton, James L. 1972. "The Demand for Cigarettes: The Health Scare and the Advertising Ban," *Review of Economics and Statistics* 54, pp. 401–11.

Hanoch, G. 1975. "Elasticity of Scale and Shape of Average Costs," *American Economic Review* 65, no. 3, pp. 492–97.

Hanusch, Horst, ed. 1988. *Evolutionary Economics: Application of Schumpeter's Ideas.* New York: Cambridge University Press.

Harcourt, G.C. 1969. "Some Cambridge Controversies in The Theory of Capital," *Journal of Economic Literature* VII (June) pp. 369–405.

Harper, M. J. 1983. "Capital Input and Capital and Labor Shares," *Trends in Multifactor*

Productivity, 1948–81, U.S. Department of Labor, Bureau of Labor Statistics, Bulletin 2178. Washington, D.C.: U.S. Government Printing Office.

Harrison, Bennett, and Barry Bluestone. 1988. *The Great U-Turn: Corporate Restructuring and The Polarizing of America.* New York: Basic Books.

Hayes, Robert H., and Ramchandran Jaikumar. 1988. "Manufacturing Crisis: New Technologies, Obsolete Organizations," *Harvard Business Review* September–October, pp. 77–85.

Hayes, R.H., and S.C. Wheelwright. 1984. *Restoring Our Competitive Edge: Competing Through Manufacturing.* New York: John Wiley and Sons.

Hayes, Robert H., and William J. Abernathy. 1980. "Managing Our Way to Economic Decline," *Harvard Business Review* July–August, pp. 67–77.

Heertje, Arnold. 1988. "Schumpeter and Technical Change," *Evolutionary Economics,* H. Hanusch, ed., pp. 71–89.

Hicks, J.R. 1946. *Value and Capital.* Oxford: Clarendon Press.

Hildebrand, G.H., and T.C. Liu, 1965. *Manufacturing Production Functions in the U.S.* Ithaca, N.Y.: Cornell University Press.

von Hippel, Eric. 1988. *The Sources of Innovation.* New York: Oxford University Press.

Hirschman, Albert O. 1970. *Exit, Voice and Loyality: Responses to Decline in Firms, Organizations and States.* Cambridge, Mass.: Harvard University Press.

Hotelling, H. 1932. "Edgeworth's Taxation Paradox and the Nature of Demand and Supply Functions," *Journal of Political Economy* 40, pp. 577–616.

Hulten, C.R., and F.C. Wykoff. 1986. "Productivity Change, Capacity, Utilization, and the Sources of Efficiency Growth," *Journal of Econometrics* 33, pp. 31–50.

———. 1981a. "The Measurement of Economic Depreciation," *Depreciation, Inflation and Taxation of Income Capital,* C.R. Hulten ed. Washington, D.C.: The Urban Institute.

———. 1981b. "The Estimation of Economic Depreciation Using Vintage Asset Prices: An Application of The Box-Cox Power Transformation," *Journal of Econometrics* 28, pp. 367–96.

Hulten, C.R. 1979. "On the Importance of Productivity Change," *American Economic Review* 69, pp. 126–36.

———. 1973. "Divisia Index Numbers," *Econometrica* 41, pp. 1017–26.

Illich, Ivan. 1981. *Shadow Work.* Salem, N.H.: Marion Boyers, Inc.

———. 1974. *Energy and Equity.* New York: Harper and Row.

Jaffe, A. 1986. "Technological Opportunities and Spillovers of R&D," *American Economic Review* vol. 76 December, pp. 984–1001.

Jorgenson, Dale W. 1988a. "Productivity and Postwar Economic Growth," *The Journal of Economic Perspectives* 2, no. 4 (Fall), pp. 23–42.

———. 1988b. "Productivity and Economic Growth in Japan and the United States," *American Economic Review* 78, no. 2 (May), pp. 217–222.

———; H. Sakuramoto; K. Yoshioko; and M. Kuroda. 1985a. "Bilateral Models of Production for Japanese and U.S. Industries," Conference on U.S.-Japan Productivity Growth, Cambridge, Mass.: August 25–28.

Jorgenson, Dale W., and M. Kuroda. 1985b. "Japan-U.S. Industry Level Productivity," Conference on U.S.-Japan Productivity Growth, Cambridge, Mass.: August 25–28.

———; and M. Nishimizu. 1985c. "Japan-U.S. Industry-level Productivity Comparisons, 1960–1967." Paper presented at the NBER Conference on U.S. Japan Productivity Growth. Boston, Mass.

Jorgenson, Dale W., and M. Nishimizu. 1978. "U.S. and Japanese Economic Growth, 1952–74: An International Comparison," *The Economic Journal* 83, pp. 707–26.

Kaldor, Nicholas. 1967. *Strategic Factors in Economic Development.* Ithaca, N.Y.: Cornell University Press.

Kallianpur, R., and S.L. Jang. 1967. "Technology and The Innovation Process in The U.S. Semiconductor Industry." Paper presented at the European Association for Research in Industrial Economics Conference, Berlin.

Kelly, R. 1977. *The Impact of Technological Innovation on International Trade Patterns.* Staff Economic Report, ER-24, U.S. Department of Commerce.

Kendrick, John W. ed. 1984. *International Comparisons of Productivity and Causes of the Slowdown.* Cambridge, Mass.: Ballinger Press.

———, and E.S. Grossman. 1980. *Productivity in the United States: Trends and Cycles.* Baltimore: Johns Hopkins Press.

Kendrick, J.W. 1979. "Productivity Trends and the Recent Slowdown," *Contemporary Economic Problems,* W. Fellner ed. Washington, D.C.: American Enterprise Institute.

———. 1976. *The Formation and Stocks of Total Capital.* National Bureau of Economic Research. New York: Columbia University Press.

———. 1961. *Productivity Trends in the United States.* NBER. Princeton, N.J.: Princeton University Press.

Kindleberger, Charles P. 1980. "The Economic Aging of America," *Challenge* pp. 35–44.

Kmenta, J., and R.F. Gilbert. 1968. "Small Sample Properties of Alternative Estimators of Seemingly Unrelated Regressions," *Journal of the American Statistical Association* 63, pp. 1180–1200.

Krugman Paul, and R. Baldwin. 1987. "The Persistence of the U.S. Deficit," *Brookings Papers on Economic Activity* 1, pp. 1–55.

Lasch, Christopher. 1979. *The Culture of Narcissism: American Life in An Age of Diminishing Expectations.* New York: W.W. Norton and Co.

Lawrence, Robert Z. 1984. *Can America Compete?* Washington, D.C.: The Brookings Institution.

Lawson, A.M. 1982. "Technological Growth and High-Technology in U.S. Industries," *Industrial Economic Review.* Washington, D.C.: U.S. Department of Commerce, Bureau of Industrial Economics, pp. 12–18.

Leontief, W.W. 1982. "The Distribution of Work and Income," *Scientific American* 137, pp. 189–204.

———. 1947. "A Note on the Interrelations of Subsets of Independent Variables of a Continuous Function With Continuous First Derivatives," *Bulletin of the American Mathematical Society* 53, pp. 343–50.

Levin, Richard C. 1988. "Appropriability, R&D Spending, and Technological Performance," *American Economic Review* 78, no. 2 (May), pp. 424–28.

Levy, Robert; Marianne Bowes; and James Jondrow. 1983. *Technical Change and Employment in Five Industries.* Washington, D.C.: The Public Research Institute.

Lichtenberg, Frank R., and Donald Siegel. 1989. "Using Linked Census R&D-LRD Data To Analyze The Effect of R&D Investment on Total Factor Productivity Growth,"

Discussion Paper. Center for Economics Studies, Bureau of the Census, U.S. Department of Commerce.

Link, Albert N. 1978. "Rates of Induced Technology from Investments in Research and Development," *Southern Economic Journal* 45, pp. 370–379.

Lund, T.R., and J.A. Hansen. 1986. *Keeping America at Work.* New York: John Wiley & Sons.

Magaziner, I.C., and Robert B. Reich. 1983. *Minding America's Business.* New York: Random House.

Mansfield, Edwin. 1988. "Industrial R&D in Japan and the United States: A Comparative Study," *American Economic Review* 78, no. 2 (May), pp. 223–228.

———. 1984. "R&D and Innovation: Some Empirical Findings," *R&D, Patents and Productivity,* Z. Griliches ed. Chicago: University of Chicago Press.

———; A. Romeo; and K. Switzer. 1983. "Research and Development Price Indices and Real R&D Expenditures in the United States," *Research Policy* 12, pp. 105–112.

Mansfield, Edwin. 1980. "Basic Research and Productivity Increase in Manufacturing," *American Economic Review,* 70, no. 5, pp. 863–73.

Markusen, Ann. 1986. "High-Tech Plants and Jobs: What Really Lures Them?" *Economic Development Commentary* 10 (Fall), pp. 3–7.

———; P. Hall; and A. Glasmeier. 1986. *High Tech America: The What, How, Where and Why of Sunrise Industries.* Winchester, Mass.: Allen and Unwin.

McFadden, D. L. 1973. "Cost, Revenue and Profit Functions," In *Econometric Approach to Production Theory,* D.L. McFadden ed. Amsterdam: North-Holland Publishing Co.

———. 1963. "Further Results on CES Production Functions," *The Review of Economic Studies* 30, pp. 73–83.

McIntyre, Richard. 1989. "Economic Rhetoric and Industrial Decline," *Journal of Economic Issues* 23 (June), pp. 483–491.

Mishel, Lawrence F. 1988. *Manufacturing Numbers: How Inaccurate Statistics Conceal U.S. Industrial Decline.* Washington, D.C.: Economic Policy Institute.

Mohen, P.A.; M.I. Nadiri; and I.R. Prucha. 1986. "R&D, Production Structure, and Rates of Return in the U.S., Japanese and German Manufacturing Sectors: A Non-Separable Dynamic Factor Demand Model," *European Economic Review* 26.

Morrison, C., and W.E. Diewert. 1985. "Assessing The Effects of Changes in Terms of Trade on Productivity Growth," U.S.-Japan Productivity Conference, Cambridge, Mass., August 25–28.

Morrison, C., and E.R. Berndt. 1981. "Short Run Labor Productivity in a Dynamic Model," *Journal of Econometrics* 16, pp. 339–65.

Mundlak, Y. 1964. "Transcendental Multiproduct Production Functions," *International Economic Review* 5, pp. 273–84.

Nadiri, M.I., and I.R. Prucha. 1985. "Comparison and Analysis of Productivity Growth and R&D Investment in the Electrical Machinery Industries of the United States and Japan," U.S.-Japan Productivity Conference, Cambridge, Mass., August 25–28.

Nadiri, M.I., and M.A. Schankerman. 1981. "The Structure of Production, Technological Change, and the Rate of Growth of Total Factor Productivity in the U.S. Bell System," *Productivity Measurement in Regulated Industries,* T.G. Cowing and E.R. Stevenson eds. New York: Academic Press.

Nadiri, M. Ishaq. 1982. "Producers Theory," *Handbook of Mathematical Economics,*

Arrow, Kenneth J. and Michael D. Intriligator, eds. Amsterdam: North Holland.

———. 1970. "Some Approaches to the Theory and Measurement of Total Factor Productivity: A Survey," *Journal of Economics Literature* 8, pp. 1137–77.

Naisbitt, John. 1982. *Megatrends*. New York: Warner Books.

National Research Council. 1986. *New Era in U.S. Manufacturing: Need for a National Vision*. Washington, D.C.: National Academy Press.

National Science Board, National Science Foundation. 1987. *Science and Engineering Indicators*. Washington, D.C.: Government Printing Office.

National Science Foundation. 1978–1982. *Research and Development in Industry, Surveys of Science Resource Series*. Washington, D.C.: NSF.

Nelson, Richard R. 1985. *High Technology Policies: A Five Nation Comparison*. Washington, D.C.: American Enterprise Institute.

———, and S. Winter. 1982. *An Evolutionary Theory of Economic Change*. Cambridge, Mass.: Belknap Press of Harvard University.

Norsworthy, J.R., and D.A. Malmquist. 1983. "Input Measurement and Productivity Growth in Japanese and U.S. Manufacturing," *American Economic Review* 73, pp. 947–67.

Olson, Mancur. 1988. "The Productivity Slowdown, the Oil Shocks, and the Real Cycle," *The Journal of Economic Perspectives* 2, no. 4 (Fall), pp. 43–70.

———. 1982. *The Rise and Decline of Nations: Economic Growth, Stagflation and Social Rigidities*. New Haven, Conn.: Yale University Press.

O'Neill, Gerard K. 1983. *The Technology Edge: Opportunities for America in World Competition*. New York: Simon and Schuster.

Pakes, A., and Z. Griliches. 1984a. "Estimating Distributed Lags in Short Panels With an Application to the Specification of Depreciation Patterns and Capital Stock Constructs," *Review of Economic Studies* 51, pp. 243–62.

———. 1984b. "Patents and R&D at the Firm Level: A First Look," *R&D, Patents and Productivity*, Z. Griliches ed. Chicago: University of Chicago Press, pp. 55–72.

Pakes, A., and M. Schankerman. 1984. "The Rate of Obsolescense of Patents, Research Gestation Lags and the Private Rate of Return to Research Resources," *R&D, Patents and Productivity*, Z. Griliches ed. Chicago: University of Chicago Press, pp. 73–88.

Pascal, Richard T., and Anthony G. Athos. 1981. *The Art of Japanese Management: Applications For American Executives*. New York: Simon and Schuster.

Pavitt, K. 1984. "Sectoral Patterns of Technical Change: Towards a Taxonomy and Theory," *Research Policy* 13, pp. 343–374.

Payer, Cheryl. 1982. *The World Bank: A Critical Analysis*. New York: Monthly Review Press.

Perez, Carla, and Luc Soete. 1988. "Catching Up in Technology: Entry Barriers and Windows of Opportunity," *Technical Change and Economic Theory*. Dosi et al. eds. London: Printer Publishers Ltd, pp. 458–79.

Perlman, Mark. 1988. "On The Coming Senescence of American Manufacturing Competence," *Evolutionary Economics*, H. Hanusch ed. pp. 343–382.

Peters, Thomas J. 1988. *Thriving on Chaos: Handbook for A Management Revolution*. New York: Perennial Library.

Peters, Thomas J., and Robert H. Waterman, Jr. 1982. *In Search of Excellence*. New York: Harper and Row Publishers, Inc.

Petri, Peter A. 1984. *Modelling Japanese-American Trade: A Study of Asymmetric Inter-dependence*. Cambridge, Mass.: Harvard University Press.

Pindyck, R.S., and J.J. Rotemberg. 1983. "Dynamic Factor Demand Under Rational Expectations," *Scandinavian Journal of Economics* LXXXV, pp. 223–38.

Pindyck, R.S. 1979. "Inter-Fuel Substitution and the Industrial Demand for Energy: An International Comparison," *The Review of Economics and Statistics* 69, pp. 169–74.

Piore, Michael J., and Charles F. Sabel. 1984. *The Second Industrial Divide: Possibilities for Prosperity*. New York: Basic Books.

Pollak, Robert A.; R.C. Sickles; and T.J. Wales. 1984. "The CES Translog: Specification and Estimation of a New Cost Function," *The Review of Economics and Statistics*, 66, no. 4, pp. 602–7.

Qureshi, M., and Romesh Diwan. 1990. "The Process of Technical Change." Mimeo.

Reich, Robert B. 1987. *Tales of a New America*. New York: Random House, Inc.

———. 1983. *The Next American Frontier*. New York: Times Book.

Reich, Robert; I. Hecker; and J. U. Burgan. 1983. "High-Technology Today and Tomorrow: A Small Slice of the Employment Pie," *Monthly Labor Review* 106, pp. 50–58.

Robinson, Joan. 1955. *The Accumulation of Capital*. London: Macmillan.

Rosenberg, Nathan, and W. Edward Steinmueller. 1988. "Why Are Americans Such Poor Imitators?" *American Economic Review* 78, no. 2, pp. 229–234.

Sato, K. 1967. "Two-Level Constant-Elasticity-of-Substitution Production Function," *The Review of Economic Studies* 34, pp. 201–18.

Scherer, Frederic M. 1988. "Enterprise Ownership and Managerial Behavior," *Evolutionary Economics*, H. Hanusch ed. pp. 137–144.

———. 1982. "Interindustry Technological Flows and Productivity Growth" *Review of Economics and Statistics* 64, pp. 627–34.

———. 1980. *Industrial Market Structure and Economic Performance*. Boston: Houghton Mifflin Company, second edition.

Schmalansee, Richard. 1972. *The Economics of Advertising*. Amsterdam: North Holland.

Schumpeter, Joseph A. 1939. *Business Cycle: A Theoretical, Historical and Statistical Analysis*. New York: McGraw-Hill.

Shapiro, Matthew D. 1986. "The Dynamic Demand for Capital and Labor," *The Quarterly Journal of Economics* 101, pp. 513–41.

Shephard, R.W. 1970. *The Theory of Cost and Production Functions*. Princeton: Princeton University Press.

———. 1953. *Cost and Production Functions*. Princeton: Princeton University Press.

Skinner, W. 1985. "The Taming of Lions: How Manufacturing Leadership Evolved, 1780–1984," *Uneasy Alliance*, K.B. Clark, R.H. Hayes, and C. Lorenz eds. Boston, Mass.: Harvard Business School Press.

Slater, Philip. 1980. *Wealth Addiction*. New York: E.P. Dutton Inc.

Solow, R.M. 1967. "Some Recent Developments In the Theory of Production," *The Theory and Empirical Analysis of Production*, M. Brown ed. New York: Columbia University Press.

Solow, R.M. 1957. "Technical Change and The Aggregate Production Function" *Review of Economics and Statistics* 39, pp. 312–20.

———. 1956. "The Production Function and the Theory of Capital," *Review of Economic Studies* 23, pp. 101–8.

Star, S., and R.E. Hall. 1976. "An Approximate Divisia Index of Total Factor Productivity," *Econometrica* 44, pp. 257–64.

Starr, Martin, ed. 1988. *Global Competitiveness: Getting the U.S. Back on Track,* New York: W.W. Norton & Co.

Stoneman, P. 1983. *Economic Analysis of Technical Change.* Oxford, U.K.: Oxford University Press.

Sveikauskas, L.A. 1987. "Research and Development and Productivity Growth," U.S. Department of Labor, Bureau of Labor Statistics. Mimeo.

———, and C.D. Sveikauskas. 1982. "Industry Characteristics and Productivity Growth," *Southern Economic Journal* 49, pp. 264–82.

Sveikauskas, L.A. 1981. "Technology Inputs and Multifactor Productivity Growth," *Review of Economics and Statistics* LXIII, pp. 275–82.

Tan, Hong W. 1985. "Human Capital and Technical Change: A Comparison of The U.S. and Japanese Labor Markets." Paper presented at the NBER Conference on Income and Wealth, on Productivity Comparison between U.S. and Japan, Boston.

Terkel, Studs. 1988. *The Great Divide: Second Thoughts on The American Dream.* New York: Pantheon Books, Random House, Inc.

———. 1972. *Working.* New York: Pantheon Books.

Terleckyj, N.E. 1982a. "R&D and U.S. Industrial Productivity in the 1970's," *The Transfer and Utilization of Technical Knowledge,* D. Sahel ed. Lexington: Lexington Books, pp. 63–69.

———. 1982b. "R&D as a Source of Growth of Productivity and Income," Working paper. Washington, D.C.: National Planning Association.

———. 1974. "Effect of R&D on the Productivity Growth of Industries: An Exploratory Study," Washington, D.C.: National Planning Association.

———. 1963. "R&D: Its Growth and Composition," National Industrial Conference Board, Studies in Business Economics, No. 82, New York.

Theroux, Paul. 1985. *The Kingdom by the Sea.* Boston: Houghton Mifflin Co.

Thirlte, Colin G., and Vernon W. Ruttan. 1987. *The Role of Demand and Supply in the Generation and Diffusion of Technical Change.* London: Hardwood Academic Publishers.

Thurow, Lester C. 1984. *Dangerous Currents: The State of Economics.* New York: Vintage Books.

Tireman, John. 1984. *The Militarization of High-Technology.* Cambridge, Mass.: Ballinger Press.

Toffler, Alvin. 1985. *The Adaptive Corporation.* New York: McGraw-Hill Publishing Co.

———. 1980. *The Third Wave.* New York: William Morrow and Co.

Tomer, John. 1987. *Organizational Capital: The Path to Higher Productivity and Well Being.* New York: Praeger Publishers.

Tyson, Laura D'Andrea; William T. Dickens; and John Zysman eds. 1988. *The Dynamics of Trade and Employment.* Cambridge, Mass.: Harper and Row.

U.S. Bureau of Census. *Annual Survey of Manufacturing.* Washington D.C.: Government Printing Office. [Various Issues]

———. *Census of Manufactures.* Washington, D.C.: Government Printing Office. [Various Issues]

———. 1988. *Statistical Abstract of the United States 1988.* Washington, D.C.: Government Printing Office. [Various Issues]

U.S. Bureau of Economic Analysis. 1987. *Survey of Current Business*. Washington, D.C.: Government Printing Office. [Various Issues]

U.S. Congress, Office of Technology Assessment. 1982. *Technology, Innovation, and Regional Economic Development*. Report. September, Washington, D.C.

U.S. Department of Commerce, International Trade Administration. 1984. *US. High-Technology Trade and Competitiveness*. April, Washington, D.C.

————. 1983. *An Assessment of U.S. Competitiveness in High-Technology Industries*. February, Washington, D.C.

U.S. Department of Labor, Bureau of Labor Statistics. 1989. *The Impact of Research and Development on Productivity Growth*. Bulletin 2331: September.

————. 1985. *Monthly Labor Review*. Washington, D.C.: Government Printing Office. [Various Issues]

————. 1983. *Trends in Multifactor Productivity, 1948–81*. Bulletin 2178. Washington, D.C.: U.S. Government Printing Office.

————. 1982. *Productivity Measures for Selected Industries, 1954–81*. Bulletin 2155. Washington, D.C.: Government Printing Office.

U.S. International Trade Administration. 1988. *U.S. Industrial Outlook*. Washington, D.C.: Government Printing Office. [Various Issues]

————. 1984. *U.S. High Tech Trade and Competitiveness*. Washington, D.C.: Government Printing Office.

————. 1983. *Assessment of U.S. Competitiveness in High Tech Industries*. Washington, D.C.: Government Printing Office.

U.S. National Commission on Excellence in Education. 1983. *A Nation At Risk: The Imperatives For Educational Reform*. Washington, D.C.: Government Printing Office.

Uzawa, H. 1962. "Production Functions with Constant Elasticities of Substitution," *The Review of Economic Studies* 29, pp. 291–99.

Vandyopadhyaya, Chandana. 1987. *Productivity and Technical Change: U.S. High Tech Industries*. Ph.D. Thesis, RPI, Troy, New York.

Vanek, J. 1977. *The Labor Managed Economy*. Ithaca, N.Y.: Cornell University Press.

Vinson, R., and P. Harrington. 1979. *Defining High-Technology Industries in Massachusetts*. Boston, Mass.: Department of Manpower Development.

Vogel, E. 1979. *Japan No. 1: Lessons for America*. Cambridge, Mass.: Harvard University Press.

Williamson, Oliver E. 1975. *Markets and Hierarchies: Analysis and Antitrust Implications*. New York: Free Press.

World Bank. 1988. *World Development Report, 1988*. New York: Oxford University Press.

Young, Allen. H. 1989. "Alternative Measures of Real GNP," *Survey of Current Business* 69, no. 4, pp. 27–34.

Zellner, A.M. 1963. "Estimators for Seemingly Unrelated Regression Equations: Some Exact Sample Results," *Journal of the American Statistical Association* 58, pp. 977–992.

————. 1962. "An Efficient Method of Estimation of Seemingly Unrelated Regressions and Tests for Aggregate Bias," *Journal of the American Statistical Association* 57, pp. 585–612.

Author Index

Subject Index

About the Authors

ROMESH DIWAN is Professor of Economics at Rensselaer Polytechnic Institute. He is the author of numerous books and articles on economics, productivity, and competitiveness, including *Essays in Gandhian Economics, Productivity and Technical Change in Foodgrains,* and *Alternative Development Strategies and Appropriate Technology: Policy for an Equitable World Order.*

CHANDANA CHAKRABORTY is Assistant Professor of Economics at Montclair State College. She has presented numerous papers at economics conferences and has published articles in *Economics Letters* and *Eastern Economic Journal.*